D0832118

Video for Change

WITNESS <www.witness.org> uses the power of video to open the eyes of the world to human rights abuses. By partnering with local organizations around the globe, WITNESS empowers human rights defenders to use video to shine a light on those most affected by human rights violations, and to transform personal stories of abuse into powerful tools of justice. Over the past decade, WITNESS has partnered with groups in more than 60 countries, bringing often unseen images, untold stories and seldom-heard voices to the attention of key decision-makers, the media, and the general public—catalyzing grassroots activism, political engagement, and lasting change.

Video for Change

A Guide for Advocacy and Activism

Edited by
Sam Gregory, Gillian Caldwell,
Ronit Avni and Thomas Harding

Pluto Press

LONDON • ANN ARBOR, MI

In association with

WITNESS

First published 2005 by Pluto Press
345 Archway Road, London N6 5AA
and 839 Greene Street, Ann Arbor, MI 48106

www.plutobooks.com

Copyright © WITNESS, 2005

The right of the individual contributors to be identified as the authors of this work
has been asserted by them in accordance with the Copyright, Designs and Patents Act
1988.

British Library Cataloguing in Publication Data
A catalogue record for this book is available from the British Library

ISBN   0 7453 2413 4 hardback
ISBN   0 7453 2412 6 paperback

Library of Congress Cataloging in Publication Data applied for

10   9   8   7   6   5   4   3   2   1

Designed and produced for Pluto Press by
Chase Publishing Services Ltd, Fortescue, Sidmouth, EX10 9QG, England
Typeset from disk by Stanford DTP Services, Northampton, England
Printed and bound in Canada by Transcontinental Printing

Contents

Figures and Tables

FIGURES

TABLES

Acknowledgements

This book is dedicated to the human rights organizations who work with WITNESS around the world, for their bravery, courage and commitment in their continuing struggle for human rights.

This book has benefited from the input and experiences of current WITNESS staff, including Hakima Abbas, Matisse Bustos, Sara Federlein, and Tamaryn Nelson, as well as the many talented interns and volunteers who have worked with us over the years. We are also grateful to the members of the WITNESS "pod" who reviewed drafts of the book in July 2004—including Pat Aufderheide, Kat Cizek, Joanna Duchesne, Mallika Dutt, Lilibet Foster, Sandrine Isambert, Tom Keenan, Tia Lessin, Meg McLagan, Liz Miller, Richard O'Regan, and Fernanda Rossi. Many other video advocates worldwide, too numerous to mention or single out here, shared their experiences and expertise at different points in the process, and their input is reflected in the shape and content of this book. We thank them all.

Stephanie Hankey, Darius Cuplinskas and John Peizer at the Open Society Institute initially funded the training modules that became this book—WITNESS particularly acknowledges them. We also thank all the other steadfast supporters of WITNESS over the years, including the Ford Foundation, the Omidyar Network, the Skoll Foundation, and the Glaser Progress Foundation, as well as numerous other foundations and individual donors around the world.

At Pluto, Anne Beech has patiently shepherded first-time editors through to publication.

Among the editors, Sam thanks Larry, for loving patience over too many long days, and WITNESS partners for their efforts for justice: particularly Joey Lozano, as well as the staff of Burma Issues, who remain a constant inspiration.

Gillian Caldwell thanks Louis, for his love and for his willingness to stay home and nurture our kids while she was out trying to change the world. She thanks Steve Galster, for introducing her to video advocacy. And she thanks her parents, for modelling a commitment to making the world a better place.

Ronit Avni thanks the thousands of courageous civilians combating inequality worldwide who model human agency and the capacity for good. Your daily acts of courage, humility, purpose and compassion amidst great suffering inspire, obligate and transform. Thank you.

Thomas Harding: For my kids Kadian and Sam, who accompanied me so patiently during my early days of video activism. Thanks to Anne who said "yes" again. And of course to DH.

Foreword

Back in 1988, I went on tour with Amnesty International's "Human Rights Now!" Tour, which was to celebrate the 40th anniversary of the Universal Declaration of Human Rights, making people aware not only of their civil and political rights, but also their entitlement to food, shelter, health care, education, employment and much more. We managed to persuade Bruce Springsteen, Tracey Chapman, Youssou N'dour and Sting to join us, and toured over nineteen countries.

The experience of meeting many survivors of human rights abuses, and listening to their stories was very moving and there was no way I could walk away from their requests for help. Some were living in fear, being regularly threatened and harassed, some had witnessed their family being murdered, and some had suffered terrible tortures. In many instances the perpetrators went unpunished.

However, in many ways what most shocked me was that many of these human rights abuses were being successfully denied, buried, ignored and forgotten, despite many written reports. But, it was clear that in those cases where photographic film or video evidence existed, it was almost impossible for the oppressors to get away with it.

For that reason, when we had our Reebok Human Rights Foundation annual meeting, I proposed that we begin an initiative to supply human rights activists with video cameras. (The Reebok Human Rights Foundation was set up after the Human Rights Now! Tour to give awards to extraordinary young people (under the age 30) for courage, commitment and compassion in human rights work.)

It was however in 1992, after the videoing of the Rodney King beatings in Los Angeles, that the Foundation realized the potential impact of video cameras in human rights work. Paul Fireman and the Reebok team generously agreed to get behind this initiative, and Michael Posner of the Lawyers Committee for Human Rights offered us a home within his offices. Thus, WITNESS was born.

Over thirteen years later, the original mission of WITNESS remains true. We've come a long way since our early focus on solely providing video cameras to human rights groups. We're an independent organization with a rigorous application process for partnership, and provide our partners with hands-on training in video advocacy. We broker relationships with political leaders and journalists to ensure tactical distribution of our partners' videos. We also show their videos on our website, on television and at film festivals worldwide to make sure they get seen by audiences everywhere. Since our inception, we've collaborated with more than 200 partners across 50 countries, who have together created a living archive of more than 2,000 hours of important footage. That's a lot, but it's nothing compared to the overwhelming demand and potential for our support. To address this need, we've recently begun to provide short-term training to an even broader array of non-affiliated social justice groups with the dream of creating a global movement of activists equipped with these powerful tools.

I hope that the innovative work of Gillian Caldwell's extraordinary team at WITNESS and all the remarkable groups discussed in this book will inspire not just human rights activists, but others committed to social justice to really embrace the use of all that video and computer technology can do.

In this age, when the mass media rest in fewer and fewer hands, we must have strong, vital, independent voices if we ever want to hear all the story, or seek for justice. We have an incredible opportunity to change lives.

The UN Declaration of Human Rights laid down what any person might reasonably expect, yet there are remarkably few people who enjoy these rights. With cameras in the hands of activists and meaningful distribution of those images, we will witness what really goes on in this world and hopefully want to change it.

Peter Gabriel
July 2005

Introduction

This book is an invitation—an invitation to discover the potential of a simple video camera and the power it holds to spark social change. Every day, all around the world, activists draw upon video in creative, strategic ways and use the results to ensure that silent voices are heard and important reforms are made. In this book we will show you how they do this, and how you can do it too.

There has never been an easier time to start using video to make a better world possible. Video cameras have gotten ever cheaper—they're now integrated into cell phones—and editing software comes prepackaged with many home computers. Since the early 1990s, the increasing availability and affordability of technology has fueled the world of social justice video activism. The movement has also been strengthened by new vehicles for online and offline distribution, by novel ways to get around the traditional gate-keepers of media, and by the proliferation of nongovernmental organizations and people's movements asserting their rights, voices and identities, particularly in the Global South.

Pioneering organizations like Appalshop in the US, the Chiapas Media Project in Mexico, CEFREC in Bolivia, the Drishti Media Collective in India, Undercurrents in the UK, Labor News Production in South Korea, INSIST in Indonesia, and innumerable others, have made video an integral part of campaigns focused on human rights, environmentalism, corporate globalization, and indigenous rights. Online, individuals and collectives, including the global Indymedia movement started in Seattle in 1999, have made the World Wide Web a free and open venue for new information and new stories. With access to production and distribution democratized, many more people are now able to participate in the tradition of video and filmmaking to document and challenge prevailing social ills. In doing so, these new media activists are furthering a time-honoured tradition that has included the pioneering social documentaries of the 1930s, the cinema verité experiments of the 1960s, and the indigenous, community, and alternative media movements of the 1970s, 1980s, and 1990s.

These chapters will walk you through the process of "video advocacy." By this phrase we mean the use of video as an essential *tool* in social justice activism—one that can be deployed as strategically and effectively as more traditional forms of "advocacy" referring to the range of ways to exert pressure for a defined goal of change, including persuasion, relationship-building, lobbying, organizing, and mobilizing.

We will draw on the inspiring real-life experiences of social justice video advocates worldwide—groups that have worked with the human rights organization WITNESS where I work, and a range of other well-known and lesser-known figures in the activist universe. Throughout you'll find an emphasis on the emotional and empathetic aspect of video, on its humanizing ability to communicate across boundaries. We also stress the need for collaboration within organizations and among outside allies to more successfully facilitate the production and use of video. And, we value foresight and planning to ensure that video builds on other complementary activities and helps to achieve a common goal. We don't make the assumption that television broadcast is necessarily the aim of most video productions. In fact, we show the challenges that you will likely face in trying to get your video broadcast and fill you in on alternative methods for effective distribution.

You do not need any prior experience with video or activism to benefit from this book—only an interest in making video an effective, fulfilling dimension of your social justice work. "Video" is our shorthand term for a range of audiovisual media of different formats, lengths and purpose, from feature documentaries and short films to video clips, public service announcements, and raw footage. We speak often of organizations, since we have generally seen video work best in campaigns when embraced by the advocacy and communications strategy of a group, collective or movement. But video can, of course, still be a powerful medium for the individual. It's just as important for these activists to identify likeminded allies to help with the process.

It's important to remember that technology is neither a positive nor a negative tool. It's what you do with technology that counts. If we look at video imagery coming out of the Iraq war and into the mainstream and alternative media, it has shown both the controlled, pre-censored imagery of the "embedded" journalists and the uncensored voices of ordinary Iraqis and American soldiers speaking out about the conflict and the life-destroying effects of war. It has on one hand exposed the human rights abuses of Abu Ghraib and on the other facilitated distribution of the obscene scenes of beheadings conducted by rebels and insurgents.

A number of chapters in this book were initially conceived as training materials for the human rights organization WITNESS <www. witness.org>, and many of the stories detailed here, as well as the approach we take, come from the WITNESS experience. WITNESS is a US-based organization that puts video cameras into the hands of human rights defenders worldwide and provides training and support so they can create lasting change by using powerful imagery and testimony from the frontlines of human rights struggles to connect with, and then move to act, audiences both near and far.

WITNESS' work is grounded in partnerships with human rights groups around the world. Our current partner organizations focus on issues including child-soldiers in the Democratic Republic of Congo, juvenile prison reform in the US, massive displacement and human rights abuses in Burma, slave labor in Brazil, and torture and impunity in Mexico. We are working with these groups on specific advocacy campaigns for periods of one to three years. In each case, we have worked with them to identify how video can bring a unique and critical component to their campaigns for change.

With WITNESS' assistance, these partners prepare and make use of video in ways that will complement—not replace—other more traditional forms of advocacy. The partners clearly identify the audiences they need to reach through their individual stories and voices. They draw on video's unique power to bring these stories as well as the visual "evidence" of a situation, directly to a human rights decision-making body, a government policy-maker, a community, or the global public. We then share these experiences and best practices as broadly as possible among our partners and other networks of social justice media-makers and users.

In our experience, the most critical stage of making an effective video is planning (followed by planning and more planning) based on a clear understanding of why you are choosing to invest in the project. If you don't know why, and for whom, you are making an advocacy video you will limit your ultimate effectiveness. In Chapter 1, "Using Video Advocacy," Gillian Caldwell, who has been the Executive Director of WITNESS since 1998, draws on her experiences working on a pioneering campaign against the global trafficking of women to talk you through the essential questions to ask as you prepare to make a video.

Safety and security is another subject raised by Gillian's experience with the trafficking campaign filmed undercover in the former Soviet Union. In mainstream production for broadcast, there is often a tremendous focus on ensuring the safety of journalists, producers and crew, and on following proper consent procedures. When you are filming for social justice work, however, you need to seriously consider a range of potential risks not only to yourself, but also to the people you work with and those you film. These risks may come before, during or even long after you film, and are at the core of the first of three chapters (Chapter 2, on "Safety and Security") by Katerina Cizek, a leading social justice filmmaker from Canada, who co-directed the award-winning film *Seeing is Believing: Handicams, Human Rights and the News*.

Part of the planning process outlined in the "Advocacy" chapter involves paying careful attention to your audience and to the stories that will engage that audience. A film to "rally the troops" will require a different approach than one required to persuade a committee of impatient, time-pressed and sceptical legislators. This idea of "Storytelling for Advocacy" is at the heart of Chapter 3, again by Katerina Cizek. She writes about how to think through a story that will move, engage, persuade or shame a given audience into action. In the same chapter, she also walks us through the steps of preproduction—the practical and logistical stage of filmmaking that occurs once you have identified your audience and story.

When WITNESS begins working with its partners, there is often an assumption that filming is a mysterious process, best done only by professionals. Within hours of picking up a camera, our partners realize that this is not the case. It is simple and intuitive to develop the basic skills of video. Demystification of the process is the goal of the next chapter in the book, Chapter 4, "Video Production: Filming a Story," written by Joanna Duchesne, who was for many years the audiovisual producer for Amnesty International in London, with additional writing by Liz Miller, who teaches video production at Concordia University in Montreal. They offer simple guidance and exercises to help you progress from single shot to sequence, and explain the importance of using different types of shots in the editing process.

Editing—the process by which the components of a video come together to form a satisfying, compelling whole—remains a more complex technical skill than filming. But regardless of whether you develop your own expertise with editing software, understanding the concepts behind editing and the needs of an editor are critical steps for any filmmaker. As you look at how the material you filmed fits together, and how certain ethical issues reverberate from the filming through to the editing process, you will enhance your own ability to create powerful footage. In Chapter 5, "Editing for Advocacy," by Katerina Cizek, we look at the technical process of editing and the particular constraints you face as an ethical filmmaker and activist dealing with issues of consent, how style and substance contradict and reinforce, and the use (and impact on you and others) of violent or disturbing imagery.

Since advocacy is all about persuading an audience to act, an advocacy video has value only if it gets seen. In this book's remaining chapters we look at how distribution can be targeted to a range of audiences. Using video as evidence is not an easy process in most courtrooms at the national and international level. Often your usage will be constrained by the rules of evidence, the need to maintain a clear chain of custody, and the impossibility of cross-examining a videotaped witness. Former WITNESS Program Coordinator Sukanya Pillay walks us through the pitfalls of using video in legal contexts in Chapter 6, "Video as Evidence," and offers inspiring examples of when it has been used successfully.

In the final chapter, Chapter 7, on "Strategic Distribution," Thomas Harding, author of the *Video Activist Handbook* and the co-founder of Undercurrents, shows how to effectively distribute video when resources are scarce but you know exactly whom you want to reach. He discusses how to use community screenings, how to ally and network with partners, and how to go direct-to-decision-makers or use (or create your own) mainstream and online media. He emphasizes the need to choose the right tactic for your intended audience and paints various scenarios for using your video: in the office of a legislator, on public television, or in community screenings—all of which can have a cumulative, multiplying effect.

In the Appendices we include forms and checklists that you may need, as well as a copy of the "Video Action Plan" that WITNESS gives its partners to guide them through the thinking process of using video for advocacy. We also provide resource lists of other helpful places to go for information, and a clear glossary of terms.

The stories we tell here by no means cover all the creative uses for video, nor the wide variety of groups using video in effective, transformative ways. But we do hope that the innovative work discussed in this book will inspire you and other defenders of social justice to embrace its use in your work. Since video advocacy is an ever-evolving field, we would love to hear about your experiences with video and welcome your feedback and suggestions at <videoadvocacy@witness.org>.

Sam Gregory
WITNESS Program Manager

1

Using Video for Advocacy

Gillian Caldwell

In 1995, I was working as an attorney doing civil rights work in Washington, DC. A friend returned from a trip to Siberia, where he had been investigating the illegal trade in tiger pelts. Undercover, and in the midst of discussions on a sale, the traffickers had offered to sell him women. He asked me if I wanted to help him do something about it. I said I would spend some time after-hours researching the issue and see what I thought about getting involved.

Two weeks later, I resigned from my job as a civil rights attorney and camped out at his office, telling him that I would wait tables if necessary until we raised the money to support our proposed campaign into the illegal trafficking of women for forced prostitution out of Russia.

And so, my adventure in video advocacy began. Just over two years later, we released the film *Bought & Sold: An Investigative Documentary About the International Trade in Women*, a documentary based on our investigation, which received widespread media coverage, including BBC, CNN, ABC, *New York Times*, and *Washington Post*—and significant results internationally in terms of policy change.

Bought & Sold integrated an unusual mix of video. There was undercover footage shot with miniature tie cameras in meetings with the Russian mafia—gathered while we posed as foreign buyers interested in purchasing women to work as prostitutes. And there were conversations with women around the world who had been forced into the sex trade. Additional interviews with counselors and advocates helped frame the key issues surrounding trafficking and conveyed recommendations to policy-makers.

What made *Bought & Sold* influential internationally was that it was ground-breaking in the information it revealed in a powerful visual medium. At the same time it could be used in screenings before a broad array of audiences, including law enforcement, NGOs working to meet the needs of women, girls and women at risk for recruitment, and a range of policy-makers worldwide.

1

Figure 1.1   Undercover footage shot for *Bought & Sold* (Global Survival Network/ WITNESS)

Video has several strengths that convinced us that it was worth the considerable time, energy and resources required to integrate it into our work. We recognized that video could elicit powerful emotional impact, connecting viewers to personal stories. It can illustrate stark visual contrasts and provide direct visual evidence of abuses. It can be a vehicle for building coalitions with other groups working on an issue. It can reach a wide range of people since it does not require literacy to convey information. It can help counter stereotypes and assist you in reaching new, different and multiple audiences, particularly if broadcast is a possibility. And it can be used in segments of varying lengths for different contexts.

But even given its strengths, video isn't right for every campaign or organization. For one thing, it is a very time-consuming and potentially expensive endeavour. Additionally, at WITNESS we often talk about whether or not an issue lends itself to being conveyed convincingly with images and compelling human stories. Are the images accessible, or are the risks and difficulty of obtaining them obstacles you may not be able to overcome? When assessing whether to use video, even more important than the strength of the images themselves is the power of the stories they help convey. A video is only as powerful as its ability to touch the people that watch it, to connect them to the experience of the people portrayed in the film, and to motivate them to get involved to make a difference. Do you have access to the people and the stories you will need to make your video compelling, engaging, and powerful?

This chapter provides a brief strategic overview of some of the key themes echoed throughout this book and helps you begin to analyze whether and how you may integrate video into your advocacy work. I will draw on my own experiences between 1995 and 1998 in launching the video advocacy campaign on trafficking in women, and on the experiences of many other social justice video advocates around the world. I also recommend you look at the "WITNESS Video Action Plan" (see Appendix I) for a more formal step-by-step, question-by-question guide to the process of incorporating video into your advocacy.

*   *   *

So, to begin with, when we talk about "video advocacy," what do we mean?

"Video advocacy" is the process of integrating video into an advocacy effort to achieve heightened visibility or impact in your campaign.

Figure 1.2   Women interviewed for a film by RAWA, filmed in Afghanistan shortly after the fall of the Taliban (RAWA/WITNESS)

"Advocacy" is the process of working for a particular position, result or solution. For example, in an environmental context, you might advocate to prevent the construction of a sewage treatment plant in a poor neighborhood. In a human or civil rights context, you advocate to stop a woman from being stoned to death for infidelity to her husband or to press for a change in laws to enhance women's rights. In a community context, a group may mobilize support for the construction of a new school.

All these efforts represent different kinds of advocacy, and each advocacy campaign requires its own analysis of several important factors to lay the groundwork for success. For example, who is in the best position to help you get what you are looking for? How can you be most influential with that audience? What arguments, stories or evidence should you present? At what time and in what place?

When considering whether or how to integrate video into your advocacy work, the process can be broken down into five key steps:

- Step 1: Define your goals.
- Step 2: Talk to other people who have worked on the issue you want to tackle. What has worked, what hasn't, and why?
- Step 3: Analyze your style and strengths, and identify your allies.
- Step 4: Define your audience and think through how to communicate your message to them—your format, style and the "messenger").
- Step 5: Decide on a level of involvement and start planning production and distribution.

Step 1: Define your goals

By 1995, trafficking in women for forced prostitution had been going on for centuries, but trafficking out of Russia into Asia, Western Europe and the US was a new and growing business in the wake of the fall of the Berlin Wall. We knew that written and video exposés on trafficking from Asia and Latin America had been generated, but noted that they had not received adequate attention from the US government or the international community. We hoped that a campaign focused on an area of strategic interest to the US (that is to say, the former Soviet Bloc), and the introduction of powerful undercover investigative video, would garner fresh attention for the problem on a global level. Our first goal, then, was to address a fundamental ignorance about the scope and dimensions of the human trafficking industry, which was valued to be as lucrative as the international trade in drugs and guns. We wanted to educate government and a broader public about the issue.

A second related goal was to campaign for laws and law enforcement responses to trafficking that would ensure that women were treated fairly in the legal process. For example, we wanted to be sure they were offered adequate support in a language they could understand, that they received a stay of deportation and time to consider whether to provide testimony against the trafficking rings, that they were offered witness protection where necessary, and that they received assistance to meet their basic needs in terms of housing, counseling, health care and other support once trafficking was identified as the underlying problem.

A third goal was to increase funding to support locally based organizations in Central and Eastern Europe that could provide education and support to women at risk, or already caught in the trafficking system.

All these goals were thoroughly analyzed and understood before we began our investigation and our filming—and we referred to them continually throughout the process to be sure that our original aims coincided with our newly gained perspectives and experience and that we were gathering compelling arguments for making the changes we were recommending.

The first question to ask, then, when thinking about a video advocacy strategy is: *What problem are we trying to resolve, and what solutions will we be proposing?* For example, in a human or civil rights campaign it is important to determine early on whether changes in the legal system are required or whether, instead, the campaign is about addressing the failure of the system to enforce or comply with laws already on the books. In most cases, there will be national as well as international laws, treaties and conventions that prohibit the abuses you have identified, and the focus of your campaign will be on documenting and highlighting the violations taking place and pressuring the responsible parties to take action to stop the abuse. In other instances, the solution to your problem may not lie in the legal system but in community solidarity or collective action, or in persuading particular individuals that it is in their best interests to behave or act in a different way. It is in the process of bringing the human experience of a situation or problem to life, and in presenting it powerfully to key audiences, that video can play an important role.

Step 2: Talk to other people who have worked on the issue you want to tackle. What has worked, what hasn't, and why?

As I mentioned above, our early research revealed that several other documentary films had been produced on trafficking, with a focus on the experience in Southeast Asia, but that those films had not generated the responses advocates were looking for on a national or international level. Perhaps cynically, and perhaps realistically, part of our assumption was that a documentary video that highlighted the experience of Caucasian women trafficked from Russia would generate greater public attention and visibility within US government circles, and that once we got their attention we could educate regarding the broader global problem. We also noted that there was a relative lull in advocacy on trafficking within the US at the time.

It is very important to get a sense of the "landscape" surrounding the issue you want to address. Very few successful advocacy campaigns occur in isolation—many individuals and organizations, often from different parts of the world, play a role in influencing the course of events.

Community groups and nongovernmental organizations often fail to collaborate as effectively as they could or should—whether because of competition for scarce resources, personality differences, ego, or political differences regarding recommendations for reform. Wherever possible, learn from the work that other advocates are doing and find ways to reinforce each other with the video material you produce. The more tactical and collaborative you are in your thinking around problems and solutions, the more likely you are to succeed—and the more allies you will have developed who are vested in using your video to help advocate alongside you. In our case, we researched and communicated with dozens of key organizations already working around the world to address the problem, and we learned from their experiences. We involved them in the process of producing our video by conducting on- and off-camera interviews and soliciting their advice on key recommendations for reform. The inclusive process of production we developed helped to solidify their connection to the video as a resource they could use to support their work.

Step 3: Analyze your own style and strengths, and identify your allies

It is important to be as objective and clear-sighted as possible in analyzing your style and strengths. In our case, we were a small, underfunded start-up. There were two of us working together on a very ambitious, multinational campaign—and my colleague was only working part-time on it. We had no reputation or experience in the national or international community on the issue. In fact, we didn't even have nonprofit status in the US and our sponsor for tax purposes was the Marine Mammal Fund, a group with a history of working on trade in endangered species. Needless to say, it wasn't easy to establish our credentials for conducting an undercover investigation on the Russian mafia!

It was therefore clear from the outset that we would need to take a highly collaborative approach to our work. There was no sense in reinventing the wheel, since so much important policy work and analysis had already been done. And we needed credible allies. The point was to draw on the strong groundwork that had been done by international coalitions such as the Global Alliance Against Trafficking in Women. We found the international community very receptive to our requests for interviews and information, and rarely came across what can sometimes be described as "territorial" behavior among nonprofit and nongovernmental organizations. Your approach is very important, and of course influences the response you receive.

The strength of the material we researched, the insatiable media interest in it, and the added credibility we gained by recruiting several well-placed experts as part of our advisory committee, opened the necessary doors and landed us in the autumn of 1997 with the ear of top advisers in the Clinton administration in the US, when we helped them craft the first multi-agency task force on trafficking. We were also able to work with our colleagues in the movement to draft a resolution for the late Senator Paul Wellstone that became the basis for a bipartisan Trafficking Victims Protection Act that passed the US Congress in 2000. And we became the only NGO partner for the Open Society Institute/Soros Foundation on a regional initiative in Central and Eastern Europe to train, fund, and support NGOs to work on trafficking.

What helped make our distribution campaign internationally successful was our commitment to involving a range of key players throughout the process—they reviewed scripts and rough cuts and their voices were heard and reflected in the final product, so they felt a sense of ownership and began using it in their work.

It is very important at this stage of your thinking to assess where your strengths lie. Questions like: Are we a formally organized NGO or a people's movement for change? Do our strengths lie in our access to grassroots communities that can be mobilized, or do we have credibility and access to the "halls of power"? Do we use a litigation-based approach, a popular protest strategy, a lobbying strategy, or some combination? Do we work best in coalitions or independently? Who are our key allies?

For the more established organizations, a style and reputation may precede you, which will help define your approach to using video in advocacy. If your constituency is grassroots, consider drawing on that strength to produce something that can be used to educate and activate a broader audience. If you tend to have more influence with well-placed officials and governing bodies, consider developing a piece that would educate, inform and motivate them toward your intended goal. Ideally, you can outline a video production that will speak to multiple audiences. No matter what, research well, collaborate as much as possible, and while you should have a series of clear, achievable goals in mind, don't forget to dream. In the end, our accomplishments exceeded our wildest expectations.

Step 4: Define your audience and think through how to communicate your message to them

In our campaign on trafficking, we had numerous audiences and allies in mind. We wanted to reach a global international public, women at risk for recruitment, organizations working to educate people about the problem, government authorities around the world, and intergovernmental bodies such as the United Nations.

It is very important to be clear about your key audiences from the beginning of any campaign for change, and this is certainly no less true where you are planning to integrate video. One of the basic premises of communications strategy is that you need to have a clear, concise message, and you have to identify your intended audience before you can craft the message. Having a clearly defined audience makes it easier to shoot and construct a compelling argument using video. But remember that some of the most powerful video advocacy campaigns successfully speak to multiple audiences at once, or in a sequence using a variety of materials for different settings. Analyze your situation carefully to determine how to proceed.

So, how to define your audience? You must decide which audience has the most influence on the change you seek, and whether that audience is accessible to you, or whether you will first need to seek alliances or work with an intermediate audience.

Once you have identified your audience you need to be sure you know what you want them to do, and how they will be convinced to join the effort. If there is a direct appeal to get involved, decide who should encourage them to take action. Recognize what will be appealing, persuasive or intriguing to them—in terms of factual information conveyed, the people interviewed or featured, and experts you may include for commentary. You also need to understand who you'll alienate and repel as you make these choices. For a more detailed analysis of this process, read Chapter 3 below.

Once you have identified your key audiences and goals and crafted your message, you can prepare a distribution plan drawing on some of the strategies outlined in Chapter 7. You should think carefully about the appropriate timing to get your video to your audience, and the most appropriate messenger or "bearer" of the news—is it you or your organization or should the approach and the delivery be by someone else? All this should be ready, at least in draft form, before you begin the process of producing or selecting a video for use in your advocacy campaign.

Step 5: Decide on a level of involvement and start planning production and distribution

In launching a campaign that uses video, there are many varying levels of involvement in the actual filmmaking process for an organization to consider. An organization with limited resources may choose to use an existing film in their campaign, since video production is always more time consuming and expensive than web or written communications.

If more resources are available, you could also team up with a filmmaker who is producing a film on the issue and offer support either in the form of guidance, connections for filming and interviews, and/or funds.

The third option is to take on the actual production of a film yourself. In the case of *Bought & Sold*, we made the decision to produce a 42-minute film, making it the centerpiece of our campaign. But it took us two years of working around the clock to produce it, and in the end we had filmed over 150 hours of videotape! Making a documentary-length film is an immense undertaking in terms of time and financial resources, even though the cost of production has been reduced by the development of digital video and laptop editing technology. Organizations and individuals new to making film are taking on the task of learning about filmmaking as well as the task of furthering their knowledge of the issues they choose to cover. So it is often larger organizations that choose to tackle this scale of video productions themselves. Taking this route requires extensive planning and committed human and financial resources. For more details, see Chapters 3 and 4.

If you do decide to commit to production yourself, you will need to determine the length and whether you will generate different language or content versions of your piece. It is not always necessary or even advisable to produce a documentary of 40 minutes or longer—many successful campaigns have been supported by videos of between five and twenty minutes in length. In fact, a 15 to 20 minute video is often the perfect length to introduce a group to the key issues and to connect them to the human struggles involved. From there, the advocate can help direct and engage them in addressing the problem.

When you are thinking about using video as part of your advocacy, and whether you have decided to produce your own work or utilize videos produced by others, there are numerous ways you may consider integrating video into your campaign for change. Remember that none is mutually exclusive and you may want to work with a variety of them to reach or communicate with different audiences. Often timing will be crucial—look at the case study below about the psychiatric hospital in Paraguay and the cumulative impact of using video in the legal setting and on the news. Thomas Harding also opens his chapter with an example from his own experience of how you can tap into multiple distribution opportunities and secure a greater effect.

Using videos for organizing communities and allies

Video was used successfully by the Ella Baker Center for Human Rights in California, together with WITNESS and other allies as a tool to mobilize youth audiences to pressure Alameda County in California to stop its plans to build a "Super-Jail for Kids." *Books Not Bars* is a 22-minute video that documents the inspiring youth-led movement against the growth of the US prison industry, particularly in California. The video is particularly geared toward youth of color, who are disproportionately victims of the human rights abuses highlighted in the video, to encourage them to participate in the grassroots campaign. WITNESS and its partners developed an Action Pack to accompany the video that provided examples of tangible ways for youth to participate in the movement to reform the prison system, and created extensive Lesson Plans for high school students that examine incarceration-related issues within a human rights framework. As a result of two years of collaborative campaigning by The Ella Baker Center and other groups, the grassroots campaign successfully derailed the "Super-Jail for Kids" proposal.

With an appropriate distribution network and accompanying screening materials such as information packets, handbooks or action packs, many video lengths, styles and formats can fit a local audience.

Communities using video in a "participatory" context

Participatory video has most often been used in the context of development, as a way to help document and convey the way in which a community identifies solutions to the challenges it faces. Although WITNESS has not used this methodology, many other development and rights organizations have effectively done so. For example, here is a description of its use in Tanzania by the local development organization "Maneno Mengi," cited in the book *Making Waves*:

Consider this scene at the Kilwa fish market in the Mtwara Region of southeastern Tanzania: the image shows a group of fishermen accusing the district executive director of not sharing the collected tax with the marine environment fund and the village. "This is the truth. Money is collected, but the way they use the money is bad, as you can see. First he does not know himself what he collects, and then we don't know what we should get. That is how they grow big stomachs, while we are becoming very thin."

The discussion goes on as if the camera was not there; people have gotten used to having the camera inside the circle, as another participant. Nobody looks at the camera; nobody modifies the wording or the attitude to please the camera. This is one of the participatory video sessions organised by Maneno Mengi and it is only one step in a long process of using video tools to help a community better understand a social or economic development initiative.

The final product, *Utuambie Wananchi* is a "video digest," short report on how the interactive process developed over a period of several months. But this is neither an end result nor the main objective, only a way of sharing with others the process in an encapsulated form. The real objective of Maneno Mengi's work is in the interactive participatory process.[1]

Around the world, video is increasingly embraced as a tool to support education, reinforce cultural identity, and encourage organizational and political participation. In a participatory video process, members of the community film and watch and use the video they are shooting, and the *process* is generally considered more important than the *product*, as demonstrated by the Maneno Mengi experience. This is a very different proposition from having an outside organization or filmmaker record video and construct a story that is then used by members of the community to educate and mobilize around issues they are confronting.

Streaming video footage on the Internet with associated advocacy campaigns

A trailer from Michael Moore's record-breaking documentary *Fahrenheit 911* was streamed on the net and circulated by numerous groups throughout the United States, including the advocacy group <www.moveon.org>, as part of a very successful effort to encourage people to attend the film's premiere and to get involved in voter registration drives for the 2004 presidential elections in the United States. Getting footage on the Internet provides exciting opportunities for advocacy work, especially when supplemented by advocacy components such as background materials, relevant links and resources and a call to action. See the WITNESS Rights Alert online video broadcasts at <www.witness.org> for numerous other examples. Bear in mind, however, that the Internet audience that can view your footage online is limited to those who have fast enough connections and computers to stream or download video, and to hear audio. For that reason, the Internet can be a useful way to reach sympathetic international audiences with high Internet connectivity, or to reach a diaspora or exile population. But it may not be the best strategy for reaching remote rural populations in developing countries, or other communities that may be offline. For more information, see Chapter 3.

Presenting focused, action-oriented video to government, corporate or NGO decision-makers

Amazon Watch, a campaigning environmental NGO, produced the *Camisea Project*, a film that vividly illustrated the damage inflicted on habitats and local communities by a Peruvian gas pipeline. Under mounting pressure from environmental and human rights groups and members of Congress, and after viewing footage shot by Amazon Watch of land already devastated by the pipeline, the board of the taxpayer-supported Export-Import Bank of the United States rejected $1.3 million in financing for the project.

In many cases reaching a key government committee, NGO or business decision-maker will be critical to your advocacy. Many top decision-makers are not regularly exposed to the voices of those affected by the abuses and problems their constituents may be clamouring about. Bringing these voices directly into their offices can be powerfully effective when combined with well-prepared background reports and concrete, realistic recommendations on how to resolve the problems presented. In my experience, it isn't always the number of eyeballs that see the video, but which ones. So targeted screenings before key decision-makers have often generated the strongest results in our partners' advocacy campaigns.

Video presented as evidence before a national court, regional body, or international tribunal

Mental Disability Rights International (MDRI), a leading organization working for the rights of people with mental disabilities, collaborated with WITNESS in late 2003 to prepare a video submission to the Inter-American Commission on Human Rights (IACHR), exposing the dehumanizing conditions at the Neuro-Psychiatric Hospital in Paraguay. The IACHR is part of the pan-Americas legal system. The video focused on two teenage boys, Jorge and Julio, who were locked in isolation cells for over four years, naked and without access to bathrooms. Their cells reeked of urine and excrement and the walls were smeared with feces. In December 2003, MDRI filed an emergency petition before the IACHR requesting intervention on behalf of the boys and 458 others at the hospital. Along with a legal brief, MDRI submitted video documentation of conditions at the facility. Following this, for the first time in its history, the IACHR approved urgent measures to protect the lives and physical integrity of those in psychiatric institutions—a precedent that can now be cited in other countries in the region.

MDRI and WITNESS subsequently brought the issue to the general public by streaming the video on their websites and by collaborating with *CNN en Español* on a follow-up story. After this exposure, the President of Paraguay and the Minister of Health personally visited

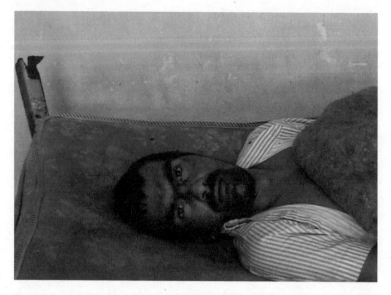

Figure 1.3   Documentation from inside a psychiatric facility, shot by Mental Disability Rights International (MDRI/WITNESS)

the hospital. They removed the director of the hospital from his position and created a committee to investigate the issue.

As you can see, your unedited, or edited, footage may be admissible and powerful as a source of evidence in a court of law or a less formal judicial process. But in order for it to be used, you must be familiar with the procedural requirements of the institution you hope to address. For more detail, see Chapter 6.

Submitting video reports before a United Nations treaty body, special rapporteur or working group

WITNESS supported Human Rights Alert, a group in Manipur, north-eastern India, to provide the UN Working Group on Forced and Involuntary Disappearances with videotaped eyewitness testimony, primarily from family members, about the forced "disappearance" of Sanamacha, a young boy abducted by the Indian government on suspicion of involvement in Manipur's secessionist movement. The UN representatives were visibly moved by the family's grief, and by the credibility of the eyewitnesses' version of events. Although they were familiar with the pattern of disappearances in Manipur, the power of an individual story to supplement accumulated facts and figures was undeniable, and the Working Group made a renewed call for action to the Indian government. Following this and other pressure at the local level, the Manipur State Government constituted a Commission of Inquiry to look into the case.

Video reports for the UN or other inter-governmental bodies can be structured in different ways: as a background documentary on the particular issue addressed; as a complement to a written "shadow report" submitted by an NGO to a UN treaty oversight committee; as direct, unedited testimonials by victims of a violation; or as raw unedited footage of an actual violation or event. In most cases, you will want to provide the material in tandem with written documentation, and link the video content directly to the arguments made in the written submission regarding violations. Bear in mind that opting for this approach will require that you organize screenings of your video report along with question-and-answer periods that can properly inform the UN treaty body or other intergovernmental body viewing your piece. You will need to review the calendars of the relevant UN bodies to determine the appropriate timeframe for your proposed screening or submission. More detail on this process can be found in the online "Video for Change 2000" manual in the training section of <www.witness.org>.

Producing a video public service announcement (PSA)

The Coalition for an International Criminal Court collaborated with WITNESS to produce a powerful PSA mobilizing people to pressure their governments to ratify the International Criminal Court (ICC) statute. The PSA incorporated stark footage of crimes against humanity across the twentieth-century. It was produced in English, French and Spanish in 30-, 60- and 90-second lengths and was broadcast in countries where governments were perceived to be "influenceable" and strategic in terms of ensuring the creation of the ICC. The ratification campaign was ultimately a success and the ICC is now in operation.

A short (generally 30-second) PSA can be an effective tool in your campaign to mobilize a broad audience around an issue. But remember that producing a PSA can be an expensive exercise because it is usually advisable to collaborate with someone experienced in producing commercials and publicity material. Remember also that it is a good idea to identify potential outlets for broadcast, or for widespread grassroots distribution through a civil society network, before you expend the resources to produce a PSA. In many television

markets around the world, major private networks charge high fees
to broadcast a PSA, or exclude PSAs deemed "political" in nature.

Producing a longer-form video documentary

In India, activist media-makers at the Drishti Media Collective, working
with Dalit (so-called "untouchables") rights activists at the Navsarjan
Trust in Ahmedabad, produced the documentary *Lesser Humans*—
55 minutes showing the degradation and disdain experienced by
Bhangis, a particular class of Dalits. As well as collecting other people's
feces, these "manual scavengers" are obliged to remove dead animal
carcasses and clean cowsheds. Shown across India in hundreds of
screenings, with over 5,000 copies distributed, it shocked audiences
with its direct portrait of the conditions Bhangis face and their own
well-articulated understanding of the societal structure holding them
back, contrasted with statements by officials showing their lack of
concern, as well as the endless commissions of inquiry and legislative
initiatives that had never been implemented.

Longer-form documentary storytelling (for instance producing
a 30-minute, 45-minute or feature-length documentary film) can
be an effective way of educating a broad public via broadcast and
public screenings. However, be sure to factor in the extensive cost/
time required, and the difficulty in securing broadcast. If you do not
have a potential broadcast outlet, consider whether the benefits are
worth the investment and financial resources required. A broadcast
on a minor channel, or one that is not targeted to a key audience,
may not be worth the effort. Also note that to produce a one-hour
documentary, a film-maker may shoot 80 hours of raw footage. The
more detailed your list of shots prior to shooting and the more you
prepare for your interviews, the less raw footage you will need to
shoot to achieve the same length for your final piece. For more detail
on this process, see Chapters 3 and 4, and for more discussion on
the challenges of securing a broadcast for advocacy-oriented video,
see Chapter 7.

Video as source for news broadcast and as an archive for news media

In 2000, WITNESS initiated a regional capacity-building project with
long-time partner Joey Lozano—based in Mindanao, in the southern
Philippines—to train the indigenous coalition NAKAMATA to use
video as a tool for documentation and advocacy. In the summer of
2001, NAKAMATA was documenting its process of peacefully and

legally pursuing ancestral land claims when three indigenous leaders were murdered, others attacked, and a village razed. While the local authorities failed to act on the attacks, Lozano and NAKAMATA were on the scene with video cameras, documenting, gathering evidence, interviewing and recording the crime scene. *Probe Team*, the top Philippines investigative news show, aired NAKAMATA's footage on national television where it was seen by millions. The footage also proved to be pivotal evidence to the Philippine National Bureau of Investigation. Under pressure from local and international sources and responding to WITNESS' international call to action via the website, they finally conducted a thorough investigation. In early 2002, murder charges were pressed against three individuals and two arrests were made. The two suspects in the NAKAMATA murders are currently on trial in the Philippines.

As this example reveals, your high-quality unedited footage of a violation can at times be the only source of news or evidence available about an important event. In those cases, you may want to provide copies of your raw footage to local, national, regional and international broadcast outlets in a packaged format, showing the

Figure 1.4   NAKAMATA films the assassination of one of its leaders (NAKAMAŢA/ WITNESS)

This will provide evidence of what actually happened. In the past there were incidents when we were harassed and yet it was us who were summoned to court.

Figure 1.5   NAKAMATA leaders in the Philippines use video documentation (NAKAMATA/ WITNESS)

highlights and providing background information in writing as well as biographies and contact information for potential spokespeople.

However, be aware that the feasibility of getting footage on local news will vary by your location; in parts of the world where media is government controlled it can be impossible to get challenging videotape broadcast. In other parts of the world where media is heavily privatized and commercial, the media may shun substantive coverage of social issues. Furthermore, getting footage on international news channels such as CNN is usually very difficult, and may depend on whether or not your material relates to the cause or issue of the moment. Rather than try to convince a television producer to do a story around your particular issue, you may try to place raw footage on television as source material for another related story. In that case, you may be less likely to see your advocacy intent and story retained in the final piece, but you may be able to obtain some fees for licensing the footage if you choose to charge for it.

A more detailed analysis of storytelling for different audiences is included in Chapter 3, while Chapter 7 focuses on practical tactics for reaching your audiences and using video in advocacy.

To summarize, there are five key steps to take when considering integrating video into advocacy:

- Step 1: Define your goals.
- Step 2: Talk to other people who have worked on the issue you want to tackle. What has worked, what hasn't, and why?
- Step 3: Analyze your style and strengths and identify your allies.
- Step 4: Define your audience.
- Step 5: Decide on a level of involvement and start planning production and distribution.

Once you have done that, and presuming you are as excited as we are about the possibilities of using video in your work, consider a variety of options for engagement—and remember that the strongest campaigns often use video in multiple formats and forums:

- Using video as a grassroots educational or organizing tool in your community or with solidarity groups elsewhere.
- Streaming video on the Internet with associated advocacy campaigns.
- Presenting focused, action-oriented video to key decision-makers.
- Submitting video as evidence before a national court, regional body, or international tribunal.
- Submitting video reports before a UN treaty body, special rapporteur or working group.
- Producing a video public service announcement.
- Engaging in a participatory video.
- Producing a video documentary.
- Using video as source for news broadcast.

Now that you have a brief overview of the ways in which you might consider integrating video into your advocacy work, read on for more detail on the process. Once you have digested the information we provide, you may also want to review the sample WITNESS "Video Action Plan" contained in Appendix I of this book and use it as a guide to plan your own video advocacy campaign.

NOTE

1. Alfonso Gumicio Dragon, *Making Waves: Stories of Participatory Communication for Social Change* (New York: The Rockefeller Foundation, 2001), pp. 283–4.

2
Safety and Security

Katerina Cizek

I think being a human rights advocate goes with the reality that you may put your life at risk. One can be abducted or murdered at any time, and justice may not be achieved. I always think that whatever I can attain in the field, no matter how little, would be of great help. This optimism keeps me going. I always share this kind of perception and optimism with those I work with. By sharing a common vision, we draw strength, inspiration, and courage.

The longer we live, we always say, the more we can accomplish. We become stronger when we think as a single group, not as separate individuals.

Joey Lozano, a veteran WITNESS partner, member of its board of directors and trainer, has dedicated his life to using video for documenting human rights violations in the Philippines. He has survived several assassination and abduction attempts in his efforts to assert indigenous land rights, and to investigate corruption and environmental degradation.

Welcome to the "Safety and Security" chapter, which features user-friendly tips for social justice advocates preparing to shoot video in dangerous environments.

This chapter is intended to be a starting point for discussions and to provide comparative examples that can help you make the best choices for your own circumstances. It is not meant to be a definitive list. Rather, it provides some commonsense practical safety measures.

While you may not be able to eliminate risks, you can anticipate and minimize them. This guide draws on the experiences and resources of seasoned WITNESS partners, videographers, journalists and human rights defenders from around the globe. We explore concrete strategies for preserving the safety of people filmed and of human rights defenders while recording violations. We also raise ethical issues that need to be addressed when working in potentially dangerous conditions.

The chapter is divided into three parts: Preparation, In the Field, and After Filming. There are also five "Top Ten Tips" from knowledgeable filmmakers and activists from around the world. The "Resources" chapter below contains further suggested readings and information about organizations, all of which are accessible via the Internet.

PREPARATION

Preparation is crucial to doing good human rights work and to getting good footage, as well as to staying safe and ensuring the safety of those you film.

Perhaps the most important factor to consider is whether you and your team will be *going in* to an area to film, or whether you will be filming *within your own community*. This distinction will affect many of the safety and security decisions you make.

While *going into* an area may present immediate and critical dangers to you and your team, ultimately, you most probably can leave the area and resume your life. Filming *within your own community,* however, may create risks for you that last for months, sometimes years. Both situations may have long-term impact on community members—those who chose to participate, and even those who have nothing to do with your video project.

In this chapter, we aim to address both sets of circumstances: *going in* to an area, as well as filming *within a place* where you are based. To begin with, we look at conducting preliminary research, risk assessment, issues of trust, deciding whether or not to go undercover, preparing documentation and equipment, planning entry and exit strategies, and learning from others' experiences.

Knowing yourself and your organization

Before we examine risks and how to avoid them, ask some key questions of yourself and your organization. Some of these may be questions you confront daily if you work in a conflict zone or an area with high levels of risk; others may be related to this specific issue you are starting to work on.

- How much risk are you and your group willing to take, and have you really considered why you are doing it? It is vital to know your own limits, and assess what in your life you are willing—and not willing—to risk.
- Who else could be affected by your actions? What about your family, children, or colleagues? What about the community

where you will be filming? What about the possibility of short-term or long-term damage to a cause you are fighting for?

Be very clear about your assignment, what you wish to achieve, and what you may risk or lose in the process, using the "Risk Assessment Checklist" below. Discuss in detail within your organization what the group boundaries are and how each member will fit into the picture. If you are working within an organization that is using video for the first time, make sure that you have a broad and informed discussion within the organization about what the potential risks are and how these can be mitigated. Know that irrespective of how well prepared you are, there will always be an element of risk and uncertainty.

Anand Patwardhan has been making political documentaries in India for nearly thirty years. He warns:

Never begin to "enjoy" danger. Danger is sometimes a necessity imposed by circumstance; it is certainly not something worth seeking out for its own sake. On the contrary, you owe it to your cause to stay alive. We have too many martyrs—too many Gandhis and Guevaras. Now we need success, not martyrdom. So run like a coward [to tell your story] rather than stand up and die. There is no shame in wanting to live. We do love life; that is why we fight for a better world. Save yourself. Also save your tape or film. You are the witness whose pictures must talk.

Risk assessment checklist

Key question:
Do you even need to use video at all? Is video the best strategy? Consider using other forms of media: print, still photos, or audio only. Video can present dangers that may not be worth the risks.

Preparation for filming in any potentially hostile environments should include a risk assessment, if only a mental one. This develops an initial awareness of likely hazards and the precautionary measures needed to avoid or reduce them.

Likely hazards can include:

- Threats or violence against filmmakers or people filmed, either during filming or at a later date
- Being discovered while filming covertly or without official permission
- Detention/arrest/kidnap of people filming or people transporting footage

▶

- Failure of security arrangements for information and material during filming and at later point
- Inadequate communication around consent and safety issues of those filmed

Precautionary measures:

- Planning and research
- Suitable equipment
- Clear protocols for consent
- Personal security
- Information security
- Competent people
- Communication arrangements—before, during, after filming
- Emergency arrangements for yourself and people filmed—during and after
- Clear exit strategy

Knowing the situation

There are always many sides to a conflict. Know the terrain, and think carefully about the situation in which the filming will take place. If you are not from the community where you are filming, getting as much information about the players, the relationships, and conflicts is key. Sensitize yourself to complicated relationships within a community, some of which may seem counterintuitive. For example, drug traffickers in Rio de Janeiro, Brazil, "protect their residents" to promote and protect their trade.

Furthermore, be aware that conditions change. You may have had a good trip to a region a year ago, but things can deteriorate rapidly. Check out current conditions. If you are traveling internationally, there are several resources worth checking out: the US State Department, as well as the British Foreign Office, and the equivalents in Australia and Canada, provide useful travel safety assessments. Consult also with locally based human rights groups who are closer to the ground and ask for their advice. They will usually be able to provide a much more nuanced understanding of the specifics of a situation than the travel advisories.

Even if you are arriving in an area with less preparation than you had hoped for, think about consulting people who will be familiar with the specific threats in different areas—for example, drivers of hired cars or public transport who know the word on the street and have direct experience of travelling to particular areas. However, remember to be careful before you reveal details of your work to strangers.

You need to understand the law and the authorities of the region you are filming in, as well as the general attitude towards journalists or human rights advocates. What are the regulations concerning photographic and video equipment? What is illegal to film? Are journalists respected or are they a target for violence and harassment? How free is the press? What risks do human rights documentors or social justice campaigners face?

Tia Lessin is a US-based filmmaker:

> I was detained outside a prison in New Jersey. They kept asking for the tapes. I refused, because there are no laws against what I did. I knew my rights, and I kept demanding that my rights be respected. Eventually, I was let go, and I got to keep my tapes.

Ronit Avni, who works with Palestinian and Israeli peace workers and filmmakers, recommends paying attention to implicit assumptions:

> Equipment could be misunderstood as weapons in places where suicide bombers operate. Understand the milieu you are working in. For example, a Palestinian-rights activist should be cautious strapping hidden camera equipment to any part of their body, as it could be misconstrued as a bomb.

Joey Lozano describes how a smile has gotten him out of tight situations:

> It's very important to understand the cultural tradition of people in particular regions. For example, in the Philippines we have this very strong affinity for family. Once, a friend and I were arrested by the army. They were all drunk. "This could be the end of me," I thought. They looked menacing—the alcohol, the smell. They tried to pull us into the building. I said: "No, do it out here." The interrogation lasted four hours. Finally, a staff sergeant came. When he paused, I butted-in to ask if he was a married man: "Where is your family? Do they live with you?" He really softened. He missed his kids. He started opening up with family talk. That saved me and my friend. No matter how menacing soldiers look … when you mention family they soften up. If they hadn't, that would've been goodbye for me. You really have to know these

kinds of techniques to be with the oppressors. To be nice with them, but not forget your mission with the oppressed.

Planning what to get on tape

Once you have decided you want to use a video camera as part of your work to defend human rights, you should use the ideas discussed in Chapters 3, 4, and 5 to map out what you will need, and ensure that the material you are gathering is targeted to an audience and with a goal in mind. With a shotlist—your checklist of the video and audio footage that you want to gather—you can start to assess which filming—of who, what, where—will be more risky.

This risk assessment may also affect the order in which you plan to shoot. High-profile interviews with authorities may compromise further shooting, so try to get lower-profile shooting out of the way first. You might want to interview the police/politicians last –because once they get a sense of what you are doing, they may prevent you from filming anything else. However, as with any strategy, evaluate this approach with others who have experience in the same situation—how quickly will your filming project come onto the radar of authorities, and how will this affect your ability to film lower-profile interviews and higher-profile interviews, as well as your ability to keep your footage secure?

Worst-case analysis

Sam Gregory of WITNESS recommends doing a "worst-case analysis" before embarking on any potentially dangerous project. He suggests a systematic approach to identifying what could happen: "You assume the impact if your worst enemy saw this material. Determine the boundaries of what can and cannot be said. It's important not to scare-monger, but it's crucial to be aware of all potential risks." Imagine, for example, if the tapes were taken via a subpoena in a legal investigation and all your material was available to the other side in a legal case.

Frank Smyth, of the Committee to Protect Journalists, recommends: "Never underestimate the ability of bad guys to torture and kill people. So prepare for every contingency."

It is essential to walk through all the potential hazards with your collaborators and subjects so that everyone involved participates with full and informed consent. (For more, see "informed consent," p. 42 below.)

Who should film?

Consider who is in the best position to film in a high-risk context. If someone is well known as an activist, a leader, or a "troublemaker," they are not always the most appropriate person to hold the camera.

Frank Smyth says the best person to collect evidence is often

someone that no one notices. One of those people who enter a room and no one turns their head. When they leave, no one can remember what they look like, perhaps didn't even notice they were there in the first place. Obviously, not a charismatic leader.

In an investigatory context where you may need to elicit information from unwilling interviewees, Anand Patwardhan recommends sending out people that your interviewees have never seen to do the talking:

Pretend to be a technician and not the director. Pretend to be a foreign crew. A few gringos into the mix can help, but this differs from occasion to occasion. Play by ear what the best profile is. [In some cases] sounding irritable and bossy [may be] more convincing.

Building trust: Subjects, team, and network

Trust is a central element to your work. It begins with you and the people you film, but it also includes the team of people you work with directly as you prepare to film, edit, and distribute. It also may involve your family, your colleagues, local scouts, and friends, and even international connections to watch your back and to provide support if you are in trouble. Remember trust is always a two-way street—there is no inherent reason for people in positions of vulnerability to trust you. Both human rights organizations and newsgathering organizations are regularly infiltrated by intelligence agencies. They may also not always represent the situations they cover with full integrity or with due attention to the security of the people they work with.

Trust, loyalty, and confidence can be complicated and multi-layered, especially when using video. How do you make an assessment and navigate difficult trust issues without endangering yourself and others?

The following four case studies showcase the importance of trust. The first story involves navigating multiple layers of trust, but primarily focuses on the filmmakers' relationships with their subjects. In the next story, we look at how a filmmaker might unwittingly endanger team-members. The third case looks at how team-members may betray you. Finally we look at how important it is to have a strong network of trustworthy people as part of a larger "team."

Case study: Trust between you and your subjects

In the 1990s wars had devastated the Balkans—and consequently, all notions of trust. Then, to make matters worse, the media descended on the refugee camps, and created a whole new level of mistrust: network producers running around in search of news-clips, in time for the dinner-hour news, "I need a 17-year old woman who has been raped and who also speaks English—quick!"

South African sociologist/documentary filmmaker Mandy Jacobson and her Croatian/American co-director Karmen Jelinic set out to make a film that explored the real story of mass rape behind the "media revictimization" plaguing the area. They wanted to create a film that could contribute to the true reconstruction of people's lives. The resulting documentary, *Calling The Ghosts*, chronicles the journey of two women, Jadranka Cigelj and Nusreta Sivac, childhood friends and legal professionals, who, after surviving Serbian concentration camps, take on the mission to make rape an internationally recognized crime of war. Through their brave efforts, their torturers were indicted by the International Criminal Tribunal for the Former Yugoslavia.

But when the filmmakers began, Mandy says,

> Trust was a big question throughout the making of the film. We had a lot of justifying to do, to prove that we were different than the rest.
>
> For one thing, we took a long, long time before switching on the camera. Karmen [the co-director] spent seven months with the characters before filming, and we allowed them to interview us, as much as we interviewed them. In fact, we saw their initial mistrust of us as healthy.

"We made all sorts of mistakes all along the way," Mandy remembers. She says that, at first, they brought in an outside cameraman, who had done excellent work in South Africa. But he was not accustomed to the slow pace of this particular project, and got frustrated. "In the end," Mandy says, "the story wasn't locked up. Our central characters weren't signed on. They weren't ready to film." So the cameraman went home, and the filmmakers eventually found a local Croatian cameraman, who was better suited to dealing with the difficult subject and pacing of the film.

"He turned out to be a great feminist himself, and because he was from the area, the women also came to trust him," she says. But when it came time to film in Belgrade, the capital of Serbia, the Croatian cameraman was scared by the implications (going into "enemy territory"), and the filmmakers had to find another crew to shoot those scenes.

The characters' mistrust of the media wasn't the only problem. After Mandy had spent several months in the region, she went to Belgrade and then returned to Croatia. Her subjects did not welcome her with open arms. "My main subject was scared that during my visit to the Serbian capital, I had been duped by the Serbian propaganda."

In advocacy media, the key question for trust, Mandy finds, is "how do you keep your subjects as active participants, from the beginning through to the actual distribution phase?"

Mandy remembers that she felt some real measure of trust had finally been gained only three years into the filming, when the central subjects finally entered the International Criminal Tribunal courtroom in The Hague. "At that moment, they became lawyers again, not just victims. They had found a political context in which to locate their personal pain." The cameras were still rolling, following a story of courage, strength and the power of transformation.

Case study: Interpreter protection
How trustworthy are *you*? Human rights advocates need to consider carefully the implications for the people they interview directly, but they also need to consider the people they employ, or from whom they seek support. This may include local fixers, interpreters, drivers, or even those who provide the team with food or accommodation, especially people working in such situations as war or conflict zones, courts of law, prisons, or police operations. How will you protect these people from the consequences of your actions?

Most of us have heard of "witness protection programs," where investigators and police help protect witnesses who have provided evidence against criminals. But very few investigations—especially those probing war crimes—have properly considered the need for "interpreter protection" for people who provide language assistance in an investigation, whether it be the police, UN, media, human rights advocates and even, by extension, filmmakers.

According to Roy Thomas, a peace operations training consultant,

> Interpreters often know of information that is of value to the intelligence organizations of warring parties. Furthermore, they are associated with foreign institutions that not everyone supports... Unfortunately, these professionals are often abandoned to their sad fate.[1]

Thomas examined UN-led investigations in the Balkans and his own experiences in Afghanistan, and found that after the investigators had left the area, interpreters had been threatened, interrogated or even killed by opposing sides of warring factions. He urges that interpreters be considered as vulnerable as witnesses themselves.

Case study: Suspicious soundman

If you are working with a set of people who are recruited for a particular video, make sure to do thorough background checks. If you do not feel comfortable working with someone, do not risk compromising your security. Even within an organization there may be risks involved in sharing too much information on a video documentation project—make informed decisions about who needs to know the specifics of who, what, where and when you are going to film. Trust your instincts and the informed advice of others who have experience.

If you develop uncertainties during filming, take time to assess. Always consider that people may have divided loyalties, be under pressure from, or may rely financially on the very powers that you are trying to bring down.

One filmmaker, working on an exposé of poor working conditions in factories, became suspicious of a sound person whom she had hired at the location of the shoot during sensitive interviews. The filmmaker decided to fire him. He, in turn, refused to give up the audio backup tapes to the crew for several days, but finally surrendered them. Later, government officials began inquiring about the secret shoot, and confirmed that the sound person had passed on copied audio tapes of the interviews to them.

Case study: International "phone tree" network

Having a solid, trustworthy network of people also involves creating local, regional, national, and international support networks that can help protect you and the people with whom you are working. Who can you turn to in case of trouble? Have that list ready for yourself, your crew, and someone you trust at home. This list should include local, regional, national, and international contacts with current phone (and mobile) numbers. This list should include people who can make things happen in emergency situations. If you are in a high-risk situation you can schedule a daily call to confirm your safety, and ask that steps be taken if you do not check in.

When Frank Smyth, a veteran war correspondent, was abducted in northern Iraq in 1991, his mother had a complete phone list that she called to bring media and political attention to his cause. The list included influential politicians and support groups, which all swung into action. Eighteen days later, Smyth was released.

The right documentation

"Anticipate the worst-case scenario and be prepared for it," says Tia Lessin, a US filmmaker. "At the risk of being alarmist, be prepared! It is irresponsible to send yourself and a crew out without doing your homework."

Tia recommends creating a mission checklist. This list should include all relevant information about you and your crew, and a copy of it should be left at home with someone trustworthy.

A good mission checklist will consist of:

- Photocopy of passports and identification cards
- Photocopy of all travel documents
- All relevant medical and insurance information
- First aid kit
- Full itinerary
- Emergency contacts locally and at home
- Map of region, with weather data and latest updates on locality-specific security concerns
- Local emergency info (e.g. hospital, embassy, bank)
- Serial numbers of all equipment
- Money for emergencies (rental car, flight etc.)

In situations of risk, you should reach an agreement with your colleagues about whether you intend to fully identify yourselves, or whether this is likely to generate further risk. If you decide that you identify yourself if asked, carry with you as much documentation as possible, including passport, visa, and proper accreditation. Ask supporting organizations for letters of introduction, press credentials, and any kind of paperwork that can legitimize your position.

Knowing your equipment

In Chapter 4 we discuss how to choose the right equipment for the project you are working on. Here are some tips to consider in choosing your equipment if you are filming in high-risk situations:

- Understand all aspects of how your camera operates (on/off, focus, light, sound, charging batteries etc.), before entering any potentially high-risk situation where you will need to be focused on the filming. Practice filming in fast-changing situations, and review the "filming a one-off event" section of Chapter 4 (p. 159).
- Practice shooting while not looking and without a tripod.
- Practice filming stable wide shots that capture the whole context of an incident.
- Learn how to use the LCD screen rather than the viewfinder, holding the camera less obviously.
- Consider covering the red record light with black electrical tape, or setting your camera so the red light does not come on. Or carry a small cloth that can cover the body of your camera and protect it from sight as well as from the sun.
- If you are going to film using a hidden camera or from an unusual angle—e.g. with the camera in a bag you are carrying—learn how to operate your camera and get the best-quality and best-composed image you can, given these limitations.
- Consider using a format that is not commonly used in the country where you are filming, so that there will be some delay in reviewing the material if it is seized.

Choosing to go undercover

Going undercover involves taking on a false or alternate identity and essentially deceiving the people you film and/or others around you, with the goal of extracting evidence or information. It can have very serious consequences.

Choosing to go undercover requires making a very careful assessment of the personal risks involved. Undercover filming is likely to increase the risks—during and after filming. Clear emergency and communication backup plans are crucial.

There are also legal risks that either your footage will be inadmissible if you are seeking to use it in a legal context (the criteria for this will vary depending on the country and jurisdiction), or you may face legal action for filming someone or something without consent or permission.

In the end, regardless of how secretive you've been during your shooting, you will need to be completely honest with your audience about how you obtained your footage. What will their reaction be? A backlash may take the form of public disapproval—or the disapproval of your target audience—for perceived illegal or inappropriate techniques.

By going undercover, you may suffer retaliation against your reputation, your person or in a court of law. It may be worth it, to ensure a story gets out—but be aware of the risks.

Case study: Backlash to *The Torture Trail*

The Torture Trail was a 1995 British television documentary, which exposed the involvement of the British government and British companies in the illicit trade of instruments of torture (electro-shock batons) to repressive regimes.

To make his film, director/producer Martyn Gregory assumed an identity as middle-man working for arms dealers. He secretly filmed his negotiations with several British companies, including British Aerospace (BAe). BAe, Europe's biggest "defense" contractor, offered to sell Gregory millions of dollars worth of electro-shock batons—an offer that it later confirmed in writing.

However, after the documentary aired on television, instead of investigating the British role in the arms trade, the British government turned against the messenger: the filmmaker himself. Conservative government ministers in Parliament condemned Gregory, and criminal charges were brought against him because of the methods by which he collected his evidence. Ministry of Defence police arrested Gregory and charged him with "incitement to break the Firearms Act" and "handling illegal weapons." These offences carry a maximum penalty of five years in prison. (The police said they had spotted Gregory handling an electro-shock baton in his film as he mingled with top business executives who were offering to sell them to him.)

Yet, three ministers, including the Deputy Prime Minister, inadvertently undermined the government's offensive against Gregory. They replied to viewers who had written to the government to protest the revelations in *The Torture Trail*. These replies were not protected by parliamentary privilege as the attack on Gregory in Parliament had been. In their letters the ministers alleged that the program was "'contrived" and "scaremongering," and suggested that Gregory had persuaded the British companies to "offer to supply goods for the purpose of making a story that otherwise did not exist."

Gregory sued for libel, and won an apology from the government in the High Court. The government also acknowledged that the program was "properly researched," and paid him $100,000 damages and costs. It was the first and only time a journalist has won a libel action against the British government. Two years later, the Ministry of Defence dropped the criminal charges against the filmmaker.

Gregory spent considerable time, effort, and money fighting to reclaim his reputation. This battle was the subject of his 1996 film, *Back on the Torture Trail,* which examined the British government's reaction to the issues raised in the original documentary and how it had deflected demands for an inquiry. The second film also showed how the British trade in electro-shock batons was continuing as usual, despite the scandal surrounding the first documentary.

The *Torture Trail* documentaries inspired years of Amnesty campaigns against British involvement in the torture trade. Eventually, nine years later, in 2004, the government made illegal the practice of "brokering" the sale of torture weapons that Gregory's films had exposed.

Case study: Not "libel" but fraud

Will the public and even a court of law question your moral authority about going undercover, thereby deflecting from the issue you aimed to target? In this case in the USA, journalists were scrutinized for their undercover methods.

Following up on a tip about unsanitary food handling practices at a major supermarket chain called Food Lion, ABC, a major US network, sent in two reporters in 1992. The journalists lied to get jobs with Food Lion in order to videotape, using a hidden camera, food handling practices at the stores. After the exposé aired, instead of facing the accusations of food safety violations, Food Lion sued ABC for trespass, breach of loyalty, and fraud. It did not sue for libel.

Food Lion undermined ABC's reporting methods with a side-door legal strategy focusing on the falsification of employment applications and the failure of the workers to fulfill their assigned duties. In 1997, the jury supported Food Lion's argument and decided on a US$5.5 million punishment.

An appeal court eventually reversed the verdict, ruling that Food Lion did not prove all the elements of a fraud claim, especially because it sidestepped a libel case.

Nonetheless, for over five years, the case roused public debates around honesty and transparency in newsgathering methods.

Preparing to go undercover

> **Key questions**
>
> Are you aware of all the risks involved in going undercover? What kind of retaliation may you or others face? Is it worth the potential jeopardy? Might your methods backfire in attaining your advocacy goals? Is there any other way you can obtain the information that would involve less threat?

Going undercover may involve preparing a false or alternate identity, as well as learning how to film covertly. Both can be time-intensive processes that should not be hurried.

Arranging to take on an.alternate identity can take a lot of time and effort. What do you need to make your false identity work? How long do you need to maintain the identity, and what do you need to do to keep your story straight?

The length and intensity of the undercover mission will determine how much preparation is required. Sometimes, changing your clothes and "fitting in" is enough. For example, in the Philippines, Joey Lozano pretended to be a miner to get inside a gold mine and document human rights and environmental violations:

I looked like a mine laborer. I wore a dirty shirt, denim pants, a T-shirt, and then I wrapped my camera in a T-shirt, put it in a cement bag, and got through the checkpoints. I did that for about a week. I'd go back in the early morning and then pull out before dark came in the next day. I made friends with some laborers, and then I was able to make my film. It was shown on *Inside*

Story, which was at that time the number-one TV magazine program in the Philippines.

One filmmaker decided to create an official "spin" about the subject of her documentary. She wrote a film proposal describing an innocuous documentary focused on port cities around the world. This got her official film permits to enter and film in normally military-sensitive port areas in Dakar, Senegal, and Guinea-Conakry, where she documented the conditions of stowaways and the trafficking of humans on cargo ships.

Simon Taylor of the international environmental NGO, Global Witness, posed as a "ignorant foreign businessman" as he and his partner traveled the border between Thailand and Cambodia investigating the illegal timber trade for three years. "The more ignorant we were, the better," he remembers. By acting this way, Simon and his partner were able to ask many more questions without raising suspicions.

To film undercover—either with a specialized hidden camera or an adapted or hidden normal camera—you should ensure that you can handle the equipment in high-stress situations without any hesitation, and that you have practiced filming with the camera. See pp. 31 and 144 for more information.

Entry and exit strategies

There are a number of strategies for getting safe access to areas where you need to film, and for being able to film material in areas where this is forbidden or difficult.

Francisco Bustamente of MINGA, a WITNESS partner in Colombia, enters remote parts of the country by joining humanitarian missions in which the UN and other aid agencies are participating. He also enters with foreign journalists and passes for one of them. If neither scenario is possible, he enters the areas via paths through the jungle or routes little used by the armed groups.

Tia Lessin got her crew into Disney World, Florida, by arming each videographer with a makeshift "family"—each cameraperson was given a fake partner and several kids. They were going undercover to examine labor conditions in the entertainment park, and under the guise of mini-families, managed to pull 12 minutes of material from each camera before getting stopped by Disney's notoriously tight security force. One cameraman, when stopped by security, began crying, claiming that they had ruined his family's vacation—buying him enough time to pass on tapes to a waiting production assistant, who got out of the park with the material.

In recent years, several filmmakers have used the cover of being a tourist to get into regions inconspicuously. For example, one filmmaker managed to enter Sri Lanka to investigate human rights violations on the pretext that she was filming an anthropological study of ancient archaeological ruins. Another human rights group got into Pakistan by packing their camera in a car trunk full of mountain gear, maintaining that they were going mountain climbing.

Burma Issues is a WITNESS partner that works with marginalized and victimized grassroots communities inside Burma, where a brutal military regime represses its people. Often their documentors must travel through zones controlled by government forces. Every time they move into a new area, the documentors arrange a back-up rendezvous point in case of fighting. To be less conspicuous, documentors will try to dress like locals, and carry their equipment in bags similar to those the villagers use, hiding the camera underneath food or wrapping it in a swathe of cloth. They also keep the labels on recorded tapes blank, until they are in a safe camp.

Figure 2.1 Woman escaping through the forest from Burma's military (Burma Issues/ WITNESS)

Before you enter an area to film you should always know how you will leave, and have an agreed alternative strategy. Plan ahead for your exit. Know what to do with your footage once you've captured it. Know how you and your tapes will get out safely. Sometimes, you may have to separate yourself from your material.

Staying healthy

Whether you are traveling to a foreign country, a neighboring state or province, or working in your own community, health and medical issues are fundamental to staying safe. Consult a qualified medical expert about medical risks in the region, necessary precautions, including vaccinations (proof of which may be required in crossing some borders), and medicines.

Carefully consider the medical threats to those around you, and be prepared to deal with them. Also remember not to underestimate the less obvious threat. Far too often deaths in the field are caused not by war, but by road accidents. Tommi Laulajainen of Médecins Sans Frontières (MSF, an NGO dedicated to providing medical support in areas of conflict), says a crucial safety concern is vehicle maintenance: "Parts, proper care, and safe driving can save your life."

Irrespective of where you are traveling, a first aid kit containing the following is essential:

- Bandages
- Sterile sutures
- Disposable gloves
- Plastic airway device or tubing for breathing resuscitation
- Scissors
- Safety pins
- Plastic bags
- Flashlight
- Adhesive tape
- Crazy glue
- Antibiotic ointment
- Sterile needles

Be careful using basic medications, including aspirin, as some people respond negatively to certain drugs. Be sure of your own medical information (pre-existing conditions, drug allergies, prescription drugs, blood type) as well as those of your colleagues. Finally, stay healthy and fit. There's nothing worse than becoming an unnecessary burden to those around you, especially in times of danger.

Insurance and pressure to take risks

Health and travel insurance remain a luxury for many people in the world. However, if you are in a position to do so, ask employers or organizations for support. Is there anyone who might be able to insure you for medical attention or evacuation should you or your colleagues require it?

If you are documenting or reporting on social justice issues it is possible that you may be approached by media outlets to provide material to them as a freelancer. Newspapers, TV, and radio stations may be interested in you and your work in the form of stories and images. Increasingly, media organizations are relying on freelancers because it is cheaper and easier than being responsible for full-time employees.

However, in this situation, know your professional and employment rights, and do not let a media source pressure you into taking undue risks. As Tina Carr of the Rory Trust Fund, a support organization for safety and security of freelance journalists, points out, "This means that you shouldn't ever feel forced by an employer to do anything you do not wish to do. Without proper training and insurance you do not have to take any job you don't feel comfortable with." Tina insists that employers need to take responsibility for the potential human risks involved in any story, whether they are sending out full-timers or freelancers. This means proper training, proper pay, and proper insurance policies.

Filming in conflict zones

Recently, much attention has been given to the dangers facing journalists in conditions of war and conflict zones. Many professional (mostly Western) journalists are now offered training in military-style workshops covering first aid, risk assessment strategies, protection gear (helmets, bullet-proof vests, etc.), dealing with biochemical weapons or landmines, what to do in case of kidnapping, and a range of other skills.

An excellent, free guide, *On Assignment: Guide to Reporting in Dangerous Situations*, is available to download on the website of the Committee to Protect Journalists at <www.cpj.org>. This guide first addresses issues facing the journalist who "flies into" a conflict zone: health and physical precautions, emergency contingency plans, cultural, comportment, and linguistic knowledge, getting close to a story, battlefield and rules of engagement, as well as surviving captivity. The guide also has a new, extended section on "sustained risk" intended for local journalists who work in the areas they live in. It covers issues of assessing personal risk, creating contingency plans, and risks for freelancers and fixers.

Yet, the biggest danger for many social justice advocates may not be a random bullet in a conflict zone. As we discuss below, those most at risk are usually the locally based human rights activists and journalists who dare to cover the stories no one else will cover. They are often killed in reprisal for their reporting, and the real need is for institutional change, not patchwork solutions of training or involuntary exile.

IN THE FIELD

There are many different strategies for staying safe while in the field with video technology. In some contexts, being open and officially sanctioned, and having the paperwork to prove, it can make things safer. In other situations, catching violations covertly may be the only way to prevent further violence.

Now, armed with your plans, preparations, your training, and your wits about you, you are ready to begin shooting.

The camera as a shield or an incitement?

Sometimes the presence of a camera can save lives. In other situations, people with cameras are targeted for particular attention. You will need to determine how this applies in your situation.

Joey Lozano recalls, with a touch of humor, the challenges he faces:

> In many situations, when I go with indigenous people trying to recover their lands, the mere presence of a video camera saves them from outright massacre by armed men who are blocking their way. It happened many times in Mindanao [the southernmost island of the Philippines, where Joey works]. When I go out of the community, armed men just wait for my disappearance and [then] they go back and start shooting people. It's those kinds of incidents that really convince me of the power of video … especially in these kinds of life-and-death situations.
>
> The good thing is that the video can save you from being shot because those guys who hold the guns would avoid getting shot with a camera. I

imagine the indigenous people would laugh at me because it's like a Western show. It's a quick draw with the other side having guns and me with my camera—and we just wait for each other to shoot. It's a funny situation.

Figure 2.2   Joey Lozano (Necessary Illusions Productions)

On the other hand, at Burma Issues, documentors must travel between dangerous and opposing forces. One of the members says:

It's very dangerous to be caught with a camera, almost worse than having a gun. Government forces don't like filming, and information collectors. They know technology has been improved, and that video can show the truth. The opposing forces also know the power of media.

Anand Patwardhan has seen a shift in reaction to his camera:

Sometimes the camera helps. Police are much better behaved. Not so the fundamentalists these days... They have had too much bad press, and seem less inclined to live and let live, unless you can pull a fast one and pretend you are one of them. That is not as easy as it sounds.

In the US, protestors against corporate globalization have claimed that people filming demonstrations and rallies are specifically targeted for arrest or harassment by law enforcement officials.

Remembering your mission

Only film when necessary. As Simon Taylor, of Global Witness says:

> Don't document everything. You can waste a lot of time. Know what you need. The key lesson is to understand what is worth documenting and what to do with it.

Don't take unnecessary risks. For example, in certain countries simply filming military personnel or even government buildings can be against the law. Why jeopardize a mission with footage that is not relevant or useful? Also, be careful whom you talk to, even informally. Word on the street spreads fast, so remain on a "need-to-know" basis.

Protecting the people you film

Working in partnership with your subjects to ensure their security is the most important consideration in any kind of human rights documentation.

Consent

You must ensure, first and foremost, that the subject understands fully what you are doing and how you plan on using the material. Are they comfortable being associated with the issue, or any issue that may appear on the raw tapes and in the final edited version? It is a good idea to do a "worst-case analysis" in which you discuss the implications of the filmed material being seen by a range of people. See below for more information.

Communication

Be careful how you contact people you are filming in situations of danger or potential danger. Consider using a mediator, and work with your interviewees to determine what will be safest for them.

Location

Be aware of the location you choose for conducting interviews. Is it secure? Choose neutral locations where you and interviewees can enter and leave via different entrances and exits.

Informed consent

Informed consent is critical to responsible video documentation, especially for people who will remain in positions of vulnerability. The key issue in most human rights-related situations is that informed consent protects not only the person filming—i.e. that you have the legal releases to protect yourself against future legal action— but the person filmed, particularly in cases where this person has already been victimized. Informed consent is not a matter of forms and paperwork, but a question of whether someone filmed truly understands the potential impact on them, and consents to the filming and distribution with this knowledge.

As a human rights or social justice filmmaker you should consider three levels of permission and consent:

1. The legal paperwork that TV channels (especially in the US) will require, but which has limited legal standing. The legal language and the written nature of these consent forms may also be difficult for people with limited literacy or exposure to this kind of language.
2. The on-camera consents following explanation of a project. Here a person who is to be filmed hears an on-camera explanation of a project, and then states their name on camera and their agreement to be filmed.
3. The informed consent that comes from understanding possible risks and benefits of being on camera, and making a choice to be there, and to stipulate an acceptable level of risk. This may include the possibility of rescinding permission to use the footage in the future, if the level of risk increases. Usually the discussion around risks and benefits, and the process of informed consent, happens off-camera.

Sam Gregory advises that in remote communities with limited access to television and other media, it may be necessary to explain in detail the potential impact of a TV broadcast, and the fact that what you shoot may end up on TV:

Sometimes people aren't aware of the potential scale of a broadcast, or the impact it may have on privacy. You need to discuss the potential of one million people seeing the material, and you need to discuss the potential downsides, but also how one million viewers may help the cause.

Possible questions for on-camera consent

On-camera consent can include the answers to the following questions:

1. Please state your name and the date of this interview.
2. Do you understand what we are doing? Please, in your own words, explain.
3. Do you consent to your interview being included in this project, including video and (state various forms of media you may use, including print, photos and Internet)?
4. Do you know who may see the final video?
5. Are there any restrictions to using the information you provide us with or video itself that we need to be aware of?
6. Are you aware you can stop the filming process at any time, in order to ask questions or have a time-out?

See Appendixes III and IV for sample personal release forms.

This analysis of the impact of widespread distribution should take place alongside the "worst-case" analysis of the possibility of a person's worst enemy seeing the footage.

You should be upfront about who the audience may be, and into whose hands material may fall once the information goes public. You should advise subjects if you plan to use the material in any other form, e.g. as a still image in a newspaper or a book, or in a written document.

Some people may change their minds later. You have to respect that, and if you can, return to a subject before the images go public to ensure you have real consent. If possible, review the taped material with your subjects, and go step by step through the material and shots you plan to use in an edit.

Case study: Withdrawn consent

Situations and perspectives can change throughout the making of a film, and subjects may decide to withdraw their consent—during the filming itself, or later, during editing—especially after they've seen the rough cut (see Chapter 5, pp. 174–5, for more on informed consent during the editing process). As an advocate, you need to remain open to the possibility that subjects may decide to withdraw participation altogether, and that it may mean the end of your film— or a sequence or two. Very occasionally, some advocacy projects, like the one described on p. 175, result in withdrawn consent that nullifies the entire film altogether.

When Mandy Jacobson and Karmen Jelinic finished their fine cut of *Calling the Ghosts*, they had a huge argument about whether or not to show their subjects the final film. Mandy, coming from a more classic filmmaking perspective, argued that they shouldn't, and that it would compromise their "editorial control," while Karmen insisted that even though they had the subjects' full, informed consent, this was a moral question, and the participants' final contribution was crucial.

"I am glad I listened to Karmen, for we had to respect the political power of testimony," says Mandy today. It had been two years since they had finished filming, and they were surprised about which segments subjects asked the filmmakers to remove. Two women, who had originally been interviewed (their dialogue had not been used in the final film), asked the filmmakers to remove all video images of them at a refugee camp. This request meant disassembling a beautifully constructed montage sequence.

One of the principal subjects, who had revealed intimate and difficult topics in direct testimony, asked only that one sequence be taken out—that of her parents bantering about her marital status.

In the end, Mandy and Karmen confronted only minor changes. They were changes made on moral grounds, for they had already secured the necessary legal releases. Clearly, the subjects were thinking about rebuilding their lives back in Bosnia, and often filmmakers do not think about the repercussions of their work back in the communities they were filming in.

Obscuring and concealing identity

Some people may agree to be filmed, but ask that you conceal their identity or location. The identity of people on film can be deduced from a number of indicators:

- Their face is visible
- Their name is provided in the dialogue or on-screen

- Their clothing is distinctive
- Their voice is recognizable
- They refer to places, locations, or people who are identifiable and specific
- They are seen in the company of people who can be identified

There are usually two points at which you can hide the identity of someone who you have filmed—when you are filming, and during the editing process.

In general you have more options if you shoot high-quality footage in the field, and then alter it in the editing room. However, security should always be your paramount concern.

If the threat of confiscation of original material—either in transit or from an archived location—is high, it is a good idea to conceal identity during the filming process, and it may be unwise to have subjects identify themselves on camera.

Some subjects may also specifically request that you obscure their identity during the shoot, and not wait till the editing stage.

To do this you can:

- Ask the person not to mention specific names or places
- Ask them not to wear distinctive clothes
- Use strong back lighting to turn the person's image into silhouette, with them either facing the camera or in profile (see Figure 2.3)
- Film out of focus so that the person's face cannot be recognized
- Not light the person's face in a scene
- Film their hands or other part of their body rather than their face
- Film from behind them so that their face is not visible, or film them in profile
- Film them with a cap shading their eyes: eyes are the most recognizable part of someone's face (see Figure 2.4)

Be conscious of asking sensitive questions. Offer to stop the camera at any time, and to replay interviews once you finish filming to give vulnerable subjects a chance to review the material.

In the editing process there are other alternatives. These include:

Figure 2.3   During production, identity can be concealed by silhouetting an interviewee (Oxygen Media LLC/Witness)

Figure 2.4   Wearing non-distinctive clothing and a hat concealing face in an interview on forced labor conducted by Burma Issues (Burma Issues/WITNESS)

- Obscuring faces in the editing process. This can be achieved either be a digitized effect over the whole face or other identifying marks, or by placing a digital bar over the eyes only (see Figure 2.5).

Figure 2.5   A digitized face conceals identity in *Bought & Sold* (Global Survival Network/ WITNESS)

- Obscuring identifying marks in the foreground, background or on the interviewee, e.g. a logo on a shirt
- Using sound edits to remove names and place locators.
- Distorting voices to make them less identifiable
- Using only an audio track
- Not showing faces or identifying characteristics, but using other shots of hands or of a non-identifiable interview location (sometimes with the interviewee seen in extreme long shot), alongside the audio track of the interviewee

---

Case study: Protecting identities in Tibet
Tibet has been called the world's largest prison. For almost fifty years it has been under Chinese government rule.

Robbie Barnett, Lecturer in Modern Tibetan Studies at Columbia University, and one of the founders of the Tibet Information Network, says:

> Over and over again, in the last 25 years, we've seen Western journalists going in opportunistically, looking for forbidden footage to "shed light on the repression," while putting local people at risk, and exposing them to potential severe retaliation at the hands of the government

The first such documentary project came out in the late 1980s, when, seeking first-hand eyewitness accounts of torture and repression, Vanya Kewley, a British journalist, filmed and used interviews with nuns describing the torture they'd endured under the Chinese regime. Even though Kewley blurred some faces to obscure their identities in the final film broadcast on British television, other faces were shown openly. Chinese authorities were able to track down several Tibetans, who were then arrested, according to the *Guardian* newspaper. Those arrested included a nun who later said she was tortured.

Prior to the television broadcast, Robbie Barnett says he asked Kewley and the television station a few questions. He recalls:

> I asked them how they knew that the women in the film would be safe. "What measures had she taken to monitor their situation after the broadcast?" She told me the women had consented to the interviews, and that was enough for her. I couldn't convince her that so-called "informed consent" wasn't enough in this situation. But the onus was on her to prove why she "needed" to show these interviews. What purpose would it serve? Too often people are persuaded that the film will revolutionize their world, that the film will make a difference if they participate. Unfortunately, that's not the case. The extra impact of revealing their faces is minimal and is rarely worth the suffering they will endure.

Much later, Robbie heard of further acts of retaliation by the government, on a woman who had not even appeared in the film, but was tortured in prison for six months because she had merely provided the filmmaker with shelter during production.

In a similar case in the late 1990s, a Tibetan man escaped from prison in Tibet. He had been imprisoned for more than four years after he was caught working for a German woman making a secret documentary there. He said he had been beaten up and accused of being a spy. Maria Blumencron, the film's director, told the *Guardian*: "For more than four years, I lived in hell wondering what happened to my guide, and I often wished I hadn't done this film."

But Bluemencron never explained why she had needed to put the Tibetan at risk in the first place, notes Robbie: "She could have shot her film in Tibet as a tourist without employing any local people to work with her."

Recently, a 2004 Canadian project, called *What Remains of Us*, came under fire by human rights groups for threatening the lives of Tibetans. The filmmakers had secretly filmed people in Tibet watching a recording of their exiled spiritual leader, the Dalai Lama. It is a political crime in Tibet even to possess an image of the Dalai Lama. The film features close-ups of people's faces watching a laptop computer recording of the Dalai Lama's message, and their personal reactions.

The filmmakers and producers (from the National Film Board, funded by the Canadian government) insisted they had taken precautions while filming, and would now place security guards at the public screenings at film festivals, searching for cameras and recording devices at the door.

But critics remain concerned about the efficacy of this method. Robbie Barnett suggests "The security measures at these screenings were always more of a publicity hype than true protection for the people involved in the film."

"We are very concerned with how this film was shot and the fact that it is being shown," said John Ackerley, of the International Campaign for Tibet, told the *Guardian*. "The desire to show films like this often outweighs the risk to the people inside. All too often, the filmmakers' results are disastrous for the Tibetans involved."

Key question

If confiscated, will the pictures you record seriously jeopardize someone's life? Consider recording and/or transporting audio only, if any kind of visual clue might compromise your project and the people involved. Audio can now be recorded digitally, and stored on very small discs. Audio can be recorded on your video camera, or recorded and transferred to some cellphones, Walkmans, iPods, handheld computers, hard drives and laptops. Importantly, audio is much more difficult to trace than video.

Conducting a hostile interview

In some cases you may be filming interviewees who are hostile to you, your project or your community. In these cases you should take extra care with:

Timing

- Will the rest of your filming be compromised after you request this interview? (Perhaps you need to do this interview last.)
- Could your interview interfere with other decisions affecting the community?

Confidentiality for other interviewees

- Can you ensure you will not reveal information about other interviewees to your hostile subject?
- Will you be under surveillance after you request/conduct this interview, and might this endanger others?

Legal consents

- Ensuring you have the proper, signed release from your subject is key.
- Ensure that you can stand behind the description of your project that you give to the interviewee. Remember they may be taping the interview so that they have a record of it too.

Securing the interview itself could well be your first problem. There may be limited access to the subject, or you may have to go through others—even public relations departments—to request the interview. You may be faced with delays and silence. At this stage, you may need to convince the subject why it may be in their best interest to have a voice in your project.

You may need to be persistent in acquiring the interview: phone calls, letters, and even personally waiting for someone in their waiting room or office. If you can, be sure to film the process of attempting to gain an interview. The footage can work well in editing, and can be used to demonstrate that you were even-handed in seeking to represent the "other side."

Once you have access to the interview subject, you need to consider:

- Signing the legal release/consent form *before* you begin the interview.
- *Prioritizing* your interview questions—start with easy questions, but don't wait too long for the tough ones, because the interview could end at any time.

- There is essentially *one key question* in any interview—the one you want the subject to answer. Do not be afraid of rephrasing your question and asking it again if you feel their answer is not complete. Do not be afraid of repeating it, again and again.

Interview strategies vary. Sometimes it can work to your advantage to sit back and let the subject do the talking. Other times, you may need to try a more confrontational interview approach, in which you are ready with your facts and your questions, to challenge your subject, and not let them get away without dealing with the issues.

Bear in mind different visual strategies: consider including the interviewer in the frame, as audiences will see how the subject is reacting, and to whom he/she is reacting.

Surprise and ambush interviews

You may never get access to your hostile subject using the conventional routes of simply asking for an interview. If the subject is a public figure, consider using one of their public appearances as a platform to conduct a *surprise interview*. For example, a politician may appear at a school opening. Might you be able to get close enough and ask a question or two before, during, or after the ceremony?

Sometimes they will be less willing to dismiss your questions as they want to maintain their public image. By getting them on camera in a public situation you may also be able more readily to hold them accountable for what they say.

Some filmmakers have resorted to *ambush interviews*. This involves "ambushing" the subject while they are leaving their office, or at the airport, or the street. You will need to have the cameras rolling at all times, and in reality, you will probably not get many answers to your questions. Rarely do hostile interview subjects stop and talk to you on the street if they have already declined an interview in their office. But what you can get, if it is not too risky, is visual imagery that clearly says "This person refused to talk to us, even though we tried!"

Security during a hostile interview: Exit strategy

If you feel you or your crew may be under direct physical threat during or directly after the interview, make sure someone on the outside is ready to respond in case of emergency. Ideally, you will have contact by cellphone, but also arrange a deadline by which, if you do not emerge, a back-up plan kicks in. Who should be called if you do not emerge on time? What is the plan to get you out safely? See p. 35 for more.

Surveillance and routine

In areas where there is a continuous threat of abduction or assassination, change your routine constantly. Where kidnapping is rife, avoid sleeping in the same place twice and eating at the same place at the same time every day. Vary your routes. Do not inform strangers where you are going, or when.

Also be aware of potential surveillance. For example, in Ecuador, Frank Smyth noticed that an ice-cream vendor kept parking outside his house, every day, yet never sold any ice cream. "Sometimes," he says, "intelligence services are not very competent." Watch out for new people who appear in your neighborhood. If you think you are being followed or watched, ask a friend to follow you as you take a new route to work, for example, and see if anyone else is also following.

Case study: Informants next door

Burma Issues makes video films about the people's movement in Burma—examples of their work can be seen on the WITNESS and Burma Issues <www.burmaissues.org> websites. The group sends out Karen ethnic minority documentors to travel to remote communities. These villages are under the control of either the SPDC (Burmese military government) or ethnic minority opposition groups. They also travel to the temporary camps of internally displaced people who have been driven from their homes by the military. Documentors will stay in these sites for up to two weeks to collect evidence of human rights abuses.

Once they are in villages, it is a challenge to find people who will speak out. In areas under government control, the most informed individuals (the ones with an overview of the situation) don't want to be filmed/seen on video as they will be recognized; while those who are willing to be interviewed tend to be people with specific grievances. People who are most likely to talk include: people who have lost hope because they have been disabled or are elderly; people in areas under ethnic opposition control, and IDPs (internally displaced people), who will tell all, except where they're located.

People also cannot trust their neighbors. There are informants in all villages, and they will report on the presence of a documentor. In addition, the headmen of villages are obliged to report intruders to the authorities or potentially face penalties themselves.

One of the documentors notes that:

> Everything that happens in the village, the villagers should tell the SPDC. The headmen have to tell, because there are people who will tell the SPDC that people have visited even if they don't. When I visit, most times they don't tell, but sometimes in the village there are visiting Burman traders (for example, ice-cream vendors), who are not Karen [the local ethnic minority]—and they may go and tell.

In many cases a Burma Issues documentor will take subjects to a safe place outside the village to do an interview. Another documentor says: "I'll bring the villagers aside to a quiet place or inside a house... Or an opposition soldier ... brings them to me without them being directly linked to me."

People are wary of sharing information with human rights groups. They have done this before with no discernible improvement in their lives. For this reason Burma Issues says it's important to explain why the filming is taking place and who the intended audience is. Burma Issues staff will explain their organization and the video project. They explain the importance of documenting abuses, and promise that if anonymity is requested, they won't show a subject's face.

> The important thing for the documentor is to be friendly with the villager, so the relationship between the villager and the person filming will be good, and so we can get more information. Sometimes, when we are in an opposition-controlled area, we spend a week with a villager, celebrate a festival with them, and go and sleep in their house and eat with them. In this way we can increase the relationship with them. But they still worry about what will happen to both the documentor and them if they are caught.
>
> We also sometimes make an agreement with villagers that if someone they don't trust comes in to the village, they are going to lie and say that we are their brother or that we come from such and such a village. The problem here is not in SPDC areas, where Burmans cannot tell one Karen ethnic person from another, but in areas controlled by ethnic-minority allies of the SPDC, as they are also Karen and can recognize us.

Protecting your equipment/tapes

Frank Smyth says: "Try and get the information and the tapes out of the situation of immediate risk. The most dangerous time is when you have the tape."

Making the right decision about how to protect and securely transport your tapes will always depend on the local situation you face. The scenarios and tips below should help inform this decision. However, if in doubt get rid of a tape, or destroy it, particularly if it contains sensitive information or if it contains unconcealed identities that might jeopardize an individual's safety or life.

In general, carrying a spare, unwrapped tape readily accessible and half-shot, or fast-forwarded is always a good idea. This tape should contain innocuous material. If you are approached while filming and told to hand over your tape, you substitute the "dummy" tape for the tape in your camera.

One strategy for tape protection is to never let them out of your sight. Tia Lessin says:

> When I am in the field, I carry all my material with me. I do not even trust the crew to carry the recorded tapes. I carry them. I don't ever leave recorded tapes in a hotel room, in a car, anywhere. They are always on me. I have a big backpack. It's just a good habit to get into.

Joanna Duchesne, a producer and filmmaker who has covered human rights worldwide for Amnesty International, recalls:

> A few years ago, we were filming a story of a human rights lawyer who was being targeted for her work in Tunisia. The government was not keen for this story to be told. We knew that our rooms were being searched while we were out filming, and that we were being followed. I carried the tapes on me at all times, and labelled them so that they looked like tourist tapes. We knew that other film crews doing human rights stories had had their tapes confiscated by the police at the airport, so we smuggled the real tapes out of the country and carried a dummy set through customs.

Avoid labelling tapes with actual names, and separate information on people from the tapes themselves if you are transporting them in a situation of risk. Use coding and numbering that only you and someone at home base understand.

If you believe that your tapes might be erased or destroyed rather than used as evidence against you or people you have filmed, consider copying your tapes as soon as possible after filming. This can be as simple as making a camera-to-camera copy between two cameras in the field. In situations where you have a support team around you, consider having a person who acts as a "media-runner" and takes tapes to a safer location as soon as they are filmed.

In tandem with this strategy it is also possible to deploy multiple cameras—one, a larger, more ostentatious camera, and other smaller or hidden digital cameras with no accompanying crew that can search out the candid shots while the larger camera absorbs people's attention.

If you can't get your tapes out, it may be better to hide them. During the 1991 Santa Cruz cemetery massacre in East Timor, Max Stahl, a videographer, had his camera rolling while the military carried out atrocities. He then hid the tapes among the gravestones, and put a blank tape in his camera, which was later seized. Afterwards he returned to the cemetery, and retrieved the original tapes to show the world how several hundred people had been gunned down during a peaceful funeral. International awareness and recognition of Indonesian repression in East Timor hugely increased as a consequence.

Being undercover

Being undercover is often a gruelling experience, and remaining confident is key to keeping up appearances.

Joey Lozano notes:

> Don't look too different from the people you are with. Shoot as if it were a natural thing, not giving the impression that you are doing something against the law. Be on alert for any potential danger and be ready to move away when the situation so demands. Being, or looking, too brave is sometimes taken by an enemy as an act of provocation. Wearing a constant smile does wonders.

Remaining flexible and adapting quickly to circumstances can help you improve your techniques. When Simon Taylor was first investigating timber camps on the Thai–Cambodian border, posing as a businessman, he spent a lot of time talking to the "flunkies," the low-end workers at the checkpoint gates of the camp. He soon realized that it was not only getting him nowhere, it was raising suspicions. He began to understand the hierarchy. So he started "leaving the flunkies in the dust." He tried driving straight through the checkpoints, and arrogantly demanding to speak to the boss deep inside the camp. Suddenly, he was getting access to the top level, and getting exactly the information he required.

Case study: Undercover with the mafia

Gillian Caldwell (Executive Director of WITNESS, then with the Global Survival Network, now called WildAid) and Steve Galster (of Global Survival Network) conducted a two-year undercover investigation of the Russian mafia, the sex trade, and the trafficking of women (see also Chapter 1). Their investigation spanned several continents: they filmed in Moscow, Vladivostok, Germany, Hong Kong, Macau, Switzerland, Japan, and Brighton Beach. Their mission was to document all aspects of the recruiting, contract negotiation, transportation, and placement of women in the sex trade.

Before embarking on their investigation, they created an entire dummy company, complete with a press kit, business cards, PO box, phone number, and fax number—all under the name "International Liaisons." Under this company name, they claimed to deal in foreign models, escorts, and entertainers. This pretext, coupled with the right introductions, gave them access to a global network of traffickers and women involved in the sex trade around the world. They rented an apartment in Moscow, and began their mission.

"The risks were substantial," Gillian says. "We were doing this in the mid-1990s, at a time when the mafia had 'pay scales' to kill people, anywhere in the world." Should they have been discovered with the camera, simply leaving Russia would not have guaranteed their safety: the mafia's tentacles reached far and wide. Their investigations involved setting up meetings with the mafia, as well as hiring prostitutes and talking with them about their experiences. Because gender was a factor, and the presence of a woman would have raised suspicions during meetings, Steve did much of the up-front work alone.

Meetings were secretly recorded, mostly with miniature cameras inside buttonholes and ties, and microphones, strapped to Steve's body. Most of the recording devices and the long-play batteries were sewn into a wrestler's weight belt. The wires were hidden under several layers of dark clothing.

Often, they had to scout out locations (especially clubs) for metal detectors before entering with the recording devices. But that wasn't the only threat. "In one instance," says Gillian, "while Steve was in a club talking to women, one prostitute sidled up to him and started stroking him. She discovered the recording device on his belt. He said it was a gun. Luckily, in that context, she believed him, and wasn't concerned."

The secret equipment required a lot of maintenance in the field. Steve frequently had to check to make sure the audio wires had not come undone, and regularly went to the bathroom to play back tapes.

They also set up numerous meetings in their own apartment, which they had rigged with hidden cameras. Conducting meetings in the place they were staying had its advantages and disadvantages. On the one hand, it was an environment they could control (including light and noise) but on the other, it left them vulnerable, with no safe place left for retreat.

Meanwhile, Gillian was playing the official role of the company's press relations manager, but often had to leave the apartment during sensitive meetings.

Her real role in the investigation was to keep track of whether they were getting all the information they needed to make their case. She would review all the tapes and steer Steve in the right direction to make sure they got the material they wanted on tape.

It was a partnership and, naturally for Steve, the situation started to really wear on him, emotionally, psychologically. Because I had a backstage role, I had to make sure we stayed on track in terms of the material we were getting. He began feeling I was critical. We really had to find a balance to support each other, and to make sure we were not risking our lives for nothing.

Shooting in dangerous crowds

Filming demonstrations can involve several dangers, including the police/ militia or the demonstrators themselves.

"Compared to the dangers faced by people I have filmed and interviewed on many occasions, the dangers I face are minimal," says Anand Patwardan. But he does face physical danger "from time to time in riot situations. These can, at times, be minimized by using a telephoto lens and being relatively far from the action, but at times it is not possible to be far away and shoot decently."

While filming clashes between demonstrators and police, Paul O'Connor of Undercurrents, a UK-based video activist group, has been threatened with "getting shot, being run over by bulldozers, being attacked by police, army, security guards, and violent people, and being tear-gassed."

Paul minimizes risks by

having a camera buddy to watch my back. In Washington, DC, during the protests against the IMF, this proved invaluable when police were firing rubber bullets and gas into peaceful demonstrators. With a buddy keeping an eye out for rounds and police aiming at us, I could concentrate on getting the story. Having a gas mask is useful as well. A tight-fitting set of goggles and a mouth mask is probably easier to handle. A bottle of water is essential to wash out eyes.

For further information on filming in protest contexts, sites such as <www.videoactivism.org> provide extensive advice, and there is additional information in Chapter 4.

Communication—via phone and email

Stay in regular touch with someone at home, or headquarters, who knows when and from where you will call next. Consider a daily check-in call.

When using email, consider using encrypted email or use services that are server-based, such as Yahoo! and Hotmail. Use them on both ends, not just for the person in the field. Avoid using names or key words in messages, especially in emails, as they tend to trigger attention and may be noticed by email surveillance systems. Use code-words rather than real names and places.

Frank Smyth advises against encryption systems because government surveillance often looks for encrypted messages on the Internet, and most can be decoded. However, many major advocacy organizations insist on encrypted email. Organizations such as Privaterra <www.privaterra.org> provide information and training on encryption and electronic information security.

Joey Lozano has several communication strategies in place:

I keep WITNESS informed if I am in a dangerous situation so they could immediately stir international attention should something happen to me or the community. It's always excellent to maintain this kind of international relationship. Locally, it's good to establish contact with such personalities as the bishop or parish priest, if you find out that he is sympathetic to the indigenous peoples' struggle. If not, find others.

Stay in close touch with your team and follow your instincts. Simon Taylor had a simple "buddy-system rule" during an undercover investigation: if either he or his partner ever felt uncomfortable in a situation, whether it was well-founded or not, they would always back out together.

AFTER FILMING

You've successfully filmed the images you need and may no longer be at the location of filming. Now what? How you decide to use the tapes will directly affect the security of you and your subjects.

Safe records, safe tapes

First and foremost, once you have arrived in safe location, make and keep in a secure location good transcripts and logs of your material. Tapes that have no reference material rapidly become of limited value, because very few people will remember what was on them.

There are a number of additional simple steps you can take:

- Keep records safely apart from tapes to protect identities.
- Make sure to keep track of all your copies and label them with clear instructions in case they do go astray.
- Destroy rough cuts of videos where the process of obscuring identities is not yet complete, and ensure that public scripts do not reference identities.
- Keep details of where and how the material can be used—for example, only as evidence, or for private screenings.
- Avoid heat and humidity, and don't rewind the tapes unnecessarily.
- Make back-up copies of important material and store them somewhere else, preferably out of the country, and ideally in a secure, temperature-controlled archive facility.

Case study: Good tape logs mean convictions
Ondrej Cakl, a human rights activist in the Czech Republic, has been following the neo-Nazi movement in that country for over

ten years. Using a video camera, he has documented neo-Nazi demonstrations, meetings, and movements. He has lived in hiding for much of that time.

Figure 2.6   Video shot by human rights activist Ondrej Cakl showing racist harassment in the Czech Republic (Ondrej Cakl)

Some of his most important material only becomes relevant years after he has shot it. For example, when a member of the neo-Nazi organization is on trial for a violent crime, the prosecution needs to prove that it is racially motivated. With his logs, Cakl is able to dig up footage from years before, in which the person in question is attending a neo-Nazi meeting. This evidence becomes a sound basis or proving affiliation with a hate group. Without good logs, he would never be able to retrieve that kind of visual evidence.

Communication after filming

Maintain secure communications (including phone and email) after filming, and follow the same precautions you did when you were in the field. Although you may now be in a place of safety, discuss with your partners and collaborators whether and how communication will endanger those left behind.

Editing decisions and safety

Editing can radically change the meaning and context of material. Consider how "guilt by association" can threaten some of your subjects. Verify that all of the individuals contributing to the video will not be endangered if they are associated with other figures in the video. See Chapter 5 for more discussion on this.

The issue of consent is not a factor you only worry about during filming. There are many layers to consent, and many of them emerge during the editing process. If at all possible, talk it through again with people you have featured to make sure they are aware of any changes in the mission, in the editing, or in the context. Review the video with trusted allies in the local community, or with locally based groups who can provide informed feedback on the current situation and risks.

Who's in charge of editing? If you are giving your material over to the mainstream media, make sure to include caveats that will protect you and your subjects, and sign a legal contract that will hold the media to their word. Consider all the possibilities of sensationalism, getting the story wrong or half-wrong, and how it could affect the community.

Impact of broadcast or distribution on you

Broadcasting an investigation can also have a huge impact on the person behind the camera. You yourself can become a target of assault or harassment.

Anand Patwardhan says:

There is a danger of being recognized by people who are your political enemies—for example, fundamentalist groups you have infiltrated. The danger can be reduced if you keep a low profile to begin with. Don't do unnecessary TV interviews. Don't get yourself photographed by the media too often. When entering areas where danger does exist, go in broad daylight with other media people, so anything done to you would be reported. The major risks come after you have published or exposed your material. My films at times get banned by the state and involve a long legal fight. Even when they become legal, screenings have been disrupted or stopped by right-wingers and fanatics. But for every negative story of this kind there are at least a hundred screenings that went well, were useful. So the moral of the story is that it is all well worth the trouble.

Joey Lozano's most obvious danger comes when he remains in the communities in which he has been filming.

So normally, I stay home for a while—a week or two, depending on the "heat" that I had generated. But before doing this, arrangements are made with the community on what to do when something happens to them. We exchange numbers, give them directions on how to reach me or other people for refuge. If there is a need for me to go back to the community immediately, I don't follow the usual entry or exit pattern. New ones are arranged with the community. We always see to it that only a few would know when I would come or leave, and that I would always have a companion when in the area.

For people in situations of sustained risk, who live in or near the community where they film, sometimes the only way to ensure security is to leave the area or country permanently. Frank Smyth notes that, "Unfortunately, this perpetuates a brain drain, and that causes new kinds of problems in a country."

Reactions to stress and trauma

Many human rights activists and journalists do not take into account the personal emotional impact of covering violence and violations. They can experience direct trauma from witnessing violations, secondary trauma from working with people who have suffered trauma or violence, as well as counter-transference where their own painful memories are triggered by exposure to trauma. Stress, vicarious traumatization, exhaustion, and burn-out are frequent consequences of exposure to these kinds of trauma. Secondary trauma can also be experienced as a consequence of repeated exposure to traumatic imagery at a remove—for example, by a filmmaker or editor working with violent or disturbing material.

Symptoms of "secondary trauma" are often subtle, and can include irritability, fatigue, depression, cynicism, poor concentration, hyper-arousal, sleep disturbances or nightmares, weight loss or gain, emotional numbing, and feelings of helplessness, anger and insecurity as well as physical pains. Talking about memories with peers or professional listeners can help, and in many cases services exist for survivors of torture or abuse that may also help activists and journalists. Other ways to prevent and treat secondary trauma include taking adequate and regular rest periods (the most critical way to avert secondary trauma in the long term), using relaxation techniques and taking regular exercise, and developing support relationships with family and friends.

Professional counseling, says the Committee to Protect Journalists, is especially important in cases where journalists have been subject to torture or other forms of physical or psychological abuse, including witnessing the torture of others.

Joey Lozano finds strength in the conviction that his work is making a difference:

> It's a very painful experience for me to interview indigenous peoples alive, and then to come back a few months later and see them in a coffin. To me that is one of the most difficult situations I find myself in. But that same experience can be a very powerful medium to show other people and arouse anger, so people start looking into issues that beset indigenous people. In practice, I always feel that I belong to their community, that I am among them and with them. Their commitment to be with me, in return, gives me strength, and my commitment to be with them does the same to them.

Impact of broadcast distribution on people filmed

As Eric Rosenthal, who documents human rights abuses of people in psychiatric institutions around the world with Mental Disability Rights International (MDRI), puts it: "Victims of human rights abuses are in danger. Often, whomever did it to them the first time—once you release an image of that victim—can do it a second time."

Sometimes, Eric has ended up not using certain images at all, for fear of reprisals on the subjects. In one case, he did not have enough evidence to ensure the perpetrators of the crime would be removed from the scene, so he did not use any of the material he had recorded.

When Gillian Caldwell and Steve Galster edited their film, *Bought & Sold,* they decided to digitize the faces of the women as well as those of the organized crime figures. They did this to provide safety to the women and the investigators. "We were doing the investigation to document the methodologies of trafficking," points out Gillian. "We were not doing it to provide specific information to law enforcement."

Beyond safety, other dangers can seriously affect subjects long after images have been used.

Eric Rosenthal notes: "Some subjects fear social stigma once the public has seen them in compromising and dehumanized situations, such as being naked and institutionalized." For example, women in Kosovo who have been institutionalized may be disowned by their families, simply for the shame they cause the family for being placed in an institution.

Rosenthal also notes that his organization, Mental Disability Rights International, has been criticized for showing degrading images of people with disabilities, in any context. These critics worry that it only serves to create another danger—the perpetuation of stereotypes. A similar danger exists with using sensational or graphic images—you may induce a fatigued reaction of impotence from the viewer, or the need to shock may have a human cost on the person filmed. You need to evaluate whether this kind of imagery is helpful or harmful, and you have to weigh up and consult with the survivor or victim on the potential damage.

However, Eric Rosenthal also says you need to evaluate *who* is doing the criticizing:

> Most individuals with disabilities detained in institutions want their photographs used. It is much more often the mental health authorities who object to our use of photos, and their use of "privacy" arguments are usually a cover for their desire to cover up abuses at their facility.

When Binta Mansaray teamed up with Lilibet Foster to make *Operation Fine Girl*, a film about the use of rape as a weapon during Sierra Leone's civil war, she wanted to make a firm statement. She did not want to digitally obscure any of the faces of the women and girls interviewed, because she wanted to send the message that the women had done nothing wrong, that they had nothing to be ashamed of.

Decisions are not always clearly right or wrong, but your choices always send out messages that affect people's lives and reputations in concrete ways.

Case study: One photo, irreversible damage

Médecins Sans Frontières (MSF) provides emergency medical assistance to populations in danger. On one occasion, the MSF press office arranged for a Western journalist to visit one of its missions in an area of severe conflict between two ethnic groups. The journalist, while seasoned, was not debriefed before leaving the area. A few days later, an excellent article appeared in his national newspaper on the other side of the world. Unfortunately, the photo accompanying the story showed MSF handing out boxes to only one of the ethnic groups.

A copy of the article and photo quickly made its way back to the region, and within a week, the mission was being harassed and threatened by the other ethnic group, and accused of being "one-sided." Despite all attempts to prove (using official mission records) that they were handing out materials equally to both sides, the mission had to withdraw the entire operation. One photo in a newspaper on the other side of the world had damaged its reputation irreversibly.

Dealing with sustained risk and long-term impact

As Frank Smyth cautions, "the vast majority of journalists killed in the last decade did not die in the crossfire of war. Instead, they were hunted down and murdered, often in direct reprisal for their reporting." Similarly human rights and social justice advocates are often at risk in every moment of their lives, not just when they are in the field documenting. Those most at risk are people who live and work in the communities they are investigating. However, most locally based journalists, "non-professionals," and human rights activists—especially those living in remote areas, –have limited or no access to training and institutional support.

> Corruption is the number-one killer [says Frank]. And the reality is that local journalists holding political and economic elements accountable, in isolation, are at enormous risk. In ninety-four percent of murdered-journalist cases, the perpetrators get away with complete impunity. What we need—ultimately— is functioning civilian judiciaries.

The effects of a shoot can last for years, even decades. Be aware of these potential risks, and be prepared to deal with them.

Case study: When people risk their lives to get the truth out

In the Eastern Congo, in 1999, local workers for the Christian Blind Mission (CBM), began warning their head office about a potential disaster unfolding. They telephoned David McAllister, then working for CBM in Nairobi, and told him what they were seeing: severe hunger, villages and crops destroyed, and hundreds of displaced people from neighbouring villages flooding the area. The local CBM workers, who wished to remain anonymous, very wisely recognized these conditions as signs of impending war in the region. This was the beginning of war in the Congo, whose impact has cost over three million lives to date.

At the time, McAllister says, "We found it very difficult to get the attention of the world press." So the local CBM workers picked up amateur video cameras (cameras they had been using to make videos for funders) and began filming horrific images of slaughter—the first images of the war in the Congo to get out of the country:

> We were able to get this on video—horrific video—and once the media saw the macabre sights of women and babies slashed open with a machete, this is what galvanized action.

McAllister called a press conference to release the graphic video, and all the major media players showed up, including CNN, BBC, Deutsche Welle, and others. Soon, the images were playing on TV around the world. McAllister says:

> I know that Mr Mandela [then President of South Africa], he was contacted, and he telephoned Mr Kofi Annan [Secretary-General of the United Nations]. It went to the very highest levels, this I know. These videos went to the highest levels—so it did have an impact.

Meanwhile, back in the Congo, the amateur videographers were in increasing danger:

> It became very dangerous for our local colleagues to keep working in the local communities; too dangerous. After a while, they said, "I need to get away, I can't accept the danger any more." So the videos won't show that, but one must remember that the people who filmed this are from the community and are known as the ones who filmed and blew the whistle.
>
> To this day, years later, we are still involved in the long-term care of the people who put themselves at risk in filming. We brought the videographer who took the original footage, and his wife and kids, to Nairobi a couple of years ago. Unfortunately he lost twenty members of his extended family last year [in the war], and so, when we knew his mother and sisters were in a house in Bunia that was being surrounded by members of the other ethnic group, we sent a plane in for them too.

Using international pressure

If there is continued and dangerous pressure on you or your subjects after you have exposed an issue, Frank Smyth suggests that international pressure can be very useful. The politics of shame and embarrassment can still carry weight. "If it's a country that has a reason to respond to international pressure (due to outside aid or investment) there's a good chance you can make things happen." Media attention, and organizations such as human rights advocacy groups, religious groups, and lobby groups, may also help.

TOP TEN SAFETY AND SECURITY TIPS

How did they do it? We asked five seasoned filmmakers and activists to share their own tips, drawn from their professional and personal experiences.

JOEY R.B. LOZANO *uses his personal video camera to assert indigenous land rights, and to investigate corruption and environmental degradation. He also writes investigative features for the* Philippine Daily Inquirer. *Joey's investigations began in 1986, when he helped the US investigative program, ABC 20/20, uncover the "Tasaday hoax," a highly successful fraud to pass off local tribespeople in the Philippines as a newly discovered Stone Age culture. He soon embarked on his own, probing into illegal logging, gold mining and land-grabbing. His exposés quickly made him the object of repeated assassination and abduction attempts, in a country that is one of the more dangerous places to do human rights and media work. Since 1986, over 40 Filipino journalists have been murdered in the line of duty. Joey and Renee Lozano, also a community worker, live in South Cotobato with their five children.*

Joey R.B. Lozano's top ten tips for security

1. You are not Superman, out to liberate a people. Recognize that you are a mortal, with your own limitations. When you do that, the art of being safe becomes a normal part of planning when you go to a dangerous assignment.
2. Develop trusted contacts at the local, national, and international level. Let them know where you will be, and when to expect your return. Leave contact addresses.
3. Gain acceptance for what you do from your family members or trusted associates. This will give you additional courage to move

on, and shoulders to cry on later, when failures or accidents happen.

4. Always bring lots of identification cards (press card, social security number, etc.) that you can afford to lose but nonetheless are helpful in identifying who you are. Never bring ID that might just increase the heat on you.

5. Develop a happy disposition. This helps take out the fear in you and makes you easily accepted by others.

6. Be culturally sensitive, especially in indigenous peoples' communities. Belong to them, for that is your guarantee that they will protect you.

7. When in depressed communities, avoid being an additional burden (e.g. by demanding better food and accommodation), or else you may end up being given away by your host community.

8. Bring along multivitamins and first aid kit/medicines, just in case.

9. Of course, check if you have your complete equipment and accessories before entering the area and devise means to keep them safe.

10. Act normally when you shoot, not so showy as to attract attention, and be able to easily mix with people around you.

Optional: Believe in divine interventions! *Deus ex machina … that is, if you believe in somebody more powerful than human beings.*

TIA LESSIN *produces and directs social issue documentary television and film. She has worked on three of Michael Moore's films, including as supervising producer of both* Fahrenheit 9/11, *the winner of the 2003 Cannes Palme D'Or, and the Academy Award winning documentary* Bowling for Columbine. *She was coordinating producer of* The Big One.

Tia won the Sidney Hillman Prize for Behind the Labels: Garment Workers on US Saipan, *a collaboration with WITNESS about indentured servitude in the garment industry on a US territory in the Pacific. She has been twice nominated for Emmy Awards for her work on the satirical television series* The Awful Truth. *Tia was field producer of the PBS series* Surviving the Bottom Line *and associate producer of the Academy Award-nominated* Shadows of Hate, *distributed free to high schools around the country as part of the Southern Poverty Law Center's Teaching Tolerance curriculum. She has contributed segments to National Public Radio, NOW with Bill Moyers and National Geographic Television, and has produced two music videos.*

While shooting video she has been detained by the New Jersey State police, Iraqi Secret Service agents, the private police force at Disneyland, and by corporate security guards throughout the US.

Tia Lessin's top ten tips for security

1. Take seriously your own safety and that of your crew. Get the appropriate medical shots for the region and obtain medical travel insurance; carry a copy of your passport, visa, IDs, medical history, and emergency contact info as well as for your travel partners and crew members; use seat belts in vehicles; drink only bottled water when traveling to rural areas.

2. Be discreet. Don't say anything on phone lines that would compromise your mission or your sources. Be aware that conversations in public places may be overheard and act accordingly. Unless it's useful to be identified as a journalist or filmmaker, keep a low profile with your equipment; use regular luggage bags instead of professional cases. Be aware that people you talk with (and employ, such as drivers, guards, crew and fixers) may be questioned about your activities.

3. Protect your confidential sources. Keep your tapes and tape logs separated; don't allow your sources to say their names on tape if they want their identity concealed; write your notes in code, if necessary; be prepared to expose shot film if necessary; park your vehicle away from your source's home.

4. Protect your shot tapes. If possible, carry them with you at all times; don't leave them in cars, hotel rooms or even in private homes; carry them on the airplane or bus or train rather than checking them; arrange to hand off your tapes to a "runner" who can bring them to a safe place; be aware that excessive heat and humidity may damage tapes.

5. Understand the risks. Typically, you have the right to shoot on public property, but know where public property stops and private property starts; if shooting police stations, jail exteriors, government buildings, factories (even from public property) leave that till the end of the shoot; don't take your tapes with you when you film in risky situations.

6. Prepare to be questioned. Review your "story" with your crew and translators in anticipation of interrogation by security forces if you are approached by the police, military, or other "security" forces. When confronted, discreetly eject your camera tape and replace it with a blank or dummy tape, and take down the badge numbers and names of the officers who are detaining you. Always carry the contact numbers for a human rights lawyer who can help defend you in an emergency. Be courteous but firm with local authorities.

7. Know the local conditions where you are shooting. Get weather forecasts, and have maps on hand. Carry a list of local hospitals, international embassies/consulates, and other journalists and NGOs in the area.

8. Legitimize yourself and your mission. Carry press credentials; obtain a letter of introduction/assignment from a media outlet or human rights group such as WITNESS.

9. Maintain contact with "home base." Have someone there know where you are and have a full copy of your travel documents, contact info, and itineraries. Set check-in times for email and telephone with home base.

10. Don't go anywhere alone, if you can help it.

ANAND PATWARDHAN *has been making political documentaries for nearly three decades, pursuing diverse and controversial issues that are at the crux of social and political life in India. Most recently he produced the widely debated film* War and Peace, *on the peace and anti-nuclear movement in India and Pakistan. His other films include* A Time to Rise *in Delhi,* In the Name of God *and* Father, Son and Holy War, *and he has won over twenty international film awards. Many of his films were at one time or another banned by state television channels in India, and have become the subject of litigation by Patwardhan, who successfully challenged the censorship rulings in court.*

Patwardhan has been an activist ever since he was a student, having participated in the anti-Vietnam War movement; been a volunteer in the Caesar Chavez United Farm Workers' Union; worked in Kishore Bharati, a rural development and education project in central India; and participated in the Bihar anti-corruption movement in 1974–75 as well as the civil liberties and democratic rights movement during and after the 1975–77 Emergency. Since then, he has been active in movements for housing rights of the urban poor, communal harmony, and the environment, and in movements against the Narmada Dam, against unjust, unsustainable development, and against nuclear testing in South Asia.

Anand Patwardhan's top tips for minimizing risk

1. Be light and mobile.
2. Have a back-up support team that can bail you out of trouble.
3. Get national and international support.
4. Get decent digital equipment and a good microphone.
5. Learn to shoot and record competently. (There is no sense risking bodily harm to create a program that is too poor in quality to watch.)
6. Give copies of the most important materials you have shot to friends in a safe house.
7. Either be totally anonymous or very famous: nothing in between.
8. If you choose the latter approach, don't let it change your original motivation.
9. Spend forty percent of your time making your program and sixty percent doing screenings. If you don't show your film, not many others will either.

MINGA *(the Asociación para la Promoción Social Alternativa) is a Colombian human rights organization and part of the WITNESS partner network. MINGA, which means "collective work project" in an indigenous Colombian language, was founded in 1992, and is dedicated to representing political prisoners and families of victims of violence. MINGA works to protect and promote basic human rights by engaging in four projects: legal advice and representation, investigation, community education, and media relations. Its work is focused in the three rural provinces of Colombia: Ocaña, Catatumbo, and south of Cesar. Colombia is a dangerous country to be a human rights activist, and MINGA often films in heavily militarized areas (government forces, guerrillas, paramilitaries), where they are confronted by armed forces, who demand to see their filmed material.*

MINGA's top tips for security

1. Have cameras that are discreet and don't call attention to yourself.
2. Be in permanent contact with the leaders of the regions where you are going to enter.

3. Accept the security recommendations of those leaders.
4. Have a bit of luck and guts.
5. If the organization for which you work has security problems in the region where you are going, it's good to have the cover/protection of another organization so that you can pass for a member of it.
6. Know the terrain/landscape before you go in with your crew/equipment.
7. Hide the equipment as much as possible in luggage.
8. Have a mobile communication device (satellite, mobile phone, radio).
9. Always believe that a better world is possible.

GILLIAN CALDWELL *is the Executive Director of WITNESS. She is a filmmaker and an attorney with experience in the areas of international human rights, civil rights, and family law. Gillian was formerly Co-Director of the Global Survival Network, where she coordinated a two-year undercover investigation into the trafficking of women for forced prostitution from Russia and the Newly Independent States. She also produced and directed* Bought & Sold, *a documentary film based on this investigation. Gillian worked in South Africa during 1991 and 1992 investigating hit squads and security force involvement in township violence, and has worked in several US cities on issues related to poverty and violence.*

Ten things to keep in mind when doing undercover video work
(in no particular order)

1. Be clear about what information you are looking for before you go into undercover situations.
2. Be clear about your cover story and have well-conceived materials supporting it where relevant (phone, fax, business card, brochures).
3. Scout the site of any meetings in advance to determine the presence of metal detectors.
4. Be sure key allies know where you are, when, so they can follow up if you don't return when expected.
5. If you require an interpreter, choose very carefully and find someone you trust implicitly.
6. Decide in advance whether it will be a benefit or a burden to admit knowledge of relevant languages (in our circumstances it actually would have endangered the investigation).

7. Keep all batteries fully charged and check periodically during the meeting to ensure that all wires are still connected and sound is being recorded.
8. Stay well fed and well rested so that your judgment is not impaired.
9. Select the genders, races, and nationalities of your investigator(s) carefully, based on an assessment of the circumstances.
10. Try to have a safe and secure space to return to after or in between negotiations.

Kat Cizek thanks:

Ronit Avni	Robbie Barnett	Dhurba Basnet
Gillian Burnett	Gillian Caldwell	Arturo Carillo
Tina Carr	Ondrej Cakl	Sean Dixon
Joanna Duchesne	Steven Galster	Marc Glassman
Martyn Gregory	Sam Gregory	Shabnam Hashmi
Sandrine Isambert	Mandy Jacobson	Tommi Laulajainen
Tia Lessin	Joey Lozano	David McAllister
Liz Miller	Paul O'Connor	Anand Patwardhan
Erica Pomerance	Eric Rosenthal	Paul Shore
Atossa Soltani	Theeba Soundararajan	Frank Smyth
Simon Taylor	Amadou Thior	

NOTE

1. Roy Thomas, "The Critical Link 3: Interpreters in the Community," in L. Brunette, G. Bastin, I. Hemlin, and H. Clarke, eds, *Follow-on Protection of Interpreters in Areas of Conflict: Selected Papers from the Third International Conference on Interpreting in Legal, Health and Social Service Settings, Montreal, Quebec, Canada, 22–26 May 2001* (Amsterdam: John Benjamins Publishing Co., 2003), pp. 307–17.

3
Storytelling for Advocacy: Conceptualization and Preproduction

Katerina Cizek

Here, we discuss how to develop your most powerful tool: the story. This chapter examines how to build solid foundations for advocacy video, before one frame of footage is filmed, perhaps even before you pick up a camera.

First, we examine "the story" itself, and how to tell stories in advocacy contexts, as well as different story models from Hollywood to the far north. We also emphasize the importance of characters, point of view, and genre, and then address the need to clearly define your audience.

With these principles in place, we introduce the planning process of preproduction, which charts how to turn your story idea into concrete video: conducting research ("recce"), creating a film outline, preparing a budget, call-sheets, and shotlists.

STORYTELLING AND GENRE

What is a story?

Filmmaking is the art of weaving together a good story. A good story grips our imagination and takes us on a journey of discovery, through emotions, places, facts, and realities. A good story makes us care. It opens us to new ideas and challenges our ways of understanding the world. A good story gives structure and meaning to a film. Finding the right story is an essential part of the whole filmmaking process.

Peter Wintonick, a Canadian filmmaker, is currently working on a film about storytelling, and says:

I believe we are genetically wired, psychologically wired, from the time we are children, when we are sung or read bedtime stories, to look for completion. We need to attach stories to personalities, to humans. Especially during editing, both emotion and logic flow back into the construction of a story. The same material can be edited 1,000 different ways. There are many different concepts of story: In Iceland, there's a long tradition of oral stories that last four days. There are epic sagas in Kyrgyzstan. On the other hand, stories in the Western world typically have a beginning, middle and end. There are thousands of different types of storytellers around the world.

In any story, you want to create drama so that people care,' says Amy Bank, who produces an advocacy soap opera for Nicaraguan television, *Sexto Sentido*.

Conflict makes a good story, people overcoming problems makes a good story, when the hero overcomes obstacles, comes out triumphant. Not that every ending needs to be happy, but audiences want to see a transformation in the protagonist.

She adds that revealing "problems" can add to your story:

In advocacy work, we often ask how much should we portray the world through rose-colored glasses? How much to portray the messy things that are not neatly tied up? Yet storytelling needs doubt. Doubts are what you overcome.

What is storytelling for advocacy?

What makes storytelling different when you are doing it to campaign for a particular social, legal, cultural, political, or economic change? The key difference is that in advocacy, storytelling is at the service of your goal for change and your message, rather than just the story itself or the ideas of the filmmaker.

Advocacy storytelling is about effectively communicating this message to the audience and encouraging them to act. Your understanding of the people who make up your audience—and how exactly you want them to act—will define *how* you will communicate this message to them. Peter Wintonick suggests that simply making films for entertainment tends to create a passive response— *entertainment for entertainment's sake*. But when you are using video for advocacy, he says:

You want to move your audience to action. That's the difference between advocacy media and entertainment media. Entertainment is a passive experience. It's laid out by the filmmaker. A good advocacy filmmaker turns things over to the audience.

In order for your viewers to feel there is room for change, you need to leave a "space for action." How much are you including your audience in the story and the ending? After watching, will they feel detached, removed, and helpless, or included, hopeful, powerful, inspired, or outraged? Most obviously, you will need to consider the end of your video. Is your story closed off and resolved, or is there room for the story—and real life—to change? Often advocacy video will end with a direct request to viewers from a character or subject in your video, or with an individual within the video framing an analysis of why a situation is occurring and what an audience can do about it. At other times, a video will reference opportunities to learn more, and further material available for offline organizing at screenings, or distributed via the Internet. Always make your request concrete and specific, and offer an option, not just a complaint, about the status quo.

Advocacy filmmakers often create a meaningful partnership with the people they film throughout the entire life cycle of a video. This method goes well beyond (and may even go against the norms of) most conventional forms of filmmaking, because in most documentaries subjects have little or no say in the filmmaking process. Subjects sign those rights away in the conventional release form.

Advocacy storytelling has no built-in time constraints. It is up to you to decide how long your video should be, based on your understanding of your audience. Perhaps your community has a thirst for information on a subject and will watch four different videos of two hours each, full of raw, unedited, complete testimonies. Or, conversely, a 30-second powerful video may just as easily move a different audience of people to action (consider that most advertisements on television last 30 seconds!). Realistically, many WITNESS projects range from 6 to 15 minutes. Length should be determined by audience and screening venue. Remember the adage: in general, *less is more*.

One particular danger that advocacy filmmakers should be aware of is the tendency to make documentaries longer and more involved than is necessary for their target audiences in the hope of getting a television broadcast. Be realistic on your chances of getting your material on television, and choose an appropriate length for your other audiences. If you do decide to make a longer video for television, consider producing a shorter version for advocacy audiences.

Finally, telling stories for advocacy may be a serious issue, but it's okay to have a wide emotional range. It's fine to be funny. No matter how tragic or difficult the issue is, humor can help ease subjects, filmmakers, and audiences into a story. Humor is often an expression of resilience and coping. Humor can also help ease the pain.

Beginning, middle, and end

In the conventional, Western storytelling tradition of North America and Western Europe—and particularly Hollywood—the most standard way to construct a film story is in three acts. This method of building a story has become formulaic and constraining, but the general principles are worth a brief description. In moderation, and with a grain of salt, they can help to structure the broad strokes of a story. They also provide insight into the expectations of audiences who enjoy Hollywood-style films.

According to this formula: Act 1 sets up the story, and sets the action into motion. We learn "who, what, where, how and why." In conventional Hollywood script manuals, this act makes up twenty-five percent of the full running time of the film. By the end of this act, the hero (the central character) embarks on a quest.

Act 2 is the "meat" of the story. This is where the emotional or physical journey of the hero takes place. Here, the hero confronts a series of obstacles and must overcome them in efforts to fulfill the larger quest. Again, formula suggests this act is fifty percent of the running time. By the end of this act, the story reaches a climax, which is the final, most important conflict.

Act 3 is the conclusion. Here, the story comes to its resolution. The threads of the story and its conflicts are wrapped up. Often in Hollywood, this is the happy ending, such as the conventional wedding scene. Formula prescribes this act make up the remaining twenty-five percent of the film.

However, Howard Weinberg, a producer and "documentary script doctor," reminds us there are no definite rules for putting together a story:

> Experienced editors will change approaches throughout their career. The only general principle would be, basically, some form of beginning, middle and end. Surprise people! Go from what they do know to what they don't know.

Whether you believe in the three-act formula or not, the basic structure and arc of a story might involve a beginning, middle, and end:

- Beginning: Set up your story (who? what? where?), and make the audience curious. In an analytical film or advocacy-driven film you may set the stage for your argument or pose a question.
- Middle: Tell the bulk of the story; go through the arguments or evidence. Engage your viewers with a reason to care and to act.
- End: Conclude it, or "hand it off" to the audience.

Fernanda Rossi, a story consultant known as the Doc Doctor, suggests that another way to analyze story structure is in terms of whether a film is conflict- or non-conflict-driven.

In a conflict-driven film, two opposing forces create drama and move the action forward through a dramatic curve. The conflict may not be necessarily actual physical conflict on screen. It may be a conflict of interests, of personality or of ideas. These films are also often character-driven. A conflict-driven model is not necessarily dependent on the audience's interest in your particular subject/theme because it creates natural curiosity. Conflict-driven films begin with a first exposition of conflict between two opposing forces or motivations that can both be observed, and conflict escalates during the film. During the film there should be smaller conflicts and tensions, combining to help build a sense of mounting urgency. In a human rights film, these conflicts could be facets of the everyday relationship between someone who is oppressed and the oppressive force—for example, the struggles of an ordinary man to feed his family, educate his children, secure adequate housing, etc. Ordering is critical to reaching a climax and resolution.

This kind of dramatic curve is often easier to create when the film is centered on an event.

The non-conflict or narrative model is based on logical cause and effect, or on a series of self-contained events or segments that relate to different themes in your film. Here you are more dependent on how interested the audience is in the issue, and on the chronology you employ.

Respecting traditional/indigenous storytelling

There are different cultural traditions of storytelling. The three-act structure and even the concept of a beginning/middle and end are not necessarily the best or only ways to tell a story effectively.

The way a story is told—or even who tells it—can have political and cultural consequences both within the community and outside.

All communities have factions and dynamics of powers and privilege within them. Ronit Avni, the director of the Just Vision project, which works with Palestinian and Israeli peace activists, observes that "privileging certain voices might have serious implications for the whole group. It might undermine and misrepresent the community in its totality."

Sam Gregory of WITNESS adds:

> There are debates about the visual and structural language of indigenous media. We don't dictate how our partners should structure their videos—and we work with a range of groups from professional human rights organizations to community-based social movements. But we suggest to our partners that they bear their audience in mind when they film and edit, and think what will be most persuasive for them. Many WITNESS partner videos are targeted at an international audience, so that fidelity to an indigenous storytelling or visual style as such is usually less of an issue for us and for our partners. But it is an audience-based decision, provided that the decisions taken on storytelling style do not have a damaging impact in the community.

It is important to respect how a community or filmmaker may choose to tell the story. Gabriela Zamorano, who works with indigenous women filmmakers in Mexico, once witnessed one indigenous filmmaker berate another for not making "indigenous films." Gabriela asks the question, "What exactly is an indigenous perspective? That this woman chose a more conventional way of telling her story didn't make her any less indigenous."

A story can be local and universal. One of the most successful Canadian fiction films in recent history is called *Atanarjuat: the Fast Runner*. It is the first fully Inuit (a group of indigenous peoples of North America) film—created, produced, and edited by a team made up mostly of Inuit, with the film's dialogue in Inuktitut. The story is based on a traditional Inuit legend, yet the story is universal. The film has won awards and been seen around the world; it has spoken to audiences across all cultures and languages.

Role of characters

Video can put the "human" into "human rights." Real people are what people who see your film will care about—whether they agree with your analysis or not. These "characters" (the term often used in documentary filmmaking) will give audiences someone to hang on to in your story. "The message in your video comes from the characters, with whom one hopes to be working in solidarity," says Peter Wintonick. Liz Miller, a political filmmaker and teacher, also believes that

> Character-based stories have the most impact. Audiences want to know what happens to them. They want to see transformation. You can have compassion and empathy for characters that go through a process of change in your film.

In documentary, we often meet characters through interviews. Liz suggests that during editing (and filming) it is a good idea to

> Look for material that isn't overly distanced. Not just talking heads, or characters talking. Look for moments when characters aren't just *describing* themselves, but *being* themselves. How do they interact with other people? What they say versus what they show?

Sam Gregory comments that a lot of WITNESS work is testimony-based, where you encounter individuals who are telling of abuses they have suffered:

> From a filmmaking perspective, this can seem problematic, because our partners tend to shoot good testimony, but do not or cannot always shoot the context—for example, shots of "a person's life in their community" or the devastated community from which they've fled. But unmediated testimony, people being given a chance to tell their story with full eye contact, on camera—often for the first time ever—can be very powerful. These are not just talking heads. These are testimonies, where the subjects are speaking to someone and there is real intent in that communication. They are very focused on communicating what has happened to them and what they are doing about it. It's the *power of that intent* that can be very moving and very strong.

Even when we are unable to follow these individuals' lives—for example, if they are traveling through the jungle as internally displaced people in Burma—the intensity of that moment of them talking to the viewer can compensate for our inability to follow them through a traditional arc of character development.

Amy Bank says that the characters they create on their Nicaraguan television show have a very important role to play in the lives of their audiences. She suggests:

> Television creates a social relationship. Through television, people have an emotional and intellectual identification with characters. For example, statistics are not (yet) high for HIV/AIDS in Nicaragua, but there is high stigma against people who are HIV positive. One character in our television show may be the first person to admit he is HIV positive that our audiences will ever meet. If audiences grow to care and like this character, then that may influence how they think and act on HIV/AIDS issues when it becomes a real issue in their real lives.

Don Edkins, who focuses on HIV/AIDS in South Africa, a country with some of the highest rates of HIV/AIDS in the world, emphasizes the *power of relationships* in storytelling. He describes a film that looks at a relationship between *people*—rather than the "facts and figures"—around a story of HIV/AIDS.

> It's story of a 50-year old woman, who became HIV positive due to a blood transfer. She was very vocal, and she went around to different communities, to go and talk publicly about her status at every opportunity: radio, schools... Now this is a great character, but does she make a good story? She makes an excellent story when you realize that she has a very difficult relationship with her daughter, who was terribly embarrassed of her mother. The mother is open and frank, and the daughter is mortified. This kind of relationship is something that anyone can understand. Now we have dramatic content. We also have humor. We have a story audiences can relate to and care about.

Case study: Interviews vs subjects/characters

Fernanda Rossi was asked to help give shape to a film called *A Day's Work, A Day's Pay* <www.newday.com>, about welfare recipients in New York City who become leaders fighting for economic justice. When Fernanda joined the project, the filmmakers had over 170 hours of footage, with many storylines and too many characters. Fernanda watched a three-hour assembly of footage and was able to help the filmmaker think through how to proceed.

"She helped us to see that we had the dramatic arc of three people's stories. The other stories and individuals fell into place only as they related to these characters' stories. If they didn't have a connection, they were out," says Kathy Leichter, one of the directors of the film. In this case, some individuals could function as context or ideas, making points that would move the story along, while a chosen few could help humanize the story with their own life examples. Now, with three main characters carrying the emotional drive of the story, audiences could hang on to the storyline even though there were other people in the film. Because of these powerful human stories, when watching the film, audiences connect deeply with the individuals on screen and feel moved to take action on welfare reform.

Exercise 3.1: From print to screen
This exercise challenges you to think about what are the key elements and people in a story, and consider how these would translate if you were to document the story using video. The exercise is best done in a small group. Start by picking a recent newspaper article or editorial that relates to the central theme of your advocacy work.

1. Highlight the key sentences that explain the story. What are the key elements of this story? Often you will find that in a newspaper article the title and first three paragraphs gives a synopsis of the story, and then the first sentence of each paragraph following and the final paragraph fill it out and summarize the article. If you use an editorial you will also see here the point of view, argument and conclusion of the writers.
2. Go through the article and highlight the names of the people featured—these are your potential "characters." In Exercise 3.2 we will look at how to pick central characters if you have many people involved in the issue.
3. Go through the article and highlight in a different color the key images that are described—these could be activities, locations, or inanimate objects.
4. Think through some of the challenges you will face in taking this story from print to screen. Take the opportunity in a group to brainstorm together. It will be helpful to have someone facilitate the conversation, and pick some of the following questions to discuss:
    a. Where is the story taking place? Is this somewhere you can film or would you need to find other ways to show/tell the story without going to this place?

b. Who are the people in the article? Are they people you could film?

c. How could you film the images you've identified? If they are inaccessible, what are your alternatives?

d. How much is taking place in the present day? How much in the past? How will this affect the way you tell the story?

e. What might you be able to express through writing that would be difficult to show in a movie? And vice-versa?

f. Does the story have a beginning, middle, and end? Is it self-contained or open-ended?

g. In an editorial, what is the argument of the editorial—what is it asking for or arguing for? How could you express this in video?

h. How would you tell this story if it had happened 25 years ago?

i. How would you find a way to tell this story if you had no money? No ability to interview anyone?

5. If you like, choose one potential interviewee from the story, and draft a set of questions to ask them. Role-play the interview with a colleague.

Point of view, voice, and narrative form: Who tells the story and how?

Point of view describes the perspective from which a video story is being told. For example, is it told through the perspective of the lead character, or an objective journalist, or the sister of a murdered opposition leader?

But point of view is not just about the voice we hear, it is about the entire way a film is framed. Through whose eyes do we understand the events? Visually, from what vantage point do we see action unfold? Is the camera with the government soldiers as they surround a community, or is the camera inside someone's home witnessing the attack through the crack in the door?

In advocacy work, you should be thinking about your audience and your story. Which point of view will be most appropriate and meaningful for them, and which will also have the most impact in an advocacy context?

• Who will provide the guiding information in the film? Who or what will orientate the viewer and explain what is happening?

- To what extent will the presence and creative direction of the filmmakers and activists be explicitly identified within the video itself?
- To what extent are the people in your film collaborators in its construction, both during the filming and in the editing process?

One key decision on point of view is whether to use narration (voiceover) or not. If you are going to use narration, who will be the narrator and what will be the tone of the narration? "People underestimate how much the choice of the narrator influences how people react consciously and subconsciously to a film," says Sam Gregory.

If you decide to use a narrator, whom will you choose? Will you choose a subject in the film, the filmmaker, someone with a good voice, or perhaps a celebrity? A man or a woman? Young or old? A person with a regional accent or a standardized, "official" accent? Do they sound like a professional or like a "regular" person? Is it the filmmaker herself speaking? Is the tone cynical or optimistic and upbeat? All of these factors will have implications for how your audience responds to the film.

Sandrine Isambert, a former editor at WITNESS, adds a practical consideration:

> You can decide before you start shooting if you want to have a voiceover or not. If you don't want a voiceover you have to make sure you have all the information in the interviews that cover all the issues you want to talk about. If you don't have that you have to use a voiceover, because you need someone to guide you through the story. Sometimes there are subjects that are very complicated and even if you are very good at writing stories, you still need someone to guide you. You need a voiceover sometimes to provide information that you were not able to shoot.

For many filmmakers, choosing between narration and titlecards in a video is a question of aesthetics. In WITNESS' work they often choose to use titlecards rather than bringing in a narrator, and distracting an audience with questions about who the narrator is, and their relationship to the materials. Titlecards appear to be perceived as more neutral and factual than a narrator, whose ethnicity, age, gender, and other perceived personal characteristics can be deconstructed and analyzed.

In this chapter we focus on three basic film forms: narration-driven, interview-driven, and observational-verité. In many cases, your films will be a hybrid of these forms.

Narration-driven film

This uses a narrator and/or titlecards (text on the screen). A voiceover narration or titlecards explain what is happening, and the film often takes for granted the narrator's credibility. How you choose this person (age, language or accent, gender, celebrity status, relationship to issue, etc.) will affect the film's impact on the viewer. In the classic "voice of god" narrative style you have a third-person narrator, off-screen, guiding us through the film, explaining what we are seeing. It is assumed that we can trust the voice and that it is objective. The narration can also be more personal and subjective, told through the voice of someone in the story.

Narration-driven film can be the easiest to make. You write a script, shoot, and then voiceover. It is easier to change and fix too—simply change the narration in the studio. Where you don't have enough or the right interview material or visuals, you can add explanatory narration.

An example of a primarily narration-driven film is available online at <www.witness.org>, where you can view *Road to Pineapple*. This video is told primarily through the narration of the filmmaker, Joey Lozano, who describes the impact of a US development agency-supported road through indigenous and Muslim communities and lands in the southern Philippines. The road was built to facilitate mono-cropping pineapple for export and has plunged local communities into a devastating and unsustainable cash-crop economy.

Interview-driven film

This is driven by a character, or multiple characters, interviewed within the film. This kind of film is sometimes referred to as a "talking head" film, particularly when the interviews are filmed in a traditional Q&A style.

Interview-driven films can take longer to make than narration-driven films, because you will need longer to film (interviews can last hours). Logging, and transcribing, and then piecing together the logic based on your interviewees' words can be time-consuming. Changes are harder to make because you need to find solutions within the interview material itself, rather than simply rewriting narration.

A good example of a primarily interview-driven film on the WITNESS website is *Books not Bars*, which uses interviews with affected youth and activists, as well as community organizers and academics to tell the story of the burgeoning prison industrial complex in the US, and how businesses are profiting from the incarceration of minority youth.

Another example to look at is *Against the Tide of History*, where the story of the impact of indiscriminate laying of landmines in Casamance, in the south of Senegal, is told through the voices of landmine victims, activists, and government and opposition figures.

Observational-verité

This is centred on filming "life as it happens," especially situations and events that occur in a particular place, process, or situation. This is the most difficult and time-consuming kind of film to make. The observational mode suggests that we should let people and their observed actions speak for themselves. The action or the narrative will evolve in front of the camera. The filmmaker should not be intrusive or interrupt the natural process of filmmaking. The underlying assumption is that people behave as normal when the camera and the crew are simply a "fly-on-the-wall," filming whatever happens in front of the camera.

Observational-verité films can take the longest to make, as life (especially in front of the camera) changes unpredictably. Getting subjects comfortable with observational cameras can take time and trust (and often involves safety and security issues). Once shooting begins, you may not know how long your story will go on, and what direction it will take. It could take weeks, months, even years. Some filmmakers will even edit alongside shooting because of the extended time frame. The films of the director Frederick Wiseman are famed for their ability to transport viewers into different institutional settings—including prisons, psychiatric facilities and schools—to show how they operate. If you plan to use an observational-verité style his films are a good choice to watch in preparation.

Observational-verité footage can have a very strong and emotional impact, because it transports audiences most directly to 'real-life' situations. Elements of observational-verité in WITNESS films online include:

- *The MDRI video submission to the Inter-American Commission*, which shows actuality or verité footage of inhumane living conditions of patients in the Neuro-Psychiatric hospital of Paraguay, intercut with titlecards that provide a human rights frame. The footage shows the story through shocking and moving pictures: patients held in excrement-smeared cells, naked, without access to latrines, and wandering in open sewage and broken glass.

- *Rise*, a co-production with the Revolutionary Association of the Women of Afghanistan (RAWA), documents life under the Taliban in Afghanistan. Parts of the video were filmed clandestinely with cameras hidden under women's veils. The footage brutally shows the tyranny in the streets of Kabul exacted by the Taliban, including morality squads and public executions.

Figure 3.1   Footage shot inside Afghanistan by RAWA (RAWA/WITNESS)

As noted, many films use a combination of all three methods listed above. For example, *Rise* combines verité footage, interviews, and narrative voiceover, as well as innovative use of text on screen.

Exercise 3.2: Select the people to include in the video

Here you analyze a situation to work out which people to include in your video. We recommend you discuss the exercise with a colleague or friend. Below we provide a sample situation to analyze, but you could also use a story from Exercise 3.1 or your own advocacy campaign focus.

It is early evening in the city, and a man, Carlos, is walking home from work with two close friends. Carlos is a married father of two who works in a local factory. A police van pulls up and three police officers jump out and pull him inside, saying they are arresting him for involvement in a robbery. According to them, John, Carlos's former schoolmate, has told them that he committed a robbery with Carlos the night before. Carlos knows this is untrue, as he was at a family party then. When he arrives at the police station Carlos is put under increasing pressure by the police, and is eventually tortured until he confesses that he was involved, and that his two friends, Jane and Khan, were also involved in the robbery. The police leave Carlos in a cell and the next morning they say that he was found dead from a heart attack.

For fifteen years, Carlos's country has been governed by one party. This party has won a series of nominally democratic, but institutionally flawed, elections. Torture in police custody is common, and is almost an accepted part of investigative procedure. For the past ten years a campaigning human rights organization with a small staff and a strong volunteer core from all sectors of society has been confronting torture in this society, and challenging the police and judiciary to be more effective and accountable.

This organization takes up a legal case against the police as part of its work to challenge torture in society, and to secure compensation for Carlos's widow, Stephanie. They also try to engage the media in a discussion of the case.

Sit down with a colleague or a friend and discuss the different people who have a stake or a perspective on the situation. You might want to consider:

- "Perpetrators and stake-holders": What are the causes of the problem or conflict and who is responsible for this situation?
- "Experts": Who are the experts? Are they experts because of depth of knowledge or societal position, or because they have direct personal experience? Remember experts don't have to be academics; they can have a life experience that makes them an expert.
- "Protagonists/change-makers": Who are the protagonists? Who is trying to change the situation?

- "Victims/survivors": Who is affected by this situation? Who has experienced the situation and survived it?

Looking at these different categories of people, who will be effective as a spokesperson or character with the target audience you have envisioned?

Try filling out a sample form like that shown in Table 3.1. Consider including yourself and your own voice as a possible character.

Table 3.1   Select the people to include in the video

Possible characters	Perspective	Comments on potential as an interviewee
"Stephanie"	Wife of torture victim, very strong personal involvement with particular case	Still very grief-stricken; able to share her own experience and loss with the audience
"John"	Carlos's friend, tortured in same police station	Experiences some guilt about his role in implicating Carlos
"Joe"	Survived torture, very critical of the government's lack of action	Articulate, a little distant
"Anita"	Worked in the government; now part of a leading NGO coalition against torture	Sticks to party-line
"Rita"	Worked in prisons under current regime, when torture practiced; accused of involvement	Difficult to get to talk, but able to offer an insider perspective. How to make her comfortable enough to speak out?

Now look at the top three and your top choice—could you tell a story with just three of these characters, and if so, would there be any missing story elements? What do you notice about the people you have chosen to tell your story?

Look at your top choice. Could the story be told from this person's perception? Could this person be the primary character?

Genre

Style or genre will also shape the telling of your story. The following are only a selection of common genres.

- *Personal point of view*: A personal essay or perspective on an issue, often from a person directly involved, or from the filmmaker or activist. Sometimes the filmmaker will appear on camera, or the camera will follow a character through whose eyes we understand the story. Sometimes, the point of view will only appear through narration. Personal point of view is also expressed visually, through the camera work. From whose eyes are you seeing events unfold? In a "reflexive" film, the presence and involvement of the filmmaker is made clear in the actual film—he or she is not a neutral technician.

- *News-journalistic:* A news style follows the rules of mainstream journalism to represent factual information. This style prioritizes notions of objectivity, balance, presenting "both sides of the story" and neutrality. The story is often told through a "third person"—the journalist—who has collected information from a variety of sources, and interviewed all opposing sides. Facts, opinions and information are sourced directly, and information is presented in a dry, punctual format. Formats can vary from short news reports and bulletins (as short as 20 seconds), to current affairs reports (anywhere from three to 15 minutes), to longer investigative documentaries unraveling a "mystery" or conflict.

- *Journey film or central character:* Tends to involve a central character who experiences a series of encounters: filming the process of the journey is as important as reaching the final destination. This kind of film is more likely to be an observational film, although someone's journey can be reconstructed through the use of interviews, narration, and creative visuals as well.

- *Location-centered film:* Here we are in one specific location from which we do not shift. The location itself is the defining characteristic or voice in the film.

- *Survey film:* A survey film reviews an issue, and presents a thesis. Several examples, multiple interviews, experts, and situations are presented to support and/or contradict the case. For example, *The Corporation*, a three-hour Canadian documentary about the rise of the most influential institution in our times (the corporation) uses interviews with more than 40 people, case studies, reels of archives and animation as well as a narrative voice to bring together a thesis about the nature of corporations, having surveyed the world for evidence.

- *Music video*: Video that is edited and even based on music or a soundtrack for its structure and length. This genre tends to reflect the editing techniques developed by MTV. Videomakers can collaborate with musicians to write lyrics and music before shooting begins. A pioneering organization in the use of music video formats for advocacy video is Breakthrough TV (<www.breakthrough.tv>).
- *Public service announcements:* These are short, punchy, to-the-point videos that "advertise" your advocacy issue. For example, WITNESS, along with Coalition for an International Criminal Court, created a 60-second "advocate-ment" for the creation of the court, drawing on the imagery of the genocidal twentieth century. Using titlecards, dramatic music, and powerful images, they made a powerful case for a renewed commitment to a successful and effective International Criminal Court.

These are only a small range of options that may help you find the "voice" and genre in your film. Many filmmakers use one or more of these techniques.

Exercise 3.3: Who will tell the story?
This exercise helps you think through how your video advocacy issue could be covered using different film forms. It may be best to brainstorm options in a small group.

Select a particular sub-issue within your advocacy project. For example, if you were documenting police misconduct and proposing alternatives, you might focus here just on arrest practices. Now consider how you would make a primarily narration-driven, interview-driven, and observational video about the subject. Use the strengths and weaknesses analyzed above (pp. 85–7).

What would you aim to capture for an observational approach? What might be the advantages of a narration-driven or interview-driven film? What kind of larger issues can you address in voiceover, with charts and text on screen, or via more formal interviews? What might be the advantages of an observational style in terms of getting insight into the situation and unguarded discussion? What will you have to shoot if you cannot use voiceover or narration? Or interviews? Consider what are the advantages and disadvantages to both styles, depending on your advocacy goals. For the purposes of this exercise try to use one form primarily, but remember that in your videos you are likely to combine elements of all three.

Alternatively, try this exercise with the situation in Exercise 3.2. How would you portray this campaign for justice using these three different narrative forms?

Exercise 3.4: Rewrite a narration

This exercise is best done in a group, and is designed to help you see how your choice of narrator and narrative style affects the way your audience responds to a film.

Start by choosing a video that that relates to a subject matter with which you and your colleagues know well (perhaps the advocacy focus of your work). It is best if the video is not one that you have watched before. Look for something that is short and aimed at a general public.

Next, each person watching the video should select a narration point of view from among the following:

- Voice of someone in the film
- "Voice of god," third-person narration
- Their own point of view
- A popular celebrity

Now sit down and watch the video with the audio off. As you watch the video each person should note down in shorthand the narration or voiceover that they think is necessary to explain the film narrative. Each viewer has a choice about how much narration they think is necessary. Each viewer should then present their narration and participants compare notes.

To make the exercise more complicated you can also choose to vary the audience the video is aimed at. You might want to try this on the second viewing of the video, after people have a sense of how the video is structured. You should ask people to reconsider how they might change their narration if the video was aimed at an audience of:

- Government decision-makers on the issue
- International human rights mechanisms
- Community groups working on the issue
- International solidarity activism groups
- A general public viewing it online or in a news broadcast

Dramatization/uses of drama

Much—but not all—advocacy video tends to be made of documentary material, with real people telling their own stories, with life unfolding before the camera. But sometimes, filmmakers turn to evocative imagery and dramatization to tell the story in a creative way or because they have no other choice in order to cover an issue they want to film.

Ronit Avni says:

> One of the hardest questions when creating advocacy video is how to reconstruct or evoke a violation that's already happened. For example, *In the Name of Safety*, a film by Ain O Salish Kendra, a human rights organization in Bangladesh, uses evocative imagery of jail cells and shadows of guards to evoke abuses suffered by unjustly jailed female prisoners, rather than actually re-enacting the scene.

Ronit also cites Lilibet Foster, who made *Operation Fine Girl: Rape as a Weapon of War in Sierra Leone*. The film traces the devastating impact of a decade-long civil war on Sierra Leone's young women, thousands of whom were abducted, raped, and/or forced into slavery by soldiers on both sides of the conflict. Ronit explains:

> Lilibet used some interesting techniques to depict emotionally sensitive situations—blurred imagery, symbolic imagery, shots of anonymous feet running away, etc., to evoke the fear and disorientation faced by these women. This can be respectfully and powerfully done without going so far as to recreate events.

There are several further options for this kind of evocative imagery—including using archival material, photos, artwork, the appearance and disappearance of people or objects in the frame—and many of these decisions can be made in the edit room.

In her film, *A Healthy Baby Girl*, award-winning director Judith Helfand uses her own artwork to portray her emotional state after losing her reproductive organs to cancer. The film was used as an advocacy video to demonstrate the widespread and fatal impact of dangerous pharmaceutical drugs given en masse to pregnant mothers in the 1960s.

In some cases dramatization can be a major part of the film. In *McLibel* (about McDonald's libel suit against two anti-McDonald's

Figure 3.2   Motion effects and blurring are used in *Operation Fine Girl* during scenes discussing the experiences of the young women who experienced sexual violence (Oxygen Media LLC/WITNESS)

activists), Franny Armstrong had no access with her camera to the courtroom proceedings. Franny knew that in order to get at these arguments, they would need to "recreate" or "redramatize" these arguments for the film. The defendants were ready and willing to replay what they had done in the courtroom, but the witnesses on McDonalds' side would be another story. "Our advantage was that our script was already written—transcripts from the courtroom were available," Franny recalls.

> We decided we would try dramatic reconstructions, so we made a joke list of the directors we would want to approach. Ken Loach was on the top, and I was on the bottom, as I had never directed fiction. The trial was pretty famous at this point, and Ken Loach wrote back a fax. Suddenly, we had the top dramatic director in England to work on our film!

Franny then embarked on the arduous process of developing the film's script from over 60,000 pages of court transcripts. Loach then shot the key fictional sequences to Franny's film. These fictional elements make up the crucial arguments and counter-arguments in the intellectual structure of the film.

Whenever you use evocation or reconstruction/redramatization, it is important to keep in mind that "scripted" scenes may be criticized for not having remained 100 percent true to reality or may be misconstrued as an attempt to sensationalize an issue. This could lead your video to lose credibility as an effective advocacy tool with some more critical or more traditional audiences.

Although we do not extensively discuss advocacy soap opera in this book, there is much that can be learned from the experiences of shows like *Sexto Sentido*. Another good source on using fiction to persuade and influence behavior is Population Media Center, <www.populationmedia.org>.

THE IMPORTANCE OF AUDIENCE

Who exactly is your audience? As discussed in Chapter 1, understanding *to whom* you are telling your story will change *how* you tell your story. More importantly, defining what you want your audience to do once they've seen your video will also identify the story you need to tell.

How to define your audience? You must decide who your most influential audience is, what you want them to do, and how they will be convinced to join the effort. If there is a direct appeal to get involved, decide who could most effectively encourage them to take action. Recognize what will be appealing, persuasive or intriguing to them, both in terms of factual information conveyed, people interviewed, and experts' commentary. You also need to understand whom you'll alienate and repel as you make these choices.

At the most basic level, Howard Weinberg suggests you ask yourself: "Are you stirring up the troops, or talking to the unconverted?" He believes this is a key question in order to determine how you will frame your entire film. Similarly, Martin Atkin, producer at Greenpeace, also starts by dividing his audiences into two main categories:

The first is a broad, general audience outside the NGO community—a general public that knows little about the issue—and the second is other NGOs, people "within" the community, who already know a little.

Language and literacy levels of your audience are additional crucial factors for your production. If you use titlecards, subtitles, and keys will your audience be able to read them? What language would best suit the telling of your story?

At WITNESS, partners are encouraged to define their audiences very specifically to ensure they target and reach these distinct audiences with the videos they produce. The following is an elaboration of some of the broad categories of viewers and potential uses of video in advocacy.

Community audiences

Seeing your image or members of your community on a screen can generate powerful results. When videos are made to go back to the communities in which they were filmed, it can stimulate grassroots organizing, consciousness-raising, and a sense of empowerment. Joey Lozano reports: "When we play back our video for screening by community members, we seem to recover lost pride in ourselves. The video helps us recover self-esteem." Gabriela Zamorano and Fabiola Gervacio built a communications division for the Women's Commission of UCIZONI, a peasant organization in Mexico, to make advocacy videos to encourage indigenous women to join. They created three short videos and traveled to villages to screen them among the women. Says Gabriela:

> The response in the communities was phenomenal.When the women saw images of women and an entire film dedicated to indigenous women, they were surprised, because usually everything is about the men.

These are videos edited to inspire, consolidate, educate, and mobilize the communities they come from. Grassroots video editing, compared to legal or policy uses, can be much more diverse in its style, structure, and composition. Joey Lozano recommends the film be made in the language or dialect understood by the people. He also says it can be longer than films intended for an international audience, as you have a "captive audience," because they are already personally interested in the subject, and don't need to be convinced to watch, or to keep watching. In some cases you can also present a more simple series of testimonies—if they are of people within the community, people are more likely to listen to them because of the innate interest and novelty of seeing people they know, or who share their own experiences. It is always a question of audience. If you are showing participatory video made within the community to help express and move forward their own decision-making processes, it does not matter if it is poorly made or tedious to an outside audience, because it will be highly effective for its target viewership. However, if you are coming from outside to try to organize and mobilize a community around an issue then you may face more pressure to create a video to different standards.

Figure 3.3   An audience in Mindanao, the Philippines watches one of Joey Lozano's productions (Necessary Illusions Productions)

Audiences often feel comfortable relating to and discussing the issues in a film that presents individuals who are similar to them, although not familiar to them as real people. For example, several individuals courageously stepped forward to participate in *Operation Fine Girl: Rape as Weapon of War in Sierra Leone*, fully disclosing their identities and faces on camera, despite their difficult testimonies. People seeing it across Sierra Leone have related to their stories and responded overwhelmingly.

During community screenings of the 47-minute video in Sierra Leone, Binta Mansaray, associate producer of the film, reports:

Girls are sometimes troubled by the young women's decision to show their faces on the video. This gives me an opportunity in screenings to raise questions about stigmatizing victims and blaming the young women rather than the soldiers and rebels.

She points out how difficult it is to win justice if the men can count on women being too afraid or ashamed to make their accusations in open court. In other screenings in the provinces, there have been mixed audiences of ex-combatants and civilians attending. Binta describes how

> some of the ex-combatant women were emotional, and some of them cried while listening to the testimony of the girls. It took some time for them to express themselves, and when they finally mustered courage to talk, they said they were willing to come forward and explain a lot of what happened ... but were concerned about their safety.

Activist audiences

Videos intended for activists address an audience that can mobilize on behalf of an issue or the people in a film. These videos speak to people who may already be interested in the subject, and want to learn more about how they can help, or even how they can help themselves by learning from the film. They may also engage and inform an audience that is new to the issues presented. Often they can be more partisan than videos for other audiences, as they are "preaching to the converted." They use facts and arguments to support an activist position, but like all videos, they rely on passion, human relationships and emotion to really engage their viewers.

At Greenpeace, Martin Atkin has been working on their GMO (Genetically Modified Organisms) project and has produced two separate videos, one intended specifically for farmers around the world, the other for a general audience. The one for farmers was intended for use by NGOs to raise awareness in the farming community about the impact of GMOs on farming livelihoods and lives. It is called *Grains of Truth*.

> I knew that it would be emotional before I went to shoot [Atkin recalls about traveling to canola and soya farming communities throughout North America]. The testimonies were so powerful. Basically, they were about the emotional issues of financial consequences, and court cases stemming from the GMOs. I decided to let the farmers speak for themselves, with no narration. I superimposed stylized images of the prairies, of the harvest. I had in my mind's eye to make *Grapes of Wrath*—black and white stylized, with elements that had that feel.

It was unlikely that television stations would take *Grains of Truth*, because it was so "artsy." But that didn't matter. This video was intended to be viewed by other farmers. It was 15 minutes long and it was translated into Bulgarian, Romanian, Czech, Thai and many other languages. It was distributed by NGOs working with sustainable farming, and it toured the world. They encouraged people to come to the screenings by postering in villages. In some cases, the subjects in the documentary were invited to come as well, to answer questions after the screening.

An artistic, emotional approach allowed immediate connection to the plight of the farmers worldwide, and made the film accessible to multiple communities with similar experiences.

Providing historical context can help frame a specific event for activists. When Indian right-wing forces unleashed communal violence in the state of Gujarat, activist Shabnam Hashmi says she and her husband Gauhar Raza "were keen to make a political film about it." One film had already been made about the 2002 massacres at Gujarat, but Shabnam was concerned that while the film portrayed the recent events, it didn't explain where the hatred came from. She wanted to make clear that

> It wasn't an isolated incident. We needed a film which dealt with the history of the right-wing movement, to show it was a movement founded on the principles introduced by Italian Fascists. We need to show what led to the events at Gujarat.

Using archival footage, photographs and the 20 hours of footage they'd filmed themselves in Gujarat, Shabnam and Gauhar edited the film *Evil Stalks the Land*. The film is used in activist circles in India and around the world to show the reality of, and the reasons for, communal violence between Hindus and Muslims in India, and Shabnam herself has shown it at 35 screenings to date in the US alone.

> We made the film to wake people up. And the film serves that purpose. The film leaves audiences stunned. By the end, we are saying that it is the audience's duty to the next generation to save our country.

Now, the film has become part of Shabnam's own toolkit as she organizes a network of five-day workshops in districts throughout the country—including within Gujarat itself—in order to sensitize activists and NGOs about the power of right-wing forces in India.

Human rights organizations producing video pay particular attention to focusing their messaging in material for activist audiences. Joanna Duchesne, a long-time producer for Amnesty International, worked on Amnesty's global "Stop Violence Against Women" campaign, producing a video that could be of use to groups around the world working on the issue. It incorporated a set of key problems including rape, post-conflict violence, domestic violence, and honor killings, and also emphasized clear goals, including building support for women's groups, and encouraging individuals to support a range of responses to these problems. To create a tool of use worldwide Duchesne featured stories from five regions of the world, all of which focused on an aspect of violence against women, letting viewers see for themselves that violence against women was everywhere, albeit in different manifestations. To create a space for action, she emphasized the role of women as dynamic and active in responding to violence, rather than as victims, and took particular care in the last minute of the 12-minute film to frame viewers' emotional understanding with analysis provided by the brother of one of the women featured, who talks about education and awareness and appeals to viewers' sense of citizenship in asking them to act.

Legal decision-makers (local, national, international), including human rights commissions, regional commissions, courts, and tribunals

Video can appear in courts and legal settings to provide background to a case, or even as direct evidence of alleged crimes or violations. It can also be presented to oversight and regulatory bodies in tandem with other materials. In some cases, it will be presented as unedited footage, and in others it may be presented in edited format, either as an existing video that is to be submitted, or as a video prepared specifically for the legal context. In either case, these video submissions are unlikely to be described as "advocacy video"—even though they may be intended to persuade a particular audience towards a particular decision.

More and more, video is becoming part of the legal process around the world. At the International Criminal Tribunal for the Former Yugoslavia, permanent video monitors have been installed throughout the courtroom, and video is providing key evidence for genocide and crimes against humanity. In one case, video evidence clearly identified a defendant at the scene of the crime—a fact he had been denying. He was convicted and sentenced to 46 years in prison, in large part owing to this video evidence.

For a legal audience, you will be creating an evidentiary submission for a court or other legal mechanism. You should generally be very careful with your language—visual, verbal, or written—in the narration and titlecards. You need to avoid editorializing polemics or policy pronouncements. But you can substantiate a factual allegation, and develop deeper human empathy through using video.

Often it is persuasive to prepare a video that parallels and substantiates the points raised in other forms of documentation, such as a written report or another evidentiary submission. For example, as described in Chapter 1, Human Rights Alert in Manipur, India prepared a video titled *Sanamacha's Story* to accompany a written presentation to the UN Working Group on Forced and Involuntary Disappearances. Although the Working Group had already been briefed on the problem of "disappearances" in Manipur, *Sanamacha's Story* was the first time the voices of eyewitnesses to the abduction by Indian government forces, and the voices of the family grieving the loss of their son, had made their way into the United Nations, and the Working Group said they felt a newly reinforced conviction to address the case.

In other cases, human rights organizations have successfully used video to show emblematic stories and individual cases that are representative of wider patterns of abuse—in these videos, a series of interviewees discuss abuses affecting them that have also been experienced by a wider population. These figures can then be substantiated and documented in much greater detail in accompanying written documentation or oral presentation. See Chapter 6 for a more extensive discussion and examples of how video can be used in a legal context.

Policy-makers, opinion-formers, and powerbrokers

Videos targeted specifically at decision-makers can be very effective. Like videos intended for legal use, they may outline specific violations of law, but they can also go further. They may also outline possible solutions, with specific policy recommendations or suggestions, and bring personal human experience directly into the boardrooms or committee rooms full of people with the power to make a difference. In other cases you may be trying to shame them into action, or to convince them that it is in their best interests to act.

Says Joey Lozano:

> These are people who survive on votes, good public image and money and profits. If one is making a video with the intention of soliciting support from these people, one must present it in such a way that makes them realize they will lose votes, have a bad public image, or lose profits. It's like hitting them where it hurts most.

In this light, *Silence and Complicity*, a low-budget women's rights film, is a powerful example of the ability of video to affect policy and decision-makers. The film was made by two women's rights organizations, the Center for Reproductive Rights (then the Center for Reproductive Law and Policy, CRLP) and the Latin American and Caribbean Committee for the Defense of Women's Rights (CLADEM), and uses the moving testimonies of women who were mistreated and abused, to expose widespread sexual, psychological, and verbal abuse, neglect, rape, and violence against women in Peruvian government-run health facilities. The video was tied to a report of the same name published in both English and Spanish. Barbara Becker, then deputy director of communications at CRLP and the co-producer of the video, chose video for its unique emotional impact:

> Human rights reports are so legalistic in their language, and they have to be. We wanted to come up with a way to show the human face of women being abused in Latin America and in Peru in particular.

The video was shown to community groups and women's centers in Peru, to key representatives at the UN, to NGOs, to development professionals, and to international audiences at human rights film festivals. The film has changed the manner in which rape and sexual abuse cases are handled in the courts. The Peruvian government has also agreed to create new guidelines for doctors, to investigate the cases documented in the video, to include women's rights organizations in its reproductive health committees, and to begin talks with the Peruvian branch of CLADEM to improve public healthcare. Becker noted that the Peruvian government chose to negotiate rather than to have the film screened in public and diplomatic venues.[1]

Remember that some videos can be alienating for powerbrokers. The language you decide to use, the stridency with which you make your point, or the spokespeople or music you select can all limit the audiences that will be receptive to your production, and therefore may limit the usefulness of a video. Sometimes, you must make choices about your audience, knowing what the casualties will be.

For example, WITNESS collaborated with the Ella Baker Center for Human Rights, a California-based human rights organization, and Columbia University Law School to create a video titled *Books Not Bars*. The target audience for the film were young people in affected communities in California and around the US, and the primary goals of the film were to explain the prison industrial complex (where an increasing prison population is linked to increasing commercialization of the whole process of incarceration), to connect the issues of disproportionate minority confinement and corresponding lack of investment in education to universal human rights norms, and to provide positive examples of ways to engage in activism around the issues. While the video and the accompanying action pack and lesson plans are effective tools for youth organizing, it is not an effective tool for advocacy with most branches of government. The very qualities that give it appeal for youth—the use of hip-hop music and spoken word, the rapid pacing, and the choice of youth interviewees, for example—can alienate some decision-makers. However, following the success of *Books Not Bars*, WITNESS and the Ella Baker Center collaborated on a follow-up video, *System Failure*, which was targeted, with a more sober style, using of footage from government hearings, and more in-depth interviews, at parents of incarcerated youth, and at government officials.

Internet audiences

The viewers you find online will depend on where you place the video, how much content exists on the site and its degree of specialization, and the audience size and demographic it typically attracts. You can't assume that this audience will know anything about the subject— or even care about it—when they begin watching unless you are streaming your video at a website that is focused on your issue.

Videos aimed for online viewing have specific technical and content demands. Online webcasts need to be short, clear, engaging, and have a clearly defined vision and concrete ideas on how to get involved. The advantage of broadcasting online is that you can supplement it with text, links and complementary material; while a viewership is reached that is not constricted by national borders or by the need to attend an organized screening or television broadcast at a particular time. "Our online video broadcasts at <www.witness. org> reach a broad, largely North American and Western European audience, and there is the immediate opportunity online to respond and take action," explains Matisse Bustos, Outreach Coordinator at WITNESS.

Online use of video is a fairly new phenomenon, so there's little information about how engaged people remain on the web. However, in general, shorter video is likely to be more effective—WITNESS finds most viewers will spend no longer than three minutes viewing online videos. Other sites, such as OneWorld TV, <www.oneworld. tv>, use short clips and subdivide longer videos to allow people to pick and choose the parts of a longer video that interest them—or offer options for interaction and messaging around clips that interest a viewer.

It's important to understand how people arrive at a website in the first place. Matisse explains:

> We need to be honest about the challenges of online, and the need to stand out from the profusion of websites out there. That's why, for example, at WITNESS we often use celebrities to introduce or to narrate, to help draw people in.

At WITNESS, offline activity, such as current affairs, can be a driving force bringing people to the website. For example, the RAWA piece *Rise*, a video including material filmed by women during the Taliban regime in Afghanistan was frequently viewed when it was topical and compelling because of world events. *Operation Fine Girl* was featured on the Oprah Winfrey show, which brought considerable traffic to the online webcast.

In some cases the webcast is a way to engage people who may then use video offline. Through the online webcast, activist groups, schools, and universities can learn about the material, and television producers can get a sense of the material available.

Pointers to remember for online/web video

- Avoid a lot of camera movement or in-frame action
- Use straight cuts rather than dissolves
- Subtitles/titlecards don't work well, so consider dubbing, or voiceover
- Use interviews—they convey information, and they are stable shots that will stream well

- Keep it short, ideally 3–5 minutes. If longer, divide it into segments so the audience can see the whole, or parts they are interested in. Include a trailer if you are putting a longer video on the Internet
- Provide accompanying text information and stills
- Get good sound—with a slow connection, the quality of sound will be higher than the visual image quality

As we move towards a broadband universe, interactive video will fill the screens of computers as they become more like computerized TV sets. These changes will affect the technical and stylistic considerations for online video. However, for now and in the foreseeable future, there will still be a digital divide. The reality is that in most parts of the world, it's wireless technology that has broken through, and we are not yet seeing wireless technology deliver full-frame broadband video. Video makers are likely to continue to have to adapt their content for online audiences. For more discussion of the Internet as a distribution vehicle, see Chapter 7.

General audience

Most of the above categories of films can be repurposed as documentaries of varying lengths for a general public and the mainstream media. The secret here is to provide context to an audience that may know and care little about the subject. You may need to "sell" the subject itself. As in almost every kind of video, you will need to tell a strong, compelling story.

But Howard Weinberg warns that it is

> hard to tell a passionate story. You can hurt your case by overselling; even people that are sympathetic may begin to think, "That's outrageous." I often see things that make one sceptical rather than supportive. A film will be full of overstatements, yet context is missing. Visually, you need to get in close for impact, but you also have to back off.

Backing off might mean not using heavy-handed narration or titlecards. It might mean including counterpoints to a given opinion rather than a series of voices that are in agreement. Weinberg says that, for a general public, "You need to locate them: The story has to connect from what the audiences know to what they don't know."

Sometimes, videos on the same subject can be shot and edited for two different audiences. After making the video *Grains of Truth* for farmers around the world, Martin Atkin of Greenpeace produced and edited another video about the same subject in a completely different style. Unlike *Grains of Truth*, which was aimed at farmers in Africa or China, *Slice of Life* is a 17-minute video intended to publicize the issues in Canada and the USA.

Martin explains:

> It became a conventional, standard documentary. It was scripted, with sound bites, fact by fact. The treatment was like a current affairs documentary. We got a distributor and it was to be released alongside a Greenpeace report on the issue, around the time of the Monsanto Annual General Assembly in 2003. So the big TV stations may have used, for example, only 1 minute from the film, but that's how it was intended.

Similar to Martin Atkin, the producer of *Operation Fine Girl*, Lilibet Foster,needed to reach multiple audiences. As she did not have the luxury of making multiple versions she had to think through from the start her multiple audiences, and in addition how these audiences were likely to see the film—i.e. broadcast on television, privately on home video, in group screenings etc. *Operation Fine Girl* was to be shown on international television with a première in the US and would reach a broad general public this way, and then was to have an extensive use across the country of Sierra Leone as an advocacy and outreach tool to help in the peace and reconciliation process, as the country transitioned to peace after a ten- year war.

As Lilibet says:

> The essential challenge for myself and Binta Mansaray, the extremely knowledgeable Sierra Leonean with whom I worked, was to figure out how to make a film that would reach an outside audience that knew little about the history of the country and the details of the conflict yet bring to light new information for Sierra Leoneans who had lived through the war. The other important considerations were that the atrocities committed in Sierra Leone were widespread and extremely brutal, and the country is in West Africa, where there were several other countries also in various stages of conflict. For an outside audience, I therefore decided to focus on the story of only three girls and one boy who would represent every other child in their situation.
>
> I hoped that this would personalize the conflict for an audience and not leave them with a sense of hopelessness and despair for a country and people far away, who were finally on the road to peace. On the other hand, within Sierra Leone, one of the issues they were struggling with in the peace process

was the successful reintegration of the abducted children back into their families and communities. This was especially true for girls who had been impregnated and were raising what was referred to as "rebel babies." We hoped that the first-hand accounts of what took place would help to reveal that abduction was a calculated war tactic used by each side of the conflict and that they had not willingly joined the rebels to commit crimes against their own villages.

Lilibet knew that to fill out and contextualize the story, they had to find the right person, *within* the community, to interview about the history of the conflict and add enough to inform the outside audience, yet without turning off the internal audience. As she notes:

> For obvious reasons, we carefully choose who to include because for the film to be taken seriously, it was important that they be considered good, fair, knowledgeable local and international sources. To even out the information and add credibility, I also interviewed members of the rebel factions and government to get their response, members of the community running the schools where many girls came when they escaped from their captors, and medical staff who had first-hand evidence and knowledge of the physical and mental condition of the abductees.

Broadcast media

If your campaign is of interest to the media, general audiences can be reached effectively through mainstream media. This may either be through the production of a documentary for broadcast or through the provision of story material to a news outlet. In both situations, it is good to be realistic about the opportunities (it is often difficult to get airtime on the channels where you want to be), and also about the degree of control you will retain over your story. Unless you are buying the airtime from the channel, you will probably have to work with a commissioning editor at the television channel during the production of your documentary. They will exert a degree of control over your production, based on their knowledge of their own audience, and the needs of the broadcasting channel.

If you are buying airtime on a niche channel, such as local cable, it is up to you to work out what audience is watching this channel. A number of human rights organizations in South Asia and elsewhere have effectively purchased local cable time to broadcast programs aimed at a general public.

If you are providing raw material to news media, in most cases you will find that the slant on the story will be determined by the outlet. They will take raw footage or interviews from you, and frame it within their own editorial stance. You will have to decide if the loss of control over your story, and how it is framed, is worth the potential exposure for the issue. For more information on the distribution of broadcast-oriented media, see Chapter 7.

MAKING A STORY A REALITY: PREPRODUCTION

The stages of filmmaking include:

1. *Conceptualization and research*: Here you build the idea and clarify the advocacy goal (why am I making this film?), the audience (for whom am I making this film?) and the elements of film to be included (how will I make this film?). Also ask yourself, what other films have been made on this issue? What perspective do these take? How is my film different? What information do I need to research to make an informed film?
2. *Preproduction*: This stage includes preparing and researching a outline, initial script and a shooting plan, logistical planning, and fundraising.
3. *Production*: This is when the film is shot bearing in mind all the available elements including interviews, verité footage, B-roll, cutaways, interviews, graphics, archival needs, music etc. (For more detail and an explanation of these terms, see Chapter 4 and the Glossary.)
4. *Postproduction*: This stage includes the production and review of a series of versions of the video, on paper and then on screen. For more detail, see Chapter 5.

What is preproduction?

Preproduction is the stage at which research is collected and questions are asked that help to shape an investigation and story. It is best to draft an outline to clarify your story and messages. You need to pay attention to the budget, resources, and timeline. From your video outline, you can then create a shotlist, schedule, and a call-sheet.

The basics of a story: what, where, when, who, why, how?

During preproduction, you should ask yourself the following questions:

- *What* story are you trying to tell? What story are you leaving out? And why?
- *When* did the incident, event or violation happen?
- *Where* does the story occur?
- *Who* will appear in your story?
- *Who* will tell the story?
- *Why* are you telling this story?
- *How* will you tell the story?

You may find that you will have more than one answer for each of these questions.

Why are you telling this story?

For advocacy-oriented video you should be absolutely clear from the outset why you are telling your story, as both a filmmaker and as a social justice advocate. You also need to determine clearly who your audience is, and what they will find persuasive or compelling. On the basis of this you should choose the most appropriate story to tell.

How will you tell your story?

How will you tell this story? Will you be following a particular chronological order or sequence? Will you concentrate on a character, an issue, or a place? How can this story most effectively be told, and how can you ensure that it will be interesting to watch and responsible to the people who participated?

Has your story been told before?

At this stage, you may also need to do some research about other videos, films, books, websites, and other forms of media on the subject. There's no sense in reinventing the wheel, and these sources may also help develop your own project.

Preparing an outline for your video

You now have a clear goal and audience, and are developing the most effective message and messenger for this audience.

At this stage, you should prepare an outline or working script. An outline is the architecture of your proposed film—a sketch of the audio and visual elements that will make up the finished film, arranged in order, illustrating the storyline of your film. From your outline you will work out what shots you need to shoot in any given location, interview or activity. A well-thought-through outline is particularly crucial in the case of human rights and social justice filming, where there is not always the opportunity to go back and get reshoots of the material.

Preparing an outline will help you to think of what you need to tell your story in a compelling and dramatic way. You do not have to stick to it once you come to film and edit but it can act as a guide to help you think about creative ways to tell your story.

An outline format is shown in Table 3.2. You use note form, with the visuals on the left, and the audio on the right.

Table 3.2   Outline format

Picture	Sound
Crowds demonstrating outside government building	Sync sound** Narration on recent rights abuses, and government involvement
John B tells story of the night in the cell, c/a* Still photos: John B, tortured	Interview on-camera with John B, victim of torture
Action pictures of him doing interviews at place of work where he works monitoring rights violations	Narration on case; voiceover from interview with another human rights worker

Notes:
*c/a = cutaway (a shot of a detail of a location or of a person, or of a visual related to the story, which is used to cover cuts in an edit of an interview and to add impact to an interview. For more detail, see Chapter 4)
**Sync sound = "synchronous" sound recorded at the same time as the picture

You will also be considering issues of characters, point of view, and narrative structure—who is telling the story? How are you telling the story?

What audiovisual components will help you tell the story?

All video is made up of combinations of visual and audio elements. Think creatively and expansively about different kinds of sound and images. What will make this story visually interesting? Can you tell your story using different combinations of visuals and audio components? What will have most impact on your audience? What do you have access to given security, budget, and time constraints? Can you make a virtue out of necessity?

Some kinds of visuals and audio to think about:

Visuals

- Visual and audio documentation of events happening—people *doing* things, without commentary.

- Landscapes, locations, and inanimate objects that are part of the story.
- Interviews—one or more people answering questions, posed to them by an interviewer on- or off-camera who may be edited out of the final film.
- Conversations observed—people aware of the presence of a camera, but not being interviewed directly.
- Conversations or people talking to each other, with the camera unobtrusive or hidden.
- Re-enactments—factually accurate recreations of scenes that could not be filmed, or are in the past. Remember that there may be credibility problems with this in the human rights context, particularly if it is not clear why a scene could not be filmed, or needed to be re-enacted.
- Expressionistic shots—often symbolic or artistic, to represent a concept or provide visuals where you do not have access to the location, e.g. in historical interviews.
- Manipulation of imagery via slow-mo, fast-forward, motion-capture etc.
- Still photos or documents—either static or shot with the camera panning/tracking or zooming in or out.
- Text including on-screen titles, headlines, and graphics—used for creative and informational purposes, including subtitles for foreign languages. These are usually added in the editing.
- Library, news, and archive footage –this could be from a professional archive, but also personal memorabilia, and possibly material from other films. Remember footage from a commercial source is usually expensive and complicated to get permission for.
- Blank screen—causing the viewer to reflect on what they have just seen or heard, prime them for what is next, indicate a change of sequence or location, or to emphasize sounds.

Audio or sound elements

- Interviewee—you can use audio only, or audio from a picture-and-sound interview with audio only used, or both picture and audio used.
- Conversations—either recorded with the participants' knowledge or unobtrusively/secretly.
- Narration—could be a narrator, the filmmaker or a participant.
- Synchronous sound—sound shot while filming.

- Sound effects—individual sounds shot while filming, or at a later point.
- Music—this is usually added in editing.
- Silence—the absence of sound can indicate change of mood or place, or cause the viewer to refocus on the screen.

Notice that in many videos the sound and visual elements are not from the same source—in editing you will make choices about how to combine different audio and visual elements.

Exercise 3.5: Deconstruct the audiovisual components of a film
Choose a favorite film and watch it with a critical eye for the different audio and visual elements that go into it. Make a note of all that you see, using the lists above as a guide to potential components. You'll likely be surprised by the variety of different inputs that go into even the simplest film.

Writing a shooting plan or shotlist

Before actually shooting in any location or interview you will want to create a shotlist. This involves brainstorming exactly what sorts of images or shots may help to tell your story, so that when you are filming you have the shots that you need clear in your mind, while being open to the opportunities that actual filming will offer. You will want to go back to your outline and review the video and audio elements you thought about using, and see how you could incorporate these into your shooting plan.

We will come back to the shooting plan in the next chapter after we have presented more on shots and sequences.

Budget, resources, and timeline

With an outline and potential shotlist in hand, you can now do a budget "breakdown" to calculate how much time, money and how many resources you will need. With your outline, estimate:

1. How many people will you have in your crew? (Don't forget the editing!)
2. What equipment and supplies do you need?—camera, tapes, batteries etc.
3. How much time and money will traveling take (both for filming *and* editing)?

4. How much cash do you need for food and extra costs while filming (including "per diem" if needed)?
5. What interviews do you need to film? (How long is each one, and will you need to return for follow-ups?)
6. How many days do you need to film visuals, B-roll or verité, and record music?
7. How much research time will you need for archives, prerecorded music, and still photos?
8. How much money and time will you need for transcribing interviews, logging, preparing paper edit?
9. How much time and money will you need for editing time, and for editing equipment?

Even if you are not expecting to pay for any of the above, it's a good idea to have a clear understanding of exactly how much time you and others will be giving to the project.

You'll need to work out a timeline for your shoot, when and where will you be conducting interviews and filming visuals. If you are able to set times with your interviewees beforehand, now is the time to do so. Use a calendar to block out the filming time you'll require. Always add an extra hour or even two for setting up the equipment, preparing the subject for the interview, etc. Do not forget traveling time between interviews. Everything on shoots takes longer than you expect!

During the budget breakdown, you may realize that you will not have as much time or money as you would like. Now is the time to prioritize and make decisions. For example, you may only have four days to shoot, and you have planned to film six major characters. Perhaps now is the time to decide who you most want to film, and you may decide to limit your filming to only two people (making sure to film ample B-roll, visuals, and sequences). Spending more time with fewer people may actually give you more material to work with in the editing room, and a stronger story line.

A note on fundraising

You may also need to do some fundraising during preproduction. Donors will want to see written material or hear about:

1. The message of the video
2. The outline or basic script
3. The timeline

4. The overall budget and how their contribution fits in
5. How you plan to distribute the video
6. How they, as fundraisers, will benefit from participating

They may not need *a lot* of information about what you plan to do, but they need good information, to help gain confidence in you and your project. The main question they will ask themselves, if they are interested in the project, is: how realistic is the plan?

Fundraising can be as simple as collecting coins at a community gathering, or as complicated as filling out stacks of forms and applying for production funds at international agencies. In all cases, though, you need to decide whether it is worth the time spent raising the money (do you become an administrator instead of an advocate?), and whether it's worth involving yourself with any money that has "strings attached." For example, will the local government council want to hold a veto over the film before you finish and release it? Who, in the end, will control the film?

Scouting ("Recce") and pre-interviews

Depending on funds and time available, and the security situation, it can be a good idea to visit the area where you want to film—before filming. This is known as a "recce," and can be very useful. You may need to determine whether access is difficult or dangerous for anyone involved, or identify and talk to potentially good spokespeople or interviewees.

You can also save time later on by checking for any loud or recurring sounds in the area, for good interview spots, and seeing whether electricity is available to recharge your batteries. You may also need to find a reliable translator or organize local transport arrangements. You may want to scout out where you and your team will stay the night.

Many filmmakers and researchers conduct "pre-interviews" during the recce stage. Pre-interviews can be brief, and need not be recorded. Pre-interviews help determine what people have to say about a subject, and importantly *how* they say it. If you are interviewing many people, it may be a good idea to take notes that detail the basics, for your own future review.

Securing access

As an advocacy filmmaker, there will be times when you need to negotiate access to a location or place where you need to film, and where this decision-making power is not held by your allies on the project. Here you should very carefully consider how you represent yourself. Alongside the issues of what immediate or long-term danger you incur from going to this location, or from concealing your reasons to be there (for more on this, see Chapter 2), you should consider the ethical issues that possible deception may raise. You should also be aware that whatever you put on paper—in explanation to authorities, interviewees, or location owners—about what you are doing has to be something you are willing to endorse and explain down the line.

Exercise 3.6: Draft a project explanation

How you present yourself, your organization, and your video advocacy project to outsiders who are not allies on your project, can have a critical impact on your ability to use the material in the future. Done effectively it will avoid credibility issues with your audience, and legal or reputational challenges from people you have filmed.

This exercise is best done in a group, and is meant to help you identify the bounds within which you can describe your project. It can be done in two parts:

1. Use one of the situations below, and draft short explanations that you would give about the project to the following individuals: site director, location guard, family member of person filmed, a person in the facility, and a translator. Project descriptions must be honest and accurate, but should also be designed with the need to secure access in mind.
2. Take your own video advocacy project, and identify a set of people with whom you will have to discuss your project. Prepare similar 30-second explanations.

- You are working to expose systematized forced labor abuses on a natural resources development jointly managed by the government and a multinational company. You plan to call on the company to withdraw from the project, and for international human rights mechanisms to sanction the government for its action. The site is in a relatively remote area far from major towns. People from the surrounding area are obliged to clear and build roads for the project—they receive some pay, but are also obliged to work additional days, and have no choice over their participation in the project. While the government has a poor reputation nationally and internationally for human rights, there has, as yet, been no exposure of the multinational's involvement in the project or the potential rights abuses. The site is guarded by locally recruited security personnel, and by members of an army unit. The project director is a representative of the multinational, who works in close collaboration with a government official.

- You are working on a project documenting human rights abuses including denial of food, adequate medical attention and cruel and degrading treatment, against people kept in a psychiatric facility. Your goal is to secure change for the people in the facility, as well as a commitment to institutional reform. Officials at the hospital generally do not see that there is anything wrong with current conditions, or accept them as a consequence of financial constraints. The personnel at the facility are short-staffed, and lack resources. Many people have been abandoned in the facility by their families, or have lost contact with family members. Some, but not all, people in the facility have mental disabilities.

Exercise 3.7: Fill the gaps

As you develop a shooting plan sometimes you will find that a vital part of your story—either a location or interviewee—is inaccessible. At this point you have to start thinking creatively about how to compensate for this.

Imagining the two situations above—if you could not get access to the two sites how would you gather sufficient audiovisual material to tell the stories?

To give you some ideas, here is how an editor resolved an absence of images from inside California's juvenile facilities as he worked on *System Failure*, a video documenting abuses in the system.

First, he stresses the importance of ensuring there is adequate footage available to fill out the interviews that you are able to obtain outside the facility.

I can't stress enough that when you are filming talking-head interviews, the more B-roll footage of those contributors the better ... just doing daily things or walking down the streets really helps their interview. Otherwise, filming B-roll of any images that help the sentiment of the piece is just as good. If someone is talking emotively of a death, still "quiet" shots of skies, clouds, landscapes, and sunsets can help convey the impression of the person's thoughts. In the process of producing *System Failure* we got as many photographs as possible of the people filmed and their families; they really helped the people that were interviewed become more real and relatable to the audience. They could understand them as people better.

To help provide information about events that had already happened or that had been out of reach of cameras, the filmmakers also did research into any other related documents, and obtained court records, newspaper cuttings and newspaper photographs (while being aware of copyright issues).

Looking for outside sources they combed both private and public archival resources:

We also got some footage from news stations and stock library footage of the prisons we featured but also other images like beatings and cages and shackles. Two things that were vital for us were firstly, getting access to televised public access archive of the California Senate where California Youth Authority officers spoke. This way, we were at least able to use their images and testimony there to give a sense of presence in the piece. The second material that was crucial was the California Youth Authority's own authorized review as we then structured our whole film around the review's quotes.

Preparing for an interview

When you've decided you'd like to interview someone, these are some issues to consider during preproduction:

- Where do the interviewees need to be filmed?
- Does the filming pose a security threat to the interviewer and/or interviewee?
- What precautions need to be taken to ensure their safety? (preparing consent forms, determining manner of transporting and storing tapes/transcripts to ensure safety/confidentiality etc.)
- Do you need to translate consent forms?
- If it is a government/military official, do you need clearance? How far in advance do you have to arrange a meeting?
- Does the interviewee require an interpreter?
- Will the gender, culture, nationality, or vocation of the interpreter, filmmaker, or cameraperson alter the course of the

interview or negatively affect the interviewee? How can this be avoided?

- List the questions to be asked of interviewee (see Chapter 4 for more information on interviews).
- What are your options if one of these film subjects/interviewees is not available?

Preparing a call-sheet

When preparing to film, a call-sheet (see Table 3.3) itemizes the names, with addresses, email and telephone numbers, of anyone you might need to be in contact with (see Chapter 2 on preparing for dangerous conditions). This list can include:

- The crew
- The interview subjects
- Location contacts (e.g. head of medical rehabilitation center where you are filming)
- Contacts for accommodation
- Contacts in case of emergency

Tips for preproduction

- Many people have had cameras confiscated or have not been allowed to film a particular building, place, or region. They didn't realize that they needed permission. Always check beforehand.
- Always assume that you will need permission to film, whether it be with an interviewee or in a public institution, e.g. in a hospital or a refugee camp. Have a prepared consent form (see Appendices III and IV for sample forms), in a language understood by the interviewee. For more information on this, see Chapter 2.
- Getting necessary clearances and the potential cost of using archive material is often overlooked at the preproduction stage. You may be able to negotiate free usage but remember to get written clearance for any photo, sound, and image that is not yours and you want to use in your video. You can also find "archival material" during shooting. For example, does your interview subject have photos that you could shoot with your camera? What about the neighbor? The local school?
- Filming alone can be hard going, especially when you have to interview people, and think about your sound and images. The quality of your filming can be compromised in this way, so if possible arrange to have someone to help you, checking the sound or asking your interviewee questions while you concentrate on what the picture looks like.
- See also Appendix VI for a checklist.

Table 3.3   Sample call-sheet

	CALL SHEET	
	Greenland: Home Rule at Work	

Shoot Dates	June 12–29, 2001	
Title:	Home Rule at Work	
Location:	Nuuk, Greenland	
Director	Anna S.	Mobile: 32-555-5555
		Passport number: BL2345
Production Manager:	Karen S.	32-555-5555
Sound:	Melody R.	Cell: 32-555-5555
		mroul@yahoo.com
		Passport number: BL2345
Camera:	Paul R.	32-555-5555
		Passport number: BL2345
		(penicilin allergy)
Translator:	Francis D.	299-555-5555
INTERVIEW SUBJECTS		
Tine S.		299-555-5555
		Office: 555-5555
		Home: 555-5555
Jacob O.		299-555-5555
		Office: 555-5555
		Home: 555-5555
Fixer in Nuuk:	Jakob R.	299-555-5555

Tuesday June 12, 2001

6h00	S. and A. drive to Ottawa Airport
9h40	First Air Flight 868 from Ottawa to Iqaluit (arrive at 12h30)
13h20	First Air Flight 1868 from Iq. to Kangerlussuaq (arrive at 16h40)
17h35	Gr. Air Flight 511 from Kangerlussuaq to Nuuk (arrive at 18h00)

F. will meet S/A. at Nuuk airport

20h00	Production meeting

Bed and breakfast in private home reserved (cost 300 DKK/person/night)

Wednesday June 13, 2001

Reece in Nuuk
10h00	Meet with T., interview subject
14h00	Location scouting

Bed and board in private home reserved (cost 300 DKK/person/night)

Table 3.3   continued

Thursday June 14, 2001

Reece in Nuuk
10h00   Meet with J., interview subject
14h00   View archives at Greenlandic television

Bed and board in private home reserved (cost 300 DKK/person/night)

Friday June 15, 2001

DAY 1—Shoot in Nuuk
08h00   film Jacob at home, getting ready for court case with children

Bed and breakfast in private home reserved (cost 300 DKK/person/night)

Saturday June 16, 2001

DAY 2—Shoot in Nuuk
Bed and board in private home reserved (cost 300 DKK/person/night)

Sunday June 17, 2001

DAY OFF
Bed and board in private home reserved (cost 300 DKK/person/night)

Monday June 18, 2001

DAY 3—Shoot in Nuuk
Bed and board in private home reserved (cost 300 DKK/person/night)

Tuesday June 19, 2001

15h35   Gr. Air Flight from Nuuk to Kangerlussuaq (arrive at 16h30)
17h25   First Air Flight 1869 from Kangar to Iq. (arrive 16h20)
18h05   First Air Flight 869 Iq. to Ottawa (arrive at 21h03)

drive or bus home

A call-sheet can also outline the timeline of your shoot. It includes travel information, location of interviews, and accommodation. Preparing a call sheet can help concretize your shoot, even if some elements may seem obvious, or may not be confirmed at the time.

It is invaluable to have all this information in one place during your shoot—ideally in your back pocket, for easy access!

Consider preparing this list for the rest of your team, including someone who is not going into the area with you. This could be a family member, or an international partner or ally if you are filming in your own community. If such a list is considered dangerous on your shoot, find ways of disguising information.

NOTE

1. Pat Aufderheide, *In the Battle for Reality*, available online at <www.centerforsocialmedia.org>.

4

Video Production: Filming a Story

Joanna Duchesne, with additional writing by Liz Miller,
Sukanya Pillay and Yvette Cheesman

This chapter invites you to start filming with your camera as soon as you can—the more you practice, the easier it will become.

You will learn about technical aspects of your camera and equipment, different types of shots, and tips on how to film stable, well-composed, and compelling images. The chapter will steer you towards preparing your own video project, and show you how to film sequences and interviews, develop characters, and build a story. There are also exercises designed to help you try out what you have learned. Don't wait until you are confident—your skills will develop as you work.

In some cases we talk about the grammar of film and video, and conventions that are used, for example, in framing shots. Think of these as a writer would grammar—in general you should abide by them, but once you know them, you will also be able to break the rules effectively.

To produce social advocacy video, you must play many roles. As you prepare to shoot, you must think accurately and objectively like a human rights monitor, technically like a camera and sound technician, sequentially like an editor, as well as like an advocacy-driven storyteller. However, you don't need to do all these jobs—remember that most films are made with a team, and are not completely individual efforts. When you are filming, if possible have people to help you with logistics, sound, and camera (and translation if necessary), and consider hiring an editor to bring a fresh eye to the project.

THE TOOLS

Your basic kit

Your basic kit should consist of a video camera, tapes, batteries, a battery charger, headphones and relevant leads to power your camera.

Try to include an external microphone and a tripod for steady filming. RCA/S-Video or firewire cables are also useful to playback what you have filmed on a television, camera, or computer.

You may want to invest in separate lighting but this is expensive and can be hired if necessary. Most cameras function well even in relatively low light, so you will find that you rarely need specialized lighting gear.

Suggested additional equipment

- Camera case with desiccant to keep camera dry
- Waterproof jacket (if using camera in humid or wet situations) or "Pelican Case" (a hard case that protects the camera from knocks and water)
- Batteries (choose their duration based on your projected access to mains electricity)
- Tripod (either a photo-video tripod or a video tripod with a fluid head)
- Microphone(s) (see the discussion on microphones below, pp. 140–2)
- Headphones
- Windscreen for microphone (reduces or eliminates wind noise)
- Reflector Board (for more information on this see below, p. 134)
- Extended warranty
- Insurance

What are the formats of video camera?

Video cameras or "camcorders" come in all shapes and sizes. They are categorized by the type of tape they use, and by the standard on which they operate (PAL or NTSC). Most cameras are now digital, though some older cameras are an analog format.

There are two different video standards: NTSC or PAL. In general NTSC is used in the Americas and a few African and Asian countries, while PAL is used elsewhere. Brazil uses a PAL variant known as PAL-M. SECAM is an older standard that has generally been replaced by PAL. You will want to buy a camera that will be convenient for use where you plan to live or work, and one with which you will be able to easily share footage or screen footage to collaborators. You can take an NTSC camera and film in a PAL standard location but you will find that it is harder to playback the images or share them with people using the PAL standard unless you are using a specialized playback machine and television that can play both standards. Some filmmakers choose to shoot in PAL even in NTSC countries as the quality of the image is generally better.

If you are buying a camera we strongly advise you to buy a digital format like MiniDV.

Higher-quality digital and analog formats

- *MiniDV cameras*: In the last few years, digital cameras have become more and more popular. They provide higher-resolution images than older formats. MiniDV tapes are small and record in a digital format.
- *DVD cameras*: These cameras use DVD technology with the capability of recording onto a disc or memory card. This new format is still not in widespread use.
- *DVCAM cameras*: These cameras provide better quality and steadier images than a MiniDV. This format is used more and more by broadcasters. MiniDV tapes can usually be used in this lightweight camera.
- *HD cameras and 24P cameras*: New cameras that shoot in formats suited for high-definition television, and a format that is closer to analog film in shutter speed, and thus better suited for transfer to film. Both are high-quality formats, increasingly being used by documentary filmmakers.
- *BetaCam SP or DigiBeta*: BetaCam cameras are generally used by broadcasters, and provide a superior image quality. However, they tend to be very heavy, cumbersome, and expensive. Digital BetaCam or 'DigiBeta' is a high quality broadcast and editing format.

The tape formats most commonly used by broadcasters are DVCAM, BetaCam SP, and DigiBeta.

Older analog formats

- *VHS*: These cameras use the same tapes as a VHS machine. They are large and heavy to operate and the images filmed are not as good quality as more modern formats.

- *VHS-C:* These are more compact video cameras than VHS but the image quality is similar. S-VHS and S-VHS-C cameras also exist. They provide superior images and sound to the VHS and VHS-C.
- *Hi8:* The Hi8 camera uses 8 mm tapes, smaller in size, but superior in quality to VHS.

Batteries and power for your camera

All cameras can be powered via a mains connection or using a detachable battery. Camcorders have a built-in signal in the viewfinder, which will tell you if the battery is running low. If you use an LCD screen or an external mike without its own battery, you will use more power. Always make sure your battery is fully charged when preparing to film, and take an extra charged battery, and if possible, adapters that will enable you to charge your camera batteries from an automobile or other 12-volt power source.

Most batteries are now lithium/ion batteries. They do not need to be completely discharged before recharging.

Looking after your camera and tapes

Protecting your camera

Cameras do not operate well in harsh climates. Be very careful with the sun or any other heat source. If you are filming outside in the sun, keep the camera in the shade after filming. To ensure the best performance in hot, humid conditions try to keep a desiccant, like a sachet of silica gel, and replace it every 2–3 months. This will help to take a little moisture out of your equipment. A good alternative natural desiccant is dry, uncooked rice in a porous bag.

Cameras do not like sand or dust so try to keep your camera clean at all times. If you are filming in windy or sandy conditions, you can protect the camera with a cover. Take special care of the lens by cleaning it regularly with a clean cloth, and always pack your camera carefully in a clean, dry bag.

If it is raining ensure your camera is well-covered, and dried in a container with desiccant following use, as water can damage the electrical elements and rust casings and mechanisms. Watch out also for water on the lens, which will affect image quality. When filming in the rain, one or two drops of water on the lens might look innocent but they can ruin the image and make editing difficult.

You can permanently damage your camera lens if you film towards the sun or another strong light. The iris on your camera opens or closes automatically to let in the correct amount of light to record a good picture. If you expose your lens to sudden strong light, the iris may not be able to adapt quickly enough. If you need to film something with a strong light source, adapt your exposure manually to close the iris, or consider using a filter on the lens. This filter can also help protect the lens from dust.

Protecting videotapes

Like your camera, videotapes are very sensitive and must be protected from excessive heat, humidity, dust, smoke, dirt, and moisture. Always carry a tape in its case, away from direct sunlight. Store your tapes in a vertical position, like books on a shelf, and don't run the risk of recording accidentally over a tape—once you have finished filming always move the red tab on the top of your tape from "record" to "save." Keep tapes away from magnetic fields, and don't leave tapes lying on top of or close to a television, computer or video.

Labeling, logging, and transcribing your tapes

Always remember to label your videotapes, noting subject matter, interviewee names, length and date of what has been recorded. If you are in a location where it would be dangerous to reveal what you are recording, put something innocuous on the label and remember what you have filmed for labeling later. Tapes with no labels at all are often lost and can get recorded over, so, unless the situation is extreme, try to put some kind of information on the label, if only the date. If you are going into a dangerous setting pre-label your tapes before shooting—e.g. with a sequential set of numbers. Producing a log or shotlist and transcribing interviews of each tape can help you to remember where important images are, and decide how to tell your story. For a sample shotlist and transcript, see Appendix VI.

Remember:

- Protect your camera and videotapes from extreme temperatures
- Move the red tab to "save"
- Label well before or immediately after shooting

Time-codes and the date/time facility

Your digital camera automatically writes continuous invisible time-code (running from 00:00:00:00, hours/minutes/seconds/frames) onto the tape as you are recording. This is important for when you want to choose your shots and edit your story together. You can shotlist your material, identifying where your material is on each tape by time code, and the editing machine will easily be able to find shots according to their time-code (e.g. a shot begins at 00:03:03:00 and ends 00:03:15:00).

Watch out for time-code breaks

Digital cameras often cause problems at the editing stage because of what are known as "time-code breaks." Breaks can happen if the camera is turned off or the tape is removed from the camera and then replaced. In this case the time-code will revert to 00:00:00:00 at the point when you have stopped recording, leaving you without an easy way to log your material.

To make sure you have no time-code breaks while filming many cameras have "end" or "edit search" functions. The end search will wind the tape to the end of what you have last recorded. The edit search facility will allow you to choose from wherever you are on your tape, to go to the closest point from where you can film again. Beware, though, because with both these facilities you will lose a few seconds of your previous shot.

You can avoid time-code breaks during your actual filming by prerecording the time-code of a whole tape with the lens cap on. The camera will film only black but it will generate an unbroken time-code from the start of the tape to the end. When you put it in your camera again for filming, the camera will recognize the time-code and will use this existing continuous time-code.

It is also a good idea not to go back over your footage while you are filming—wait till the tape is finished, and you will run no risks of breaking the time-code.

The date and time facility

Accurate date and time information are critical if the video is needed as evidence of when an incident took place. For further information on this, see Chapter 6.

Nearly all camcorders can permanently record the date and time as you record. On most digital cameras, the date and time is recorded as digital information onto the tape without being superimposed on the picture. Because the date and time are often important, make sure that they are set correctly via the camera's menu.

THE TECHNIQUES

All videos are made up of shots, sequences, and scenes. In this section we look primarily at developing a solid grasp of the key shot types, and developing elementary sequences. One way to think about how shots, sequences, and scenes fit together is to imagine them paralleling the structure of a book, as demonstrated in Table 4.1.

Table 4.1   Shots, sequences, and scenes

Shot	Sentence
⇓	⇓
A series makes a...	A series makes a...
Sequence	Paragraph
⇓	⇓
A series makes a...	A series makes a...
Scene	Chapter
⇓	⇓
A series makes a...	A series makes a...
Video	Book

Composing and framing your shots

Framing is the way in which a scene, person, or object is placed within the image you record. Viewers are familiar with certain conventions, and it is important to realize what effect different shots have on a viewer. If you film a close-up of somebody's face, you pull the viewer into their thoughts, emotions, or words; if you film the same person from a distance, you help the viewer understand the person's context.

Remember that none of these are hard-and-fast rules that you must stick to—once you understand how they are used, then you have the flexibility to know when it will be effective to break them.

You have many options to choose from but the following are the main types of shot size to be aware of (see Figure 4.1):

- *Extreme Long Shots* (abbreviated to ELS, also called Wide Shots, WS): These shots are often used as an "establishing shot"; they orient the viewer not just to one location, but also to an overall atmosphere, context, and situation. Whenever the scene changes think about reorienting your viewers with a new establishing shot.
- *Long Shot* (LS): This shot shows a person from head to toe. Be careful with headroom: too much space above a person's head will look strange, as will too much space at the person's feet.
- *Mid-shot* (MS):
  This shot shows a person from just below waist level to just above the top of their head. This shot is often used in interviews.
- *Close-up* (CU):
  This shot shows a person from mid chest to just above the top of their head, and is ideal for important or emotional parts of interviews. You can go closer but if you are subtitling your interview, leave enough space under the person's chin to allow for text on the screen. It is better to lose the top of someone's head in a frame than their chin, especially if they are talking.
- *Extreme Close-up* (ECU):
  This shot shows detail. An extreme close-up shot in an interview might just show a person's eyes or mouth.

Figure 4.1   Different shot sizes (Taw Nay Htoo)

Rule of thirds

A good guideline for composing your shots is the rule of thirds. This means that you should imagine your frame (the image your camera takes) divided into thirds, with actions and objects placed at the intersections of the vertical and horizontal thirds. This is far more interesting to the eye. Don't place people you are filming in the middle of the frame simply because they are important. It's far better to have the horizon either two-thirds from the top of the frame or two-thirds from the bottom. And if you are filming someone standing in front of a wider scene it's good to have him or her standing slightly to the left or to the right of the frame. This permits the person to speak into the empty part of the frame—it gives them "nose-room."

Getting a good-quality image

Focus

Creating the sharpest image possible is critical. Almost every camcorder is fitted with an auto focus facility. In most situations this will ensure that what you are filming is sharply in focus—very useful if there is little or no movement in your shot.

When to use manual focus

If you are filming with multiple or moving objects in the frame, or with objects both in the foreground and background, the camcorder may be confused as to what it is meant to be focusing on and will repeatedly give you blurred images while it tries to rest on a subject. Switch to manual focus on these occasions, manually adjusting the focus to keep the key subject(s) in focus.

In low light, the camera's auto focus will often "hunt around" to locate something to focus on because it needs a reasonable level of light in order to find the lines and edges that it uses to choose a focal point. In such situations, manual focus is your only option.

Zooming and focusing

The more you are zoomed in, the smaller the range of objects that will be in focus. This is called depth of field. For example, if you are filming a wide shot of a crowd you will find that almost everyone in the crowd is in focus. But if you zoom in to a close-up shot of one person in the crowd, the focus on people in the foregrounds and backgrounds is soft. If you want to avoid this, set up your shot by zooming in *first* on the person you want. Focus on them, put your camera in manual focus mode, then pull back for your wide shot. When you zoom in to get your shot, the focus will remain where you want it.

Wide shots are almost always in focus

The depth of field you have to work with when you are on a wide shot is considerable (especially when the light is good). If you are in a situation in which there is a lot of motion and things are changing quickly, try to stay on a wide shot and get the variety of shots you need by changing your location. Many an important shot has been missed or ruined because the cameraperson was wasting time trying to get focus when they should have been getting the shot.

Remember:

- Auto focus is best where movement is limited and the light is good
- Manual focus is best with multiple moving subjects and low light
- Wide shots are almost always in focus

Exposure

All camcorders are equipped with an automated exposure system. Like your eye, the iris of the camcorder will close down or open up to let in the correct amount of light. The camcorder will automatically open up the iris or increase the aperture to take in more light, or close it down to limit the brightness. In very low light, it will "boost the gain" to give you a grainier, but still usable picture.

You can override these functions by switching to the manual iris or adjusting the gain manually, but you will have to continually adjust the iris of the camcorder yourself. When you are just starting to learn how to film it's best to leave your controls on automatic—it's easy to forget that you changed the settings when you have many other things to deal with. Remember also that the brightness of the LCD screen has nothing to do with the exposure settings.

White balance

Different sources of light produce light of different "color temperatures." Artificial lighting, such as indoor light bulbs, produces an orange tinge. Daylight is bluer in color. The human brain adjusts to these variations better than a camera can. What looks perfectly fine to your eye might look orange or blue to the camera.

Most camcorders have an automatic "white balance" facility, which will register and adjust the color temperature of the prevailing light source. In most situations you can use this. Some camcorders also have pre-set white balance positions to cope with different types of lighting. If your camcorder is like this, remember to reset these positions if the lighting conditions change. You can also set the white balance manually for any location by zooming in on a piece of white paper or other white object so that it fills the screen; and then pressing the manual white balance button. Setting the white balance manually is a good idea for interviews and in situations where there is mixed indoor and outdoor lighting, but generally it's safe to stick with the automatic white balance.

Remember:

- Artificial light gives an orange tinge; outdoor light gives a blue tinge
- Reset the white balance if you use the fixed or manual settings

Lights and lighting

Lighting is used to illuminate a subject and to create a mood, or to shape and define your subject. Hard directional light—sunlight or flashlight—will illuminate with precision but may also create harsh shadows. Soft diffused light—e.g. on a foggy day—causes a wider and softer illumination and is ideal for portraits. You will often have to work with natural light. It is also less expensive and less obtrusive.

There are a number of common terms used in describing light sources—natural or artificial.

- The "key light" is your main source of light. It is off to the side from your camera, angled towards your subject shining light directly onto them. If you have the room, keep the key light between 9 and 15 feet from a subject, and the subject several feet from the background. The key light source will be slightly above your subject and angled down for the most flattering effect.
- The "fill light" is used to illuminate the shadows created by the key, and usually is on the opposite side of the camera to the key light, so that it lights the opposite side of the person you are filming.

- The "backlight" is a defining light source—it is often used to create a rim of light to separate the subject from the background, or a person's head from the background, especially if the background is black and so is your subject's hair. It is placed directly behind and above the subject being filmed, and shines onto the back of their head and onto their shoulders.

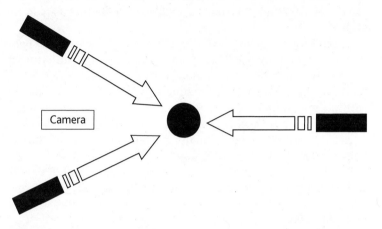

Figure 4.2 Three-point lighting set-up

Outdoor/natural light

The sun is your primary "key light" when you are working outside. Pointing your camcorder directly at a light source, especially the sun, can damage it. In general you want to keep your back to the sun or your primary light source. At the same time you don't want to position your subject so that they are squinting while looking at you or the camera.

If you position your subject in front of a strong light source the contrast may be too extreme. Especially when shooting with consumer cameras the camera may adjust the exposure to the light level in the background instead of on your subject, creating a silhouette around them. Where possible, daylight is not only adequate but also makes the picture look more "natural." An overcast day can be good for shooting, as the clouds diffuse the intensity of sunlight. However, if the sun is moving in and out of small clouds you may end up with uneven lighting.

Low and limited light

While many camcorders can record well with low levels of light, the image they produce is often of poorer quality. The camera accommodates by adding "gain" which translates to more light but a lower quality image. To let more light into your camera you can open the iris/exposure and you can also reduce the shutter speed to 1/30 or 1/60 (in NTSC) or 1/25 or 1/50 (in PAL) if you are using MiniDV.

A useful technique when you have limited light is to reflect light sources by pointing the light at the wall or ceiling and letting it bounce onto your subject, or working with the reflection of a primary source of light. One simple technique is to line a piece of cardboard with tin foil and reflect the light from the sun onto your subject. You can also use any piece of white paper or cloth, or an inexpensive reflector board. Black tends to absorb color while white tends to reflect color.

The best way to understand lighting is to begin to look at objects and people around you and to try to identify the light sources and reflections. Is it soft or hard, primary or secondary, natural or artificial, reflected or direct?

"Lighting can be used to great effect," says lighting cameraman Steen Eriksen, who has filmed in most of the world's trouble spots.

I recently filmed some interviews with some relatives of the "disappeared" in Iraq. I used a black background and shone three small lights onto different parts of the frame, so that the interviewee's face was illuminated. The effect was quite arresting and helped to convey the haunting pain of the subject matter. The use of three lights helped to diminish any potential shadows on the subject's face.

Tips:

- In low light, pictures will be of poorer quality
- Backlit pictures appear silhouetted
- Softer light is better for portraits

Holding your camera and keeping it stable

One of the best features of camcorders is that they are so portable and lightweight, but this can cause problems when trying to film steady shots. The smoothest shots will be made using a tripod or monopod, but remember that it is only a tool to stabilize the camera. Where possible use a tripod to enable you to film stable, fixed shots and movements. A monopod (a single-legged tripod that is planted on the ground for stability) will also allow you to shoot stable images even if you are frequently on the move, and stopping only for a single shot or sequence.

If you don't have a monopod or a tripod, or choose to film hand-held, some simple techniques help make your camera stable.

Grip

First, get your grip right: hold the camcorder firmly with the grip strap tightened over your right hand and use your left hand to steady the camcorder. Depending on your camera you are using, the best place for your left hand is usually under the lens, near to the other controls you may need to use, like the manual focus. Don't put your hand over the auto-focus sensor on the front of the camera.

Stability

Whenever you can, brace yourself firmly against something solid like a rock, a tree or a parked vehicle. If you are standing, support your elbows tucked-in against your chest to keep your hands stable. This may feel uncomfortable but it will soon be second nature. Keep your footing secure and your feet slightly apart. If you are filming with the LCD screen, use your chest to steady the camera. If you are kneeling down, use your raised knee to support your arm and camcorder. To film low angle shots lie down full-length with your elbows on the ground for support. You should also consider purchasing a shoulder-supported strap that will help add stability to shots.

Remember:

- Avoid camera shake
- Grip your camcorder firmly
- Support your elbows

Your first shots

Keep the image still as much as possible and hold it

When you are learning to film, take plenty of "still life" with your video camera, especially close-ups of faces and details, and stable still shots. These shots should be held for 15 seconds even if this feels like an eternity at the time.

For every camera movement you shoot, be sure to shoot at least five still shots that are stable and held for at least 10–15 seconds. In a still shot, your subject may be moving, but your camera is still or making minor movements to accommodate them.

Remember:

- Hold shots for 10–15 seconds
- Get still shots before and after camera movements
- For every shot in which you move the camera, shoot five still shots

---

Moving your camera: Pans, tilts, and zooms

Basic camera movements

There are some basic camera movements, which imitate the way we move our head and eyes. "Panning" shots are where the camera moves from one side to another, and "tilting" shots are where the camera moves upwards or downwards. "Zooms" are used to close in on a subject or pull out to show the wider context of an image. These movements are ideal when you cannot include the whole of the subject in one static shot, such as a crowd of people or a tall statue. They are also used for covering action sequences, and for showing connections between different things.

Panning and tilting

Try to hold the shot for 10–15 seconds before you pan or tilt your camera sideways or vertically. This helps the viewer establish what he or she is supposed to be looking at before the move begins. *Slowly* pivot the camera around, upwards or downwards, keeping at a constant speed. If you move too fast or do not hold the shot at the start and finish, the image may be blurred. When you stop, hold the shot for 10–15 seconds again. This may seem like a long time, but you will end up using the static shot at least as often as the move itself. By getting the three shots—the initial still shot, the pan, and then the final shot—you offer yourself and your editor choices later in the production process.

A good guideline in terms of speed for both pans and tilts is to allow approximately five seconds for an object to pass from one side of the screen to the other. Try not to move too far. A natural arc of about 90° is the most you can usually use without disorienting your viewer. Smaller is usually better. If you can't reveal everything you want in a pan or tilt of 45°, you should consider repositioning yourself so you can. A good way to ensure a smooth pan is to have your body (your feet) pointed towards the end point of the pan, and then flex around to the start point. This way you can "uncoil" your body into the pan and create a smoother, more stable pan.

Avoid "hose-piping"

Remember, however, that it is very easy to overuse these types of camera movements and end up making your audience seasick from watching too many of these shots in succession. Above all, avoid "hose-piping," which means continually panning and tilting across a subject in an effort to cover it all ("hose-piping" describes how a gardener or fireman would spray a hose of water across a bed of plants or a fire). It's much better to break the subject up into more than one shot.

> Remember:
>
> - Do not overuse pans, tilts, and zooms
> - Avoid "hose-piping" over a subject

Zooming

Zooms are achieved by manually adjusting the lens or by using a motorized zoom rocker button. The zoom creates the visual effect of moving closer to or away from your subject (sometimes called a pull-out). Hold your shot for at least 10–15 seconds before and after you zoom to give your audience time to register the scene, and to give yourself shot options in the editing room. Often, as with other camera moves, you will find that the static shot is the one you need. Make sure you have it. Remember that close-up shots taken from a camera position that is far away from the subject will amplify any slight camera shake. If you want to film a subject close-up, move nearer to it (this is called "zooming with your feet") if you can, and zoom in to create a closer shot.

If your camera has a "digital zoom" function, it is best to switch it off. This setting actually uses the camera's built-in software to "blow up" the image, but downgrades image quality, often making your shot unusable.

To zoom or not to zoom

Too many zoom shots in succession are also very difficult to watch. Usually the zoom is used to emphasize an intimate or emotional moment, or to highlight an important detail in a wider shot. With the zoom-in you can dictate where your audience's attention should be focused. With the zoom-out you can initially pick out a detail in a scene, perhaps a person's face, or disclose information that is not evident at the start of the shot. As with other camera moves, smaller is usually better. A small zoom-in for emphasis or a small pull-out for context might help your story where a larger in-camera movement would not.

Rob Brouwer is a human rights documentary filmmaker who now works for Amnesty International. He spent over a decade working as a cameraman throughout Latin America.

> I originally trained as a photographer, so when I started filming, it took me a while to really understand how to use camera movements wisely. I remember filming at a funeral procession for victims of death squads in Guatemala. Afterwards, I went to see the material being edited together. I watched as the editor used my pan of the procession, using the hold at the beginning with a voiceover to explain what was happening. He also used a static shot of an old woman crying with a voice explaining how many people had died. He said he might have used the zoom that I done because it was really effective but he needed more time for it to hold at the end. This really taught me why a static shot is needed before and after every movement.

Remember:

- Zoom in for detail, pull out for context
- Move nearer to subjects for close-ups
- Get static shots at the end of every movement
- Be careful with the digital zoom

Moving with your camera

Walking

Keep your legs bent at the knees and your body lowered all the time. This will help you avoid the rise and fall of normal walking. Create a slow motion, gliding feeling. Put each foot down softly and close to the ground. Do the same if you walking backwards. Have someone walking with you to clear the way.

Crabbing and tracking

"Crabbing" is walking sideways. Lift your feet in a slow-motion glide with your knees bent, crossing your leg behind or in front of you, letting one foot rest firmly before moving the other. "Tracking" is when a vehicle, office chair or even a wheelchair is used to get smooth moving shots. If you are sitting in something, use the armrest or your knees to steady the camera.

Remember:

- Keep your knees bent
- Move slowly, in a gliding manner
- Use wheeled vehicles for tracking

Moving with people you are filming

If people are walking in your shot and you are following them as they move, try to make sure that you leave enough space in your frame for them to "walk into." If they are walking from right to left, you should keep them more to the right of the frame so that they have space on the left to walk into. Without that space they will look as if they are pushing the picture along themselves. Too much headroom will look strange. Instead tilt down slightly and you will get a far more natural shot when there is only a small amount of space between the top of their head and the top of the frame. At the end of the shot let the person exit the frame.

Waldemar de Vries has filmed human rights stories all over Africa.

I once filmed a nun who went back to visit her church that had been destroyed by rebels in Guinea. I followed her walking into the church, keeping her face in the frame to the right, and moved the camera upwards as she looked up at the light shining through the bullet holes in the roof in the left of the frame. When I played back the material later, the footage really conveyed the destruction and the effect that it had on the nun.

Direction and continuity

Aim to collect images that when edited together will create a logical and credible continuity of events or a sense of direction that the audience will be able to understand. For example, if you are filming people walking from one place to another, you should make sure that they are always traveling in the same direction. If you don't, it will seem to your audience that they are first walking in one direction and then another. If you do decide to switch the direction from which you are observing an action make sure to use a wide shot to reorientate your viewers.

The same is true if you are filming two people talking to each other. One person will have the left side of the face favored in the shot; the other person should have the right side of their face favored. This will mean that they appear to be facing each other while they are talking. If, for example, you film both people favoring the left side of their faces, it will seem as though they are both facing the same direction. This will give the illusion that they are not talking to each other but to someone out of frame on the left.

The importance of sound

Remember, sound is at least half your story. In an interview, where the success of your footage depends on the clarity of what the person is saying, sound is more than half the story. It is the story.

Even if you have shot excellent visual footage it can be useless without good sound. *Always use your headphones*, so you can hear precisely what the camera is recording. Our hearing filters out noises that a microphone will pick up (e.g. air-conditioning or electrical hum). Without headphones you will not be aware of these noises until you are logging your footage or in the edit room. Without headphones you will also not know if your sound recording is distorting loud sounds. If you have poor sound, there is little you can do to salvage your footage.

Be aware of any sound that will interfere with interviews or general filming. You may want to have someone assist you in recording sound, especially if you are using an external mike.

Wherever your location, consider how you can "account" for uncontrollable sounds by incorporating them into the story you are telling—e.g. filming the goats that are bleating in the pen outside a home—and also make sure to record some "wild sound" or "room tone." This is 30 seconds to one minute of the "sound" of a location that can be used to cover sound editing.

Your camera's microphone

The built-in microphone on most cameras is omni-directional, which means it will pick up sound from all around, favoring the loudest.

This may be sufficient for a street demonstration or other general activity. If you have no additional microphone and you are filming an interview, move your camera as close to the interviewee as possible. The built-in microphone is highly sensitive to surrounding sound, so you want to be in as quiet a place as possible—away from the crowd or multiple noise sources.

External microphones

If you are working with a camera, you will usually have an external mike input that will automatically override the built-in microphone. Some cameras require you to manually set which mike you want to use, so be sure you know how to do this. If you have a manual for your camera, refer to it. If not, a few minutes spent switching from one mike to another while you listen with the headphones should be enough to sort it out.

Hand-held microphones

Hand-held microphones can be very useful because they enable you to get the sound source very close to a person while giving you some freedom to move your camera. These microphones are often especially tuned to the frequencies of the human voice and have what is called a "cardioid" (heart-shaped) pattern that favors sounds that are close to the microphone. These can be very useful when interviewing people or speaking to the camera in a crowd.

Directional or "shotgun" microphones

If you have a directional microphone, it will pick up sound in the direction you point it, so you can pinpoint exactly what source of sound you would like. This kind of mike is useful if you need to be flexible or, for example, have to record a number of people speaking in a crowd.

Clip-on microphones

When recording interviews, try to use a clip-on or lavaliere mike. These are very small microphones that you can attach to your interviewee's clothing, near to their neck. Although they are usually omni-directional, these mikes will pick up what your interviewee says in this position. Make sure there are no obstructing objects such as hair or jewelry, or slick fabrics, which could interfere with the recording.

Wireless microphones

In recent years, a number of relatively inexpensive high-quality wireless microphones have become available. These battery-powered microphones/transmitters, which have a matching receiver that attaches to the camera, are very useful because they allow you to pick up sound without the need for a cable or lead, and allow the camera to operate freely separate from the sound recording. When worn by a person you are following, a wireless will pick up their voice and the voices of people around them even though the camera is dozens of feet away. A wireless can also be placed in the middle of a room, or on a conference table. As with any microphone, the closer it is to the sound source the better.

There are certain situations where a wireless mike is the best or only option for getting the sound you need—e.g. if you are filming people who are moving, or where you are trying to be discreet about the filming. Be careful, however, to monitor the batteries, as they will need to be changed often. Distance, electronic interference, and physical objects can degrade or interrupt the signal. It is crucial to monitor the sound the camera is getting from a wireless.

Remember that some cameras can also use a combination of microphones simultaneously—for example, a shotgun mike and a wireless mike.

Remember:

- Learn the characteristics of your mike
- Omni-directional microphones favor loudest sounds
- Point uni-directional mikes directly at sound source, and use them when the sound source is rapidly changing
- Clip-on mikes are best for interviews
- Combine different mikes for maximum flexibility and coverage

---

Wind noise

There are a few ways to minimize the sound of the wind when it buffets your microphone. Stand with your back to the wind to shield the microphone or stand next to a natural windbreak such as a wall. External microphones can be equipped with wind-gags to help reduce wind noise. Some video cameras will have a button called "wind noise," which minimizes the sound of the wind on your video recording. If there is no such button, and your external mike protrudes from the camera, try placing a thin sock using a rubber band over the built-in microphone. It may look odd, but it will dramatically decrease the sound of the wind.

Acoustics

If you are filming indoors, always be aware of the acoustics of the room or how the sound bounces from the walls. Places like tiled bathrooms tend to reflect sound and will echo very badly. Rooms with sound-absorbent materials in them such as carpets, curtains, or soft furnishings are far better. Watch out for other sources of sound that will interfere—music playing, vacuuming, or the whir of air-conditioning. Always turn down these noise sources if you can, and if there is a really loud noise (such as a car-horn right outside or an airplane taking off) rerecord, as your audio will otherwise be unusable.

Common mistakes with sound

- Don't forget to wear headphones when recording an interview. Good interviews have been ruined because no one was paying attention to the sound levels, and didn't hear sounds like a person vacuuming in the background or air-conditioning.
- When using a uni-directional mike, always make sure that the microphone is pointed towards the person you want to hear. Some interviewers can be so concentrated on the interview itself that they wave the microphone around or in the wrong direction. If the person recording is not wearing headphones, or watching the sound levels, this may not be noticed.
- External microphones can be useless if you don't turn them on! As they override the built-in microphone, people have recorded interviews with no sound at all.
- Check your microphone battery. If possible, carry an extra battery.

Remember:

- Consider acoustics
- Be aware of background sounds
- Always monitor your audio

Exercise 4.1: What catches the eye?

If you are working in a group, this is a simple exercise to demonstrate that the idea behind filming is simple. It's all about giving people the images they need to satisfy their curiosity, and to understand a situation. All you need is a pen.

Start tapping on the table with a pen. After a few seconds, ask people what their attention was drawn to first, then what they looked at next, and then what? It is very likely that they will say:

- The pen (they looked for the focus of the action)—*What?*
- The person doing it, and up at their face (they looked for the reason)—*Who?*
- Other people in the room, or around to see if there was a reason and to understand the situation—*Where?*

This readily translates into a close-up, a medium shot and a long shot. With a few other shots—a medium shot taken from the side, and perhaps an over-the-shoulder shot (where the camera is behind the person looking over their shoulder at what they are doing), you have enough to put together a sequence with confidence.

If you like, try filming these shots with your camera and playing them back on a television or monitor, so people can see how the shots relate to what they described.

Exercise 4.2: Practice with your camera

In this exercise you will learn how to shoot a short, repetitive activity, making sure you get all the shots you need to edit a short sequence, as well as give a sense of the story. For this exercise you need: your camera, a tripod, a microphone.

Your objective is to film a person doing an activity related to your video's theme, and film this person and their environment. Choose the person you want to film carefully, as in Exercise 4.5 you will conduct an interview with them. You want to convey:

- *Where* am I?
- *Who* is the person?
- *What* are they doing?
- *How* do they feel about this work or what is their motivation for doing it? Can I understand why they are doing it?

It may be best if the person you are filming is carrying out a repetitive action, as this will allow you to film it from multiple angles and shot-sizes. Each shot should last 15 seconds and if you pan, tilt, or zoom, use only one move per shot and start and finish with a still shot held for 10–15 seconds.

There are multiple aims to this exercise. You need to make sure you have all the shots you need to ensure you can edit together a sequence (this is called "coverage"), and you also want to have a sequence that does more than this—that tells a story. For this, you need shots that convey *context*, and shots that convey the *action* and *telling details*.

Take your camera and shoot the following shots:

1. Establish the *context*: Exterior extreme long shot of the building where person is, or the place where they are working, or an exterior extreme long shot with a tilt or pan. Try a pan from the street or sky to the building/location.

   - Rehearse the shot before you record so that the shots with which you begin and end are well composed
   - Don't forget to hold the shot for 15 seconds at the end of every camera move

   Or try an Exterior/Interior—Long shot—looking through a door or a window to an interior space. If you are working outdoors, move in closer for the LS.
2. Get the *action*: Medium shots of the person doing something— sitting at desk, washing dishes, cooking, selling items, writing, watching television etc. Search for a variety of angles, and try to capture different stages of a process.
3. Get the *emotion*: Close-ups of the person's expression to convey how they feel about what they are doing. Remember that the story often comes through most powerfully in the expression on someone's face.
4. Get the *telling detail*: Close-ups of details of what the person is working with or engaged with—you might ask to get "into the shoes of that person" so that the object is shot from their perspective (e.g. in a kitchen, this could be the dishes they are washing—so ask them to move to the side and shoot the dirty dishes in a pile. Alternatively you could film over their shoulder, etc.).
5. Re-establish the *context*: Medium shot of the person still doing the same activity and finishing the task. Follow it with a long shot of the person finishing the task, and if possible walking out of the frame.

Review your footage: Congratulations! You have shot your first scene. What you might have discovered is that there is often some "directing" in documentary footage and on occasion you might set up or adjust a situation slightly. When you have finished shooting, take a look at the footage. Try to find someone who has experience with video to work with you to review the material.

Look out for:

Technical

- What is the composition of the frames? Consider the rule of thirds, headroom, and nose-room.
- Did you remember the 15 seconds rule about holding moving shots at the beginning and end, and for sticking with still shots?
- Are shots stable? Do you notice how instability is magnified with a zoomed-in shot?
- Are there any distracting elements in the frame?
- Do the foreground and the background work together or not? For example, does a potted plant in the background look like it is growing out of a person's hair?
- Is the horizon line straight?
- Where is the light source in the frame—is the light even throughout the shot?
- Did you control the filmmaking environment where you could? If there were noises disrupting the shots (dogs barking, repetitive alarms) did you either find a way to film away from them, stop them (ask to switch off the television or radio) or did you incorporate them into the story by filming them or making them into cutaways?

Conceptual

- Do you see both the context of the scene and the details?
- Try turning down the sound—is it still clear what the person is doing?

Exercise 4.3: Listening for sound
In this exercise you learn how a microphone picks up sound in a different way from your natural hearing. You will need your camera and any mikes that you plan on using.

It's very important to attune your ears and eyes to possible sounds that may enhance or interfere with your filming. Wherever you are, stop and listen to the sounds around you. Try to pick out individual sounds. It is also important to learn how your different microphones will pick up different sounds based on their recording characteristics.

First, listen for the sounds in the room you are in now. What sounds do you think will be picked up by your camera microphone? Try it out using your camera and headphones. Do you hear unexpected sounds?

Now imagine... What sounds might be picked up by your microphone in the following situations?

- A second-floor office in the center of the capital city of your country?
- A house in a rural community in your country?
- A refugee camp at midday?

Sample answers might include:

- A second-floor office in the center of the capital city of your country: The electrical hum of air-conditioning, a photocopier, or neon lights; someone typing at a computer; phones ringing; traffic noises; workmen in the area.
- A house in a rural community: Television or radio playing; animal noises; milling or pounding of grain; insect sounds, like crickets; sounds of villagers or children playing outside; someone sweeping or cleaning the house.
- A refugee camp at midday: The sound of washing at a water pump; a child crying; people chopping vegetables; a pot bubbling; crackling wood in a fire; the sound of a vehicle arriving at the camp.

Now, go with your camera and headphones to a potential location for your video.

First, use your eyes and ears and consider what sounds your microphone is likely to pick up.

Second, listen through your headphones and identify the sounds that your camera's microphone or external microphone is picking up. Try listening with different mikes—if you have an external directional mike, try it out. Think about how you could minimize unwanted noises either by:

- Selecting an appropriate microphone
- Changing the location of your shoot
- Acting to eliminate or minimize the noise
- Finding a way to incorporate it into your shooting plan

Exercise 4.4: Movement exercise

In this exercise you try acting as a live "dolly," meaning that you move with the camera while following someone. Then you try the same exercise, but you set up a shot on a tripod and the movement originates within the frame—while the camera moves, you do not change position to physically follow the person. Your objective is to use movement to liven up your filming, but not to distract the viewer from the content. You will need a camera and a tripod.

Have the person enter a new space and select a new activity. First try walking with them. Remember not to get too close. Try walking behind them, beside them, in front of them. Ask them to walk slowly or have someone with you to guide you if you are walking backward. Try to keep them in the same place in your frame and move at the same speed as them.

Reviewing your footage:

- Do you feel as if you are too close to the subject? Does it look like you are chasing them rather than accompanying them? Do they walk out of frame when you don't intend them to?
- Is the image stable? If not, review the section on "crabbing."
- If you are filming someone, do they remain in the same place within the frame as you and do you move together?

Note: When you shoot from the side or behind, you can insert a voiceover at a later moment as long as you don't see them talking.

Now try this sequence again but without moving your body. Put the camera on a tripod and have the person walk through the frame several times in different places, and with different shot sizes. Pan, tilt, or zoom to accommodate them as they cross your frame and exit it. Always allow them to exit the frame, as this will make it easier for you to cut shots together when you come to edit.

FILMING THE STORY

Keep your audience interested

The most important job of any storyteller is to keep the audience interested, and avoid disorienting them in terms of time, space, point of view, or in the narrative thread. No matter how compelling we think an issue or story is, it is our job to present that story in a way that engages the audience's intellect, their emotions, their senses of humor and justice, while not oversimplifying the issue or irresponsibly representing people or situations.

To keep them engaged, the audience should know *where* they are, *what* they are seeing, and *who* is involved. They should know whom they are listening to and what the story is. The most basic building block you have that will keep your audience oriented is the sequence—a series of shots that show the context and details of an action, person, situation, or location, presented in a way that makes sense to your audience. Your complete story is a series of different sequences, often structured with a beginning, middle and end.

Filming a sequence

Always keep in mind the story you want to tell, how you plan to establish it, and how you will introduce an issue or character. Be aware of developing the issue or the character, what has happened to them, and how you can illustrate this.

For example, if your story is to follow a forensic team sifting through evidence of a mass grave, think about beginning with an establishing shot of the area, then an introductory shot of the team and a close-up on the member of the team you will follow. Show him filling out a form, picking bones out of the soil, and trying to identify a corpse. Be sure to shoot close-up and wide shots and each step of the process.

For example, if you shoot a close-up of the bone being carefully removed from the soil, follow it with the bone being cleared of excess dirt, then the bone being placed into a plastic bag and, finally, being labeled. Sequencing your shot, and varying your angles makes the images more compelling, contextual, and realistic. You could then film an interview with the forensic scientist, asking him about what he was doing during this process, or what this evidence points to. In the editing process you could choose whether to include the sound of his voice over the images of him carrying out his work. You can tell a very different story from filming the same event from different perspectives or from what you decide to favor and what you choose to ignore.

It's always important to be thorough when filming people doing something. Take, for example, officials registering refugees at the entrance of the camp. You will want to film a variety of shots to explain the scene.

First of all, you will need an establishing shot to set the scene followed by a close-up of a sign showing the name of the camp. You may then decide to film a long shot of a refugee waiting in line. Next, you might film a mid-shot of an official sitting down and writing down the name of a refugee. You might then go behind the official and film the refugee being registered, looking at the official, then a close-up of the refugee's expression.

You might then come around to stand on the same side of the refugee and shoot a close-up of the official writing. You may then think that a long shot of the two together will help to tell the story. Try to capture the interaction from the points of view of the people involved. For a good sequence you want to capture the registration experience from the points of view of both the refugee and the official.

Remember, you don't always have to shoot "in sequence" if activities are repeated, or if it will be easier to film one aspect of a scene at one time.

Filming to edit

It is at the editing stage, otherwise known as "postproduction" that your story will come together, so thinking about what an editor needs is vital.

When you are shooting you may think you are repeating the shot too many times, but remember, an editor needs many shots to choose from. Use a variety of shots, including wide, long, mid-shots, and close-ups, as well as different angles.

The other key thing to remember is that effective editing and filmmaking is about compression of time and space. In any film we do not see every moment of an action, just the key moments that will keep us orientated. Events that take place over 20 minutes in real time, can be shown in 20 seconds in a video, and we will accept the compression. When shooting to edit you are looking to provide your editor with all the components he or she needs to compress a sequence without jarring an audience.

How shots fit together

Editing is effective when a variety of shots are put together without appearing strange or jarring to the eye. How these shots fit together depends on the content and composition of each shot. An editor always needs to contrast images, putting shots together that are not too similar or too different so that there is not a jarring "jump-cut." For example, a close-up of a person's face will not go well with a close-up of another person's face but it will look good with a mid-shot of the person sitting in a chair. An overview establishing shot of a refugee camp will go well with a more detailed shot of someone cooking, or collecting water.

The following tips are important to remember:

Follow the 15-second rule

Always film a stable shot for 10–15 seconds before you start any movement with your camera. Even if you are just shooting a stationary subject, you should always let 10–15 seconds roll. This gives the editor enough material to choose and insert a shot into a sequence.

"Bracket" your shots

"Bracketing" means shooting a subject repeatedly to get the best shot. Shooting the same subject, try to shoot wide, medium, and close focal lengths. You might want to try to zoom out, then zoom in; or pan left and pan right. Bracketing is good for experimenting with light, movement, and distance from the subject.

Shoot "bridge" shots and think sequentially

Thinking sequentially does not mean that you have to shoot in a sequential order, but rather that chronological elements should all be on the tape for the editor to rearrange into a logical sequence, demonstrating cause and effect.

For example, if you are filming a dead body being carried into a building for examination, your camera needs to follow it. Think about what has to happen to put the body into the house. These shots help the editor to edit a "sequence" and to compress a complex action into a series of shots. The links or "bridges" move your story forward in time.

Be aware of dramatic changes in the weather

If it starts to rain, and most of your shots are in the sunshine, it could be hard to edit them into a sequence. If the weather changes and time permits, "re-establish" your scene (with a wide establishing shot) in the new weather conditions. That way, the editor won't have to put one shot with rain into a sequence with five other sunny shots.

Filming characters

A dramatic and powerful way to tell your story is through one character, or a series of characters who represent an abstract story idea: for example, health care of refugees, election fraud, the "disappeared."

If you interview someone, you should always strive to go beyond the interview with your camera. Often the difference between an expert interview and a genuine character with whom people can empathize is the context you provide through additional sequences around that person. Character-driven stories depend on good action sequences showing the person doing things, and interacting with their environment. They give a character depth because we see that character in many different situations.

The method for developing character is straightforward: once you find captivating characters, stick with them. Follow them through the day, interview them, shoot their reactions to situations, shoot personal belongings, and other details of their personality.

If they go between places, film their journeys. If they cry, if they speak, if they interact with others, shoot it all. By doing this, you create character; someone who is not one-dimensional and whose individual story can ultimately tell the big story. With video, many "little pictures" can create one overall big picture. That big picture is what you want your viewers to remember, long after they have finished watching.

Remember, a character need not be a person. A character can be a physical place or event as well: a polluted lake, a deserted village, a refugee camp, or a political demonstration. These things may not be human but they still have "personality." That personality or ambience is what you should look for.

Characters and continuity

Think about what your characters are wearing because when you edit together a sequence, seeing them in different clothing may not work well. You could ask them to wear the same or similar clothing if you are filming over a period of days, or in the editing stage you may choose to use only the sound of their voice in one particular sequence.

Case study: A personal experience developing a film around a character
Once I was filming a human rights lawyer called Alirio Uribe in Colombia. He regularly receives death threats but continues to work to defend others who had been targeted or killed by illegal paramilitaries in the country.

It was important to film Alirio in as many different scenarios as possible to give a sense of how he perseveres with his life despite everything. In the video Alirio first appears in the back seat of a car, giving the voiceover a chance to introduce him. The video then cuts to a wide shot of him getting out of the car, walking into court, and in the courtroom. The viewer finds out about the case he is working on.

Driving home, Alirio talks about the death threats he receives. We then see him the next morning having breakfast with his family. His voice over these images explains who these death threats come from and why. The next scene shows him at a market with his wife and heading to a park with his family. His wife talks about the reality of having a husband who works as a human rights lawyer, living under the threat of death, and how this affects their family.

Filming an interview

Interviews are often the building blocks for documentary film. Some simple steps can ensure good interviews:

Choose a location

Remember that there are many options for where you do an interview. Traditional news programs often rely on mid-shots of interviewees in offices, or neutral surroundings (i.e. backdrops of curtains, potted plants etc.). Think about filming people in the location where what they are discussing took place, or in their home, or walking around. Often people are more relaxed when they are doing something rather than in a formal sit-down interview setting. Others will find having photos, or other objects related to their interview, near them will help them talk.

The Dutch filmmaker Heddy Honigmann does this very effectively in her film *Good Husband, Dear Son*, where she interviews the mothers, wives, and daughters of men killed in a village near Sarajevo. A woman holds a photo of her husband, another sits with the tools he used to work with, another stands in the home they built together, and this makes their ability to recall painful memories and the viewer to empathize that much easier.

You may not be able to control the location where an interview takes place, but always consider what is comfortable for your interviewee and the best technical environment for your camera. Listen for background sounds; look at the lighting and what is behind and around the interviewee. What story do they tell about your interviewee?

If appropriate and if the situation is not too emotionally sensitive, ask your interviewee to readjust glasses or change a shirt. A sloppy or strange appearance can distract the viewer from what the interviewee is saying or diminish their credibility.

Establish a relationship with your interviewee and ensure they are making an informed decision about appearing on video

In an interview, it is natural for people to feel uncomfortable and it's very important to be sensitive to their needs. Their experiences may be traumatic, politically sensitive, or they may simply be shy in front of the camera. Be aware of how cultural norms or cross-cultural communication issues (if you and the interviewee are from different cultures) are affecting the situation.

Always try to make your interviewee feel at ease before you start. Many of your interviewees may be reluctant to talk on camera, so it is your job to relax them. Always maintain eye contact and give the person your fullest attention. People often need to warm up, so start with a more general question to get the interview going. Ask each person to say his or her name at the beginning of any recording. This may seem obvious, but there may be confusion later on, especially if you are interviewing many people in a row on one tape.

In Chapter 2 we discuss the issue of informed consent. In interviews or filming with victims and survivors it is particularly important to explain the importance of consent.

Observe your interviewee

Look for physical details that reveal someone's character: callused hands, an awkward and nervous posture, lack of eye contact, animated hand gestures while speaking. These will be useful to bear in mind as you frame your shots, and also to help identify shots that you can film as cutaways to use during the editing process. Remember, unless you have two cameras, you cannot shoot two things at once. You will only be able to shoot some details after an interview or an event is over.

Observe how your interviewee reacts to the camera. If your interviewee gesticulates to emphasize meaning, you may need wider shots. People you are filming can move around while speaking. Watch for early signs of such movement, so that you can be prepared to widen your shots or move with them once the interview begins.

Frame your interview

Always remember the rule of thirds when filming interviews. In close-up shots, keep your interviewee's eyes a third of the way down from the top of the frame.

Make sure your interviewee has enough talking space. If they are looking over to the left of the frame you should move them further to the right of your viewfinder, and vice versa.

If you are shooting a series of interviews, do not always shoot your interviewees on the same side of the camera. Instead, shoot some on the left third of your frame, and the other half on the right third. These variations allow for continuity and balance in the final edit of your footage. If you know beforehand that two people will be used to make contrasting points of view, shoot one looking to the left, the other to the right. That way, you can juxtapose them more effectively.

Where should the interviewee look?

Usually you will ask them to look at the interviewer, who is placed just off to the side of the camera, close to the lens, and diagonally across from the interviewee. If you are both filming and asking the questions ask the interviewee to look towards this place rather than directly at the camera. For a more confrontational interview you may on occasion want your interviewee to look directly into the camera.

Bracket shots in an interview

Try not to shift angles in the midst of the interviewee's response to a question. Move your camera for a bracket shot while the questions are being posed or while the interpreter is speaking. Editors appreciate having bracket shots of the same person as it gives them alternatives to edit with. Capturing expressive hand movements or other visual elements also conveys a sense of your interviewee's character.

Think about your angle

If you shoot a person with too wide an angle, it can diminish them. Wide-angle interviews are good when someone is walking or explaining something that is also being shown on the camera. In interviews, a higher angle will "diminish" a person whereas a low angle will make the person seem more powerful. In most interviews it is preferable to keep the camera at eye level.

Conducting an interview: Avoid "yes" or "no" questions

Remember that you are aiming to get your interviewee to give full and complete answers that you can use to tell your story. The best way to do this is to ask open questions that do not require a yes or no in response. For example, if you ask, "Are the living conditions in the refugee camp bad?" your interviewee may reply: "Yes, they are." However, if you ask, "Can you describe what the living conditions are like in the refugee camp?" you might get a more useful answer. Open questions like "Tell me about...?" are good for getting more complete answers. Explain to your interviewee how to incorporate your questions into their answers.

For example:

Question—How long have you worked at this center?

Answer—Five years.

This will be hard to edit. Instead you should ask your interviewee to say:

Question—How long have you worked at this center?

Answer—I have worked at this centre for over five years.

Avoid bias for or against your interviewee. This does not mean you cannot be sympathetic to someone who has been traumatized or suffered a human rights violation. Being fair means being impartial to the information you are seeking. Be especially careful not to ask leading questions like "Wouldn't you say that the government is responsible for stopping the supply of food to the refugee camp?" It's better to ask, "Can you explain who is responsible for stopping the supply of food to the camp?" The first question reveals your bias and can elicit a yes or no. The latter question invites a more detailed answer.

Always keep silent during the interview. Interviewers who continually give encouraging sounds to their interviewee like, "Aha" or "I see" have ruined many answers to questions, and make it harder to edit the material. Be careful not to interrupt and disrupt their flow of conversation.

Other shots you will need: Establishing shots

In every interview, as well as recording the actual interview you need to think about situating where the story is, or the context of an interview. Often this will involve shooting an establishing shot or sequence. This shows the interviewee in the environment where they are to be interviewed, talking with their interviewer in long shot or otherwise doing something over which an audio narration could later be placed to introduce the interviewee.

"When you interview someone who is traumatized, you need to be very aware of what is happening to them," says Mariana Katzarova, who is a researcher on Russia at Amnesty International. "Especially if the person is recounting an incident or traumatic experience for the first time they may go into fine detail and relive the experience in some way. You need to be able to listen and put their needs before the interview that you are recording."

Remember:

- Think about the sound, lighting and background of an interview
- Always try to get an on-camera consent, unless there are security reasons not to
- Observe your interviewee
- Avoid yes or no answers and don't ask leading questions
- Keep silent while your interviewee answers

Cutaways, reaction shots, B-roll, and verité

Cutaways and "B-roll" are the building blocks of editing that are the most overlooked and the most vital to a successful editing process.

Cutaway

A cutaway is a shot that the camera "cuts away" to from an interview or dominant scene, to allow for explanation of the character and the context of their story. These shots also "cover" edits and help to build a sequence. A cutaway is usually a detail of the scene—in the case of an interview it could be the character's hands, for example, or the face of a person listening. Cutaways are easiest to film in situations where people are engaged in an activity and you can take a close-up shot of a detail, or when they are in an environment with other people or with many other interesting potential shots around them. An interview in a bland room makes the on-location cutaway shots difficult.

In an interview context, you may want to keep your camera fixed on the person throughout. Once the interview is over, you can ask them to remain where they are and continue speaking while you shoot some "cutaway" shots of the person's immediate surroundings, and of details of their actions. In a doctor's office you might take a close-up of his prescription pad, or a set of medical instruments sitting on his desk, or the outside of his office. In someone's home it might be shots of photos of individuals they are talking about, an object from their home country etc. If someone is clutching something as they talk you might take a close-up of their hands holding it. If they were particularly expressive with their hands, then after you have finished the interview, ask them a random question and film their hands as they answer. The key to these detail shots is that they not include the person's face so that they will be easier to edit into the interview.

If someone has been doing something while you film them—for example, preparing vegetables for a stew, or sorting through papers—you will have an easy job of shooting cutaways if you take close-up shots of this activity that can be formed into mini-sequences. These cutaway shots are short and are used in the middle of the interview to smooth over audio and visual breaks in the editing. Another possibility for a cutaway is a long shot of the situation in which the viewer cannot discern what the interviewee is saying.

B-roll

B-roll is essentially any footage that is not interview footage, and which will serve to complement interviews and help tell your story. In any filming situation you should always be looking to gather images/ footage relevant to the story—i.e. if someone were talking about life in a refugee camp you would take shots of the living conditions, of people working, of people preparing meals, of the poor conditions in the schools. These will be used to "cover" (i.e. provide visuals while someone speaks) both interviews and narration. Take shots of different sizes—wide shots that show a context, action shots with one or two people doing an activity, pans across a scene, and close-ups to show important or interesting details. These images can also show the conditions and "speak for themselves," as with verité footage. A visual sequence within your interview can both tell the story and provide a breathing space and transition. Good B-roll and visual sequences do not just provide a visual image of what a person is saying, they provide something new and complementary to the audio track of an interview, or voiceover.

Verité footage

Verité is observational footage of activities and "life happening in front of the lens." It is footage that speaks for itself without necessarily requiring explanatory voiceover or narration. An example of verité would be footage of police officers beating protesters at a demonstration, or a scene in which we follow someone walking to a village water-pump far from their home.

Weaving general images and verité scenes of reality skillfully throughout a story gives it shape, pace, and tempo. Without them, a story seems flat and filled with the "talking heads" of one interview after another.

For every action there is a reaction

Reaction shots are compelling because they put a situation, a person, an event, in greater context with its surroundings. When shooting an interview in a public space, be ready to film the reactions of crowds or individuals to what is being said. This is especially important at political rallies or demonstrations. In more intimate situations, if someone is relaying an important story, shoot onlookers responding with looks of interest, concern, tears, or happiness. Reaction is often full of emotion—it *always* conveys to your audience that what they are listening to is interesting. (If it isn't—and that's your point—nothing could convey that better than cutaways of people looking bored.) Remember that you don't always need to shoot your reaction shots during the main action or interview—they can be shot before or afterwards if people continue to behave in a similar way.

Allow the story to unfold

The moment you put a video camera in your hand, be mindful of the immediacy that your role demands. The interview can turn sour, it can start to rain, or the most compelling part of any story can begin only when you turn your back on it. The interviewee may talk about a particular incident, which you may decide would be more important to the story than other filming you have planned. Always watch out for what you can film to illustrate the story, even when the camera is turned off.

Filming events that happen only once

When filming a one-off event, you need to think as you would when filming an activity, but you will need to think, act, and react quickly to what you are seeing through the lens of your camera. Practicing filming a live event is also a great way to improve your camera skills. Sometimes you want to experience that event through one person's experience, other times you want the footage to remain more "observational."

If it is critical to ensure there are effective images of the events that are occurring then it will be best to film stable wide shots. Make sure you have the footage to establish who, what, why, where, and when. Prepare in advance for the most critical moment by shooting other B-roll and establishing footage that will help explain the key events, and that can be gathered separately, as well as by interviewing people, both before and after events, and asking them to explain what is going on. Ask simple questions like "What is happening here?" Or perhaps you want an impression after the event—how did the meeting, the event, go?

For example, if YOU are filming at a demonstration and a fight breaks out between a police officer and a protester, keep the camera rolling. Most importantly get wide shots that show the whole scene, and give an overview of the situation, and include clear indicators of where you are. Try to keep your camera stable, to ensure that you can edit this material later if necessary.

Remember:

- Cutaways and B-roll are vital
- Reaction shots help to convey interest and emotion

Filming a conversation, an encounter, or a meeting

A challenging situation is filming a spontaneous conversation between two or more people or a mass meeting with just one camera.

Here, as with when you film any one-off activity, you need to use stable wide shots to ensure you establish a setting, and that you have the best chance of catching any key moment.

For a conversation you should get in as close as possible to include the people talking in a wide shot. As you get comfortable with the rhythm of a conversation you might want to start filming just one person. When the conversation shifts to another person you can pan across, or zoom out for a wide shot. Don't worry about always getting the first words of a new speaker—in editing, the shot will often linger on the person who has just finished speaking or who is listening, and you can cover the lack of an image with a cutaway. Useful cutaways in this setting include reaction shots of other people listening—remember these, and other contextualizing or B-roll shots, don't necessarily need to be gathered at the same time as the main action.

In a meeting, acoustics will often work against you. Unless you can record your sound directly from the public address system (if the speaker is using a mike) you will need to be close to the speaker, and with a directional mike that is focused on the speaker, not the ambient noise in a room. If you can't get close enough to record good sound, consider focusing on getting good wide shots of the whole setting including the speaker and audience, as well as audience reaction shots, and then getting good interviews in the immediate aftermath. As with any other live event, a good question to ask people is—"What just happened?"—and then leave them with a silence they fill with an answer.

Filming discreetly

Every camcorder has a small red light that comes on every time you press the record button: you can disguise it by sticking masking tape over the light or by holding the camera so that your hands obscure it. Many cameras also give you the option of disabling this light.

To film discreetly, make sure the camera is on auto focus and fully zoomed out and then hold it unobtrusively as if just carrying it by your side. If you are trying to film a person, you may need to tilt the lens up slightly to avoid filming just their torso and to include their head in the shot. It is usually prudent to remove such tapes from the camera as soon as possible after you have the shots you need.

There are ethical, legal, and safety considerations to consider when carrying out filming without permission or when the person or people you are filming are unaware. Ensure you have thought these through thoroughly before you do undercover or covert filming. For more information, see Chapter 2.

Draft a shooting plan

In Chapter 3 we talked about drafting a shooting plan as a step in preproduction. Now that you have more familiarity with the different kinds of shots and how sequences are constructed you can also prepare a shooting plan for your video.

You should draft your shooting plan based on the following:

- Which people do I need to film? Am I interviewing them or following their activities?

- What interview/dialogue, establishing shot, B-roll, verité, and cutaways will I film with each person? What additional material related to that person will I need to gather before or after filming with them? What contextualizing footage for my story and the people featured do I need to film?
- Can I break this down further into specific shots and sequences?
- Is there additional sound that needs to be recorded on-site or secured elsewhere?

For example, if you were going to be interviewing a mother who lost three sons during a brutal dictatorship, and a human rights organization that has been working to uncover mass graves and document names of the "disappeared," you might want to film the following:

- Establishing shots of the country would help to introduce and tell the story of its recent history. For example, overviews of street scenes, former military headquarters, evidence of the chaos of transition or the continuing presence of military forces, e.g. checkpoints or soldiers on the street. If there is any evidence of the former regime, you might want to film this.
- The mother's home may be a good place to film an interview, with cutaways (short shots) of her looking at photos of her sons, and close-ups of the photos and of her face looking at them. Cutaways of the house and other poignant objects would also be effective.
- Provided there are no security concerns, the human rights organization's office could be a good place for an interview, including an establishing shot of the office and close-ups of files and photos of the "disappeared" and B-roll of the organization at work.
- You might visit a mass grave, or even conduct an interview with someone from the human rights organization at the site as they conduct their work. You need to ensure that this is possible, that evidence at the site is left undamaged, and that no specific, identifiable remains are in shot.

Exercise 4.5: Film an interview
With this exercise you will pull together what you have learned so far about filming interviews, as well as shooting establishing

shots, cutaways, and B-roll. Set-up an interview with the person you observed conducting an activity before. Try to do it in the location where they were doing the activity, and perhaps while they are still doing it. Bring along a volunteer to help you ask questions and to assist in sound recording. Your objective is to shoot a 3- to 5-minute interview, including cut-away shots, and B-roll to cover the interview and linked narration.

Stage 1: *Establishing shot or sequence*

Choose your location and possible interview activity using the guidelines in this chapter.

Start with an establishing shot. Typically this is a wide shot at the beginning of a scene designed to inform viewers of a change in location and to orient them to the general mood and relative placement of subjects in the scene. This shot is also often used for the visuals when a narrator is "introducing" the subject of an interview.

You can choose the following options for your establishing shot (or sequence):

- Action shot of individual in context
- A pan from the street to your subject (interviewee) in the middle of an activity
- A wide-angle shot of the environment that slowly zooms in to your subject in the middle of an activity
- Shoot an extreme close-up of an action, and zoom or cut to reveal a wider picture
- A sequence showing the person conducting an activity

Stage 2: *Shoot the interview*

- Frame your subject, thinking about composition and lighting. Ensure there is neither too much backlight nor too much glare in the interviewee's eyes. Find your medium shot and close-up, bearing in mind how much the interviewee moves or gesticulates while talking.
- Start your interview—aim to get 3 to 5 minutes of material. Be creative. If the person is doing an activity talk to them about what they are doing.
- Remember to ask open-ended questions that do not require a "yes" or "no" answer. Remember that the interviewee's answers

should be self-contained, as you will probably not use the interviewer's questions in the final video.

- Five to eight questions should be sufficient.

Stage 3: *Shoot cutaway shots and B-roll*

- Shoot cutaway shots paying attention to the person's surroundings, their body language and gesticulation and to the details of any activity they have been performing as you talked.
- Shoot B-roll and verité sequences that can complement the interviewee's answers. If they discuss a place, person or event, see if it is possible to film this. Look at what you have from your initial exercise and then decide what additional material you will need. Go and shoot this.

Reviewing your footage:

- Is the frame stable, and does the interviewee remain in frame?
- Did you use medium shots and close-ups? Are close-ups used in more emotional or personal moments? Is the transition between the shot sizes done during an interviewer's question so that it can be easily edited-out, or smoothly and unobtrusively during the interviewee's answer?
- Are questions non-biased, open-ended? Are the interview responses self-contained?
- Are the cutaways interesting in themselves, or purely functional?
- Does the B-roll you have complement and supplement the interview, or does it just "show" what the person is saying?
- Did you shoot additional material to fill the gaps from your initial filming? Is it a good fit?

Exercise 4.6: Filming an activity

With the same person, think of something that they do every day. You must communicate this visually, and will not be able to use them speaking or voiceover to explain it. See if you show this activity in 10 shots. Draw 10 shots you want to film—this is called your storyboard. Review your storyboard. Does this show the story you would like to tell?

Example: Imagine that your friend works in a crowded office, trying to sort through thousands of files on people who have gone missing or who have been "disappeared" under a repressive regime. Every day people come to their office, carrying photos, trying to locate a relative. Members of the organization will sit with them, making a file on the missing person's name and attaching their photo. Think of a sequence that will show the activity of the human rights organization. Draw 10 shots you want to film. This is your storyboard. Review this. Does it show the story you would like to tell?

To give you an example, Figure 4.3 shows how this storyboard might look visually.

Example of a 10-shot storyboard in the human rights office:

1. LS: Human rights researcher sits at desk working and looks up
2. MS: Person at other side of the desk is standing and sits down, and zoom to CU of shaking hands
3. LS: Researcher pushes seat back, stands up and walks over to a film cabinet
4. CU: Researcher's hands looking at different files and selecting a folder that says REPORT
5. MS: Person across from the desk is shown talking about something intense
6. MS: Human rights worker listens carefully and takes notes
7. CU: A section on the form
8. LS of both in the frame discussing section together
9. Over the shoulder MS of the human rights worker as the person gets up to leave and shakes hands
10. CU as the human rights worker closes the file

Think of an activity that you want to film. Try drawing another storyboard and then film based on what you have drawn.

Exercise 4.7: Capturing a sense of place
Note: A tripod or monopod is recommended for this exercise.

Your goal is to convey the feeling of a place and the community of people who live, work, and pass through there, to someone who has never been there. Go to the location and observe it at the beginning, middle, and end of the day, as well as other key moments (e.g. if there was a marketplace, the hour when it opens, or the time when the local college finishes classes and all the students go home). On each visit, stay for at least half an hour and film what happens.

- Make sure you get a range of shots and angles. What is the mood of the place? What activities are going on in the place? Who enters and leaves?
- Extreme long shots can be very important in helping to establish a place or connect scenes that take place over a period of time.
- You may find it helpful also to pick out a person whose activities are connected to the place, and follow them for part of your filming.

Sequences conveying the feeling of a place are often used at the beginning of a film, to connect scenes, or as a closing sequence.

Figure 4.3 Storyboard example: Human rights investigation (Taw Nay Htoo)

5

Editing for Advocacy

Katerina Cizek

This chapter is a guide to editing advocacy videos aimed at a variety of audiences, including local communities, international audiences, courts and tribunals, as well as an online viewership. Intended as a companion to more technically oriented video editing manuals, this chapter focuses on the unique concerns of editing video for advocacy in human rights, social justice, and humanitarian contexts. It uses case studies drawn from WITNESS partnerships and beyond to demonstrate varying approaches to creating videos designed to effect broader social change.

INTRODUCTION TO EDITING FOR ADVOCACY

What is editing?

> A film is born three times. First in the writing of the script, once again in the shooting, and finally in the editing. (French filmmaker Robert Bresson[1])

Editing, or postproduction, is the process in which a film or video's component parts—visuals, sound, word, music, and text—are woven together through storytelling and juxtaposition to create meaning. It is considered the most labor-intensive stage of the process of making a video or film. One of Hollywood's famous editors, Walter Murch, points out that editing is "something like sewing: You knit the pieces of film together."[2]

An editor's skill and creativity can make or break the quality of a video—turning amateur footage into compelling videos, or reducing quality footage into an incoherent string of imagery and sound. As there are a thousand different ways to edit any one video, no two editors will put the pieces together in the same way. Each editor strives to create a unique "'whole" that makes sense.

Editing is also about manipulation. In the "Kuleshov Experiment," an early Russian filmmaker proved that juxtaposing two unrelated images could convey separate meanings. In his experiment, Kuleshov filmed a famous Russian actor, as well as shots of a bowl of soup, a girl, a teddy bear, and a child's coffin. He then edited the shot of the actor into the other shots; each time it was the same shot of the actor. But when audiences watched, they felt that the shots of the actor conveyed different emotions, though each time it was in fact the same shot. Intended or not, editing creates new levels of meaning.

Whether it's fiction or documentary, on average there is about 25 to 50 times more material shot than will end up in the final video, and this ratio can go up to 80:1 or higher in documentaries with a lot of verité footage. You may have filmed a given event in real time over the course of many hours, but, through good editing, you can convey the same event within seconds. Sometimes you may have far less material, and then the challenge is to tell your story with limited material. This is possible too. In every case editing is a process of ellipsis. As Peter Wintonick, a media critic and one of Canada's leading documentary-makers, says: "At the basic level, editing is about time-compression, whether you are compressing an afternoon into 3 minutes, a year into 20 minutes or a lifetime of a person into 60 minutes."

It is important to know your goals, audience, and intentions going into the process of making and editing a film. Defining your vision is key, even as you recognize, as Bresson says, that a film is recreated at each stage of the process. Therefore, when making a video, it's a good idea to begin planning for the edit even before you shoot. Prepare a script and use it as a blueprint to go through the various stages of making the video. A video benefits from this early vision and clarity (for more information on this early planning, see Chapters 1 and 3). Some edits stick close to the shooting script and are highly structured, while others are more organic, drawing on what has been filmed. However, it is equally important in the edit room to follow the script and simultaneously to respond to the material you have in front of you, to let the material speak to you. This is the challenge of the edit—to balance the script and the vision with the reality of the material that exists.

Editing for advocacy: The importance of audience

How may editing strategies differ if you are editing for advocacy?

In conventional editing, the story is king. Often, conventional editors have little or no direct relationship to the people they film or to the issue. In editing for advocacy, the focus shifts to:

- Speaking to your audience
- Communicating your message
- Navigating ethical concerns
- Respecting the people about/with whom you're making the film

Certainly, developing a good story plays a crucial role in fulfilling these responsibilities, but the triangle between the subject, the editor, and the audiences becomes a delicate balance in editing for advocacy.

There are a thousand ways to edit, and another thousand ways to edit for advocacy. An audience of teenagers will respond differently than a judge sitting on a tribunal. As you explore ways to encourage your audience to "do something," you may believe your greatest strength lies in the power of art, of empathy, or the power of overt persuasion, or all three. Across the board, video images and stories have the unparalleled capacity—beyond the written word—to put a human face on any issue, on any human rights story. It is the challenge of the editor to make that story come to life (for a more thorough discussion on defining your audience, see Chapter 3).

During editing for advocacy, special attention to ethics and unique concerns is also of paramount importance. Some of the major ethical issues involved in editing for advocacy are discussed later in this chapter.

Along with a clear message and ethical guidelines, advocacy video editing requires resources: time, equipment, labor, and some money. While it is true that much can be accomplished with creative solutions (bartering, volunteers, low-budget/low-tech options), the harsh reality of filmmaking is that there are always some hard costs involved. Good budgeting and planning before going into the edit room can save you or your organization headaches and surprises (see Chapter 3 for details on how to budget).

In the following pages we will explore only some of the "editing for advocacy" strategies, by learning from the successes and failures of editors and advocates from around the world. Mostly, we hope to inspire new ways of telling stories that matter—that will bring audiences, whomever you decide they may be, to their feet to take action.

Who is the editor?

In many human rights advocacy contexts (and low-budget contexts) often the very same person who has done the filming will also be editing—alone. There are certain advantages to having a single person act as the videographer and the editor, especially when you are pressed for time. Firstly, the videographer/editor will already know the material, the issues, and the story. Secondly, editing is the best way to learn what to shoot next time. For example, many first-time videographers forget to shoot sufficient visual representations of a story beyond interviews or sufficient cutaway shots. When they reach the editing room, however, they realize how critical such footage is to the process of visual storytelling. They quickly learn from their mistakes and are better prepared for their next shoot. Another advantage is that the videographer/editor is likely to have the most direct contact with and exposure to the people and communities represented, so that he/she may bring a sensitivity to the ethical dimensions of the edit that someone more distant might not.

Howard Weinberg, a producer and documentary script adviser for political and cultural films for America's TV networks for over 30 years, recommends that organizations train several members in creating media for distribution. They can then work collectively and "mentor each other. When someone else is doing the editing, it's better than trying to do everything yourself. It's good to trade-off roles; it's less solitary. You can pick up new ideas from doing other things." In his experience, when there are two people working together, the editor is generally the one who has not been in the field, and looks at the material matter-of-factly. But, he says, "an editor can create something that wasn't there, so the producer who was on the scene keeps it honest. The relationship and dialogue between the editor and the producer/director tame the unlimited editing possibilities."

Sandrine Isambert worked as the in-house editor at WITNESS for two and a half years. While in the edit studio, she worked in various scenarios—editing material alone, as well as working closely with partners visiting from the field. She says, "It's so great to work with someone else, to laugh and to share the experience." When you are editing, "It's a constant battle to be with the individuals in your video, and to be with the viewers at the same time—to understand what they will respond to." As most audiences will only watch once, "It's ultimately about the first viewing for them, and that's a hard thing to keep in mind when you've seen the material so many times, and are deep inside the storyline, empathizing with the individuals featured."

A good editor has a lot of patience. An editor must be willing to spend long periods of time in a dark space, watching footage over and over again. Weinberg identifies a good editor as a person who can "track information, organize, and will have a sense of rhythm and flow, [who] will build story emotionally." No matter what the structure or content of the video, this ability to understand what emotional responses the video evokes at every stage is critical to the success of the project. For advocacy videos, it may also be critical to the success of the campaign or legal case at hand.

An editor has to be willing to throw weeks of work away, in the service of the video, says Franny Armstrong, a political filmmaker in the UK: "Sometimes a scene you love will have to go because it doesn't work in the larger picture. An editor can't have a big ego. They have to be willing to let go of their own creations."

An editor's work involves endless decision-making: how long to make a shot, to use music or not, what sequence to put shots in, etc. Ironically, in the end, a seamless editing job will probably go unnoticed by general audiences. Sandrine Isambert reminds us: "Ultimately, when people haven't said anything about the edit of a video, then it's probably a good edit."

Exercise 5.1: Learn to identify edits

This exercise is about getting a feel for the underlying editing. It is best done in a group.

Pick a recent film that you have enjoyed. If you have access to WITNESS films you might want to view an excerpt from the film *Books Not Bars*, and then contrast it with the film *Operation Fine Girl* to see two very different editing styles. Short versions of both these films can be seen online at <www.witness.org>.

Start by familiarizing yourself with the feel of the editing. Sit and watch the video, and tap your finger whenever there is a cut in the images. Now try doing the same thing with the audio edits. Now split the group in two, and half clap when audio changes and half clap when visual. Quickly you'll notice that they don't always happen at the same time. Challenge yourself to really listen and watch for changes, including audio cuts that may be hidden by cutaways or B-roll.

Quickly you will develop a feel for the way edits happen, their pacing, and how audio and visual edits play off of each other. Often, if you have not thought about it before you will be surprised at the number of edits within even the simplest of films.

A variation on this exercise is to have group members shout out when a different source of audio or visual material (as discussed in Chapter 3) is used.

Conceptualizing a film for a better edit

It is never too early to think of editing in the filmmaking process. Peter Wintonick, a director who began his 30-year long filmmaking career as an editor, says: "In every stage of making a film, think like an editor." This means think of your story, and how you want to tell it before you start shooting, so you are better prepared for the edit room.

Joey Lozano stresses the importance of a shooting plan and script to good editing:

> The story concept usually comes in before I do the actual shoot and it guides me in my actual shooting work. After shooting, I do the shotlisting to determine which visuals are good ones and which are not that good. Then, after that, I go back to my original concept of the story and start the script.

By thinking of your edit before you shoot, you are troubleshooting for the edit process, and refining your story. Consider the early stages as a blueprint—things can and should change, but having a vision won't hurt if you remain flexible.

Notes Sam Gregory of WITNESS:

> A common problem is that during shooting, many points of view are filmed within the community, and you may need to focus on only a few,' notes Sam Gregory of WITNESS. 'Editing decisions may need to be explained before shooting because everyone who is filmed may be expecting to be in the film. They may not realize that 25 hours have been filmed and that the final video will only be 10 minutes! So you have to explain that in the edit you will use only a fraction of the footage, and you cannot be rigidly guided by the politics of representation. Not everyone can be included, and the key figures in the film should be determined as much by their perceived impact on the intended audience as by their stature within a community or simply because they were filmed.

ETHICS OF EDITING

Moving into the postproduction phase often means removing yourself from the tangible context of filming, of being "on the ground." It may mean you need to work in a studio far away from the community, or you may begin working with an editor who has little or no relation to the subjects you've been filming. It also means devoting your time to your footage rather than the situation on the ground. For all these reasons, it means that at some level you are distancing yourself from the concrete reality of a situation, in exchange for being able to "represent" it on video.

You are also alone with the material, often for a very long time. This separates you from your audience, from the people to whom you are communicating your message.

This very process of editing presents a complex web of ethical dilemmas that may not have been present while filming. As an editor and as an advocate, one needs to address the potentially dangerous consequences of how material is handled in the edit room.

Respect the subject

Says Ronit Avni:

> It is critical to honor every commitment that has been made during the filming of a scene or an interview. It can become very tempting in the edit room to use footage that is off-limits. You need to be very clear about the parameters of the material. During editing, we have the tools to manipulate, to change words, to reconfigure viewpoints without the context. It might further the goals of the video—but it might also hurt or endanger subjects.

In an advocacy context, whether it is yours or someone else's footage, you need to understand the context in which consent was obtained. If the interview was granted under the condition that the identity not be revealed, you need to take precautions that will ensure this anonymity. For example, the technique you use to obscure their identity needs to be appropriate. Sometimes, using the digitizing effect to obscure details of a face may seem enough in the edit room, but is not enough in the community—for example, clothes and voice could reveal a person's identity as well (see Chapter 2).

Guilt by association

Necessarily, the act of editing—placing one image/sound next to or layered over another—is the act of juxtaposition. Juxtaposition can create ethical problems, back in the field or at home, of which you may not be aware in the edit room. Ronit Avni remembers one instance in which the producers of a video didn't realize the danger of juxtaposition:

> Once we edited a piece in a war-torn situation. We decided to include various parties from the political spectrum in the video. When we sent out the tape to the subjects for final approval, we suddenly got a terrified phone call. One subject, working within the bounds of the law, was terrified to be in the video with another subject considered *persona non grata* by the government. The subject insisted that WITNESS take out either one or the other interview, but keeping both in could be very dangerous. In the end we shelved the entire film.

Editing presents whole new situations of danger. Even if full consent has been given for an interview, a subject may feel threatened by the way the material is edited. "When editing for advocacy," Ronit Avni advises, "there's a great need to be committed to the safety of everyone in the film above everything else." This often differs from traditional news and documentary filmmaking, in which interviewees do not have a say regarding the other viewpoints represented in the film or in the eventual structure of the film.

Sam Gregory echoes:

> There can be a conflict between dramatic editing and ethical representation when making human rights video. How does the visual language work with (or against) what is being spoken? For example, when putting images over someone's interview, what do those images convey beyond the words spoken? You need to think about the images over-dramatizing the actual words. The juxtaposition between sound and image is crucial. Are you exaggerating what the interviewee is saying? Are you misrepresenting what they are saying—i.e. they are conveying a message of reconciliation while you are placing violent imagery over it? You have been given the person's trust not to misuse their words, and you must have that in your mind all the time.

Emotional manipulation and over-dramatization

In the editing process, an issue or subject can easily be either trivialized or over-dramatized. Both can cause ethical problems for the subjects as well as the audience. Producers can also feel the pressure to make situations look "as bad as possible" and to focus on the graphic images rather than explaining the reasons for the situation.

The tendency in the editing process may be to boost the emotion around the footage, in an effort to make it more dramatic. For example, using heavy music with slow-motion visuals and loaded, biased narration to ensure the message is clear—that a grave injustice is being represented.

While music, emotion, and drama are part of the language of filmmaking, you may need a reality check on how you use them. Are you leaning on stereotypes to manipulate your subjects and your audience? For example, many charitable organizations use images of starving children pumped up with sappy music, in efforts to tap into pity and raise donations for their missions. But what does this type of representation say about the nameless, anonymous children portrayed? What does it say about the audience?

As Sam Gregory says:

> There is the question of what message you are sending out: are you representing agency or plight, optimism or pessimism, victims or survivors? Are you making the subjects of the film look like hapless victims who need to be saved? Or are you giving voice to people... giving agency to a community as being capable of being part of the solution? It's difficult when you are looking for donors at the same time, not tapping into pity and charity. But it's a vicious cycle that perpetuates misperceptions if you start to do that. Audiences eventually feel tired and manipulated by this imagery, and if you frame the people in your video as victims you are disempowering precisely the people whose voices you want to be heard.

As the editor, you are mediating the relationship between the subject and the audience. You have the capacity to perpetuate stereotypes or to advocate for a new relationship between audiences and subjects as partners. As the socially conscious photographer Lewis Hines said of his own career: "I want to show the things that should be changed. I want to show the things that should be admired." Allow the people in your films as well as your filmmaking to speak to both.

Joey Lozano says that his approach to video-activism has changed over the years:

> If you go to a community where they only have problems, and they have no solutions, you can only come out with that kind of video, concentrating very much on the problems and maybe ending up with a grim situation. Failing to present any hope for the community can be very detrimental... In the past, in my early years, when trying to produce videos, I always fell into that pitfall

of presenting grim situations. This is more like a propaganda video, which may be useful at a certain stage, for example during the time of martial law [in the Philippines]. It was good, during that time. But it has come to a point when I think it's time to present the positive aspects, the positive struggles of people who are affected by this kind of bad situation. I think the effect, for viewers seeing this kind of video, is to inspire them to try this kind of solution that is being proposed in the video. Not to get paralyzed by situations that have been portrayed as hopeless. So it would also be good if a video can also provide a brighter side to the people's struggle.

Objectivity vs propaganda

Whether to present the other side of the argument is a key question in advocacy video. Journalistic tradition, especially in the USA, favors always showing the other side of the argument, and providing an ostensibly balanced viewpoint in which the different positions are given equal time.

Yet in many cases, video activists feel as though the "other side" (e.g. the government, figures of authority) has had enough exposure, with frequent presentation on TV, newspapers and other media. They feel the video they are making is their opportunity to give their point of view, often for the first time. Why give more time to the other side, one may think, when they have already had their time everywhere else?

Yet for some audiences, it may be very important to present "objective journalism" and let the other side speak. Gillian Caldwell says:

Doing this says "We offered the other side a chance to speak." It also says that we have gone through the procedures and mechanisms at the local level and they didn't work, for example, by going to the police and asking them why they did not act, we prove to the audiences that there is inaction at the local level, and that's why we must go higher, to national and even international levels.

In some human rights contexts this may also be relevant in proving that international action is necessary given that all domestic remedies have been exhausted.

Presenting the other side can also make your own argument stronger. Peter Wintonick points out that people often "put their own foot in their mouth." In a classic scene in *Manufacturing Consent:*

Noam Chomsky and the Media Wintonick and his co-director Mark Achbar intercut Chomsky's points with those of an opponent at the *New York Times*. Wintonick says this is one of the most powerful scenes in the video, because presenting the opposition only helped reinforce the power of Chomsky's point of view.

Audiences recognize propaganda when they see it. "If you use a sledgehammer instead of a button, this will usually be detrimental," warns Peter Wintonick. Martin Atkin, a producer at Greenpeace, agrees:

> Even though you are pushing a message, you need to be subtle. At Greenpeace, I have been trying to cut down the Greenpeace branding. Recently, we sent a team to Iraq, to investigate radiation contamination from radioactive material throughout the country. We sent a videographer and a still photographer. They had the Greenpeace logo on all equipment, on their T-shirts, on the caps. They had logos everywhere. Every shot that we edited had this in. When I tried to get this to the TV stations. They wouldn't use it. They told me "If that was a Shell, Ford or any other corporate brand logo, we wouldn't use it. So why should we use yours! Why should we give you guys a free advert?"

Gillian Caldwell counters:

> Pure propaganda is sometimes exactly what you are looking for! For example, in public service announcements (PSAs), you only have a few seconds to convey a powerful message to a broad audience. You need to make your point, and you need to make it right away. But if it doesn't resonate, if there is no human being to relate to, it will fall flat. We produced a powerful PSA calling for the ratification of the International Criminal Court statute that had a very strong impact on audiences—and it certainly wasn't a light touch.

Don Edkins, of the STEPS project in South Africa, warns:

> Now, the messaging around HIV/AIDS in South Africa tends to put people off. The billboards, the overt public service announcements, are preachy. People are tired of it, there's a fatigue. So, as filmmakers, we thought to use stories in order to not be preachy. We thought, "Let's create stories around different characters." We found that people related more to real stories. The other thing we learned was the people like their own stories from their own communities and their own filmmakers. People want to see videos from their own locations.

Old school and new school: The conventional and the cutting edge

A debate in advocacy filmmaking communities involves the issue of aesthetics, and how much to use a conventional grammar of editing. Within activist communities, there is a debate about the balance between breaking new ground and relying upon traditional aesthetics, filmmaking, storytelling techniques, and styles of production. Liz Miller asks: "How do we respectfully mainstream issues? Should we use the aesthetics of familiarity to get our message across? Does the message get lost in the process?"

Whichever way you choose to address the questions of aesthetics, innovation, and rule-breaking, the key is to understand your audience, and how you think they will respond. During the editing stage, you should plan to put together groups of individuals who resemble your target audience to "test" the material in rough cut screenings before your video is finalized. Do they understand what you are trying to achieve? Are they responsive?

For example, Stephen Marshal of GNN notes:

Many people in the "left" feel our style (editing to music, in the style of music videos with heavy montages and special effects) is giving precedence to style over content, that we are delegitimizing the issues. I think that's an excuse on their part for not learning how this media works. Our target audience is the 20–35 year olds. I have no hope for my dad's generation. It's a desktop digital revolution. Yet it's amazing how few groups actually employ the very revolutionary techniques offered up by the technology to inspire a whole new generation. The advantage of our form is that we know our audiences, on average, watch our stuff two or even three times. It's a whole different viewing experience than, let's say, the documentary form, that has one chance to get their message across — because their audiences are only watching one time. The corporations out there are all using this vibe to get the attention of the new generation, and they are working hard to get them. So we need to be as smart, we need to go after them the same way.

Gillian Caldwell observes:

GNN speaks to a very specific, but important audience. Their videos aren't going to convince the powerbrokers—but they may mobilize people who can make other kinds of impact. I think all these genres have their place and time, and that they can be mutually reinforcing even though the presentations and impacts may be very distinct.

Dealing with violent and difficult material

Invariably, when working with video in a human rights context, editors will at some point be faced with images of violence, torture, pain, and even death. What responsibilities do editors have in dealing and using this material?

Ronit Avni suggests the following guidelines:

> If the graphic imagery sheds light on the situation that a certain target audience wasn't aware of, and it doesn't exploit the people shot in the images, if there is a context then, yes, use the image. But if it's used, for example, in a music video (with no light shed on the context) just to shock and titillate then its problematic. These are hard questions, because the very aim of art is, at times, to shock and titillate. But in an advocacy context, the context needs to be provided. Will the audience learn more? How might they weigh in? Will it prompt them to do more than just watch the video?

A very graphic image, when used in the right context, can reinforce the point that the situation is grave, real, and has true consequences. "They realize that this is not Hollywood," says Sandrine Isambert. For example, in the final scenes of the video *Rule of the Gun in Sugarland,* Joey Lozano edited footage of Ananias Tahuyan, a member of the NAKAMATA indigenous peoples' coalition, dying in front of the camera. The entire video until that scene builds the context surrounding Tahuyan's murder. For years, members of NAKAMATA, a coalition of indigenous tribes in the Philippines, have been harassed, intimidated, and even murdered in efforts to suppress their legal and peaceful pursuit of ancestral land claims. The video also points out what an international audience can do to bring justice to the NAKAMATA.

Case study: Using hip-hop music and montage for advocacy

The short music video *Diamond Life* was the Guerrilla News Network's (<www.gnn.org>) first video. Edited to hip-hop music, *Diamond Life* examines the violent impact of the diamond trade on lives in Africa. The video contains extremely graphic material, in montage sequence, and has been criticized for its deliberate attempts to shock.

Stephen Marshall of GNN explains:

> *Diamond Life* was the first video we did. We wanted to create an R-rated documentary; we wanted to speak to the hip-hop culture that we are closely

connected to. In hip-hop culture, people are covered with diamonds. We wanted to convey the traumatic experiences of people in Africa who suffer because of the diamond trade. The video contains very graphic scenes of murder and torture, at the hands of child soldiers. But we were speaking to audiences that we believe are already desensitized, and we were also speaking to girls dreaming of their first diamond.

We launched our organization with that video, and we had many people come back to us and say that they will never buy a diamond because of our video. But we also heard from some teachers that kids were passing around the video just for shock effect. We are in the midst of information warfare, so it's hit or miss. No strategy is going to work 100% of the time. But our point was that despite all this violence so prevalent in our media, war itself tends to be so sanitized in the media, and we wanted to challenge that.

When you do decide to use the material, Sandrine asks: "Will the audience take it? Someone is being killed on camera. You can't soften it; you can't make it more dramatic. It's just very, very difficult." The key question is: Have you done justice to the representation of that person's life—and death?

You should also make sure to test the resulting video with individuals who are not working on the issue– people who have been documenting abuses may have lost track of how a less experienced public will react to images of extreme violence or of death. As Sandrine points out:

It's very hard, because when you work in human rights, it's not like you get used to [graphic, violent situations], but as an editor, even if you have a hard time watching these images, you have to do it. Sometimes you have to remind yourself that people are not accustomed to that kind of story—to seeing those kinds of images. You always have to try and put yourself in someone else's shoes.

Research has been done that shows that people react to violent imagery by not remembering the material that precedes a violent sequence or the audio content of the sequence itself—consider how the use of this kind of imagery in your film may affect your audience's ability to follow the story.[3]

If you decide to edit a video to include graphic material, you should also include information in accompanying screening materials that can prepare audiences for the viewing. You may also consider placing a title card warning of graphic or violent content before the film begins.

But, fundamentally, you need to ask yourself to what end is your use of violent material contributing? What message are you sending out? The term "The Trauma Vortex." has been coined by psychologist Peter Levine to describe the spiralling process of reliving trauma outside a person's normal life experience. The media can play a damaging role by sustaining the vortex, when reproducing images of violence.

Ronit Avni says:

> One of the reasons I founded Just Vision was because I wanted to show constructive models of people trying to *do something* about the violence plaguing Israel/Palestine, and not just see more images of violence, violations and victimization. Video advocacy need not simply focus on violence, on sensational imagery, on reinforcing a paradigm of victimized and victimizer. It ultimately robs everyone of their agency and dehumanizes. The world needs more live, contemporary models of civic engagement, leadership, and activism. Sensational images leave audiences fixated, addicted to violence, but further disempowered.

Exercise 5.2: Dealing with violence

The Guerrilla News Network production, *The Diamond Life* had a very specific audience in mind. If possible, go to the WITNESS website at <www.witness.org> and watch the video in the Rights Alert section. What was your reaction to how it was made? Analyze how the video is constructed, and how it deals with specific images of violence. Using this same material, imagine different ways of editing this material for a different audience. What would you personally take out? What might you like to see put in? In your view, is the use of violent material justified in this video? Discuss your feelings and reactions to the material in a group.

Psychological effects of violent material

Watching violent images repeatedly as you log, transcribe, and edit has emotional and psychological effects. Editors and others involved in the production may experience guilt, anxiety, sleeplessness, and suffer from nightmares. Sometimes these symptoms are actually components of a well-documented psychological condition known as secondary trauma, which is discussed more in Chapter 2. One common reaction is feeling that you are a witness to abuse, yet are completely powerless to stop it.

Sandrine Isambert says that editors, in any context, begin to feel as though they know the subjects intimately through the editing process. "I especially feel emotional when editing footage of refugees," she says, "because I always wonder what's happened to them."

Sandrine suggests:

> You need to take a lot of breaks. It's not always easy to be in the right mindset. With footage of war, people dying on camera, you just concentrate; you just hold your breath the whole time. You watch it over and over, and you need to stay detached, yet you are trying to build an emotional sequence. It's terribly difficult to keep the balance.

Respecting the audience, the field, the facts

A good editor respects the audience. There is often a fine line between condescension, and generosity of information. It's a fine balance to explain thoroughly, while at the same time not treating audiences as though they are inferior or lack knowledge.

Being responsible also means respecting the facts of the case. Manipulating the facts can be detrimental to your message, the subject, and the audience. Sandrine insists:

> You have to make sure your information is very accurate. You can't be wrong. Your credibility could be endangered. It's such an important issue and you want people to believe that what you are saying is true. You should double-check your sources.

As an editor, you also have responsibility to the emerging field of "human rights video" and to the broader human rights and social justice field. You are accountable to your colleagues. One bad film can affect everyone using media for advocacy—it can discredit other video-activists, by making audiences less open, more cynical.

PRACTICAL STEPS TO EDITING FOR ADVOCACY

Preparing the edit

Focus

You must begin with a clear idea, and an understanding of your message and audience. Peter Wintonick says:

Editing begins with an idea.What is the video, what are the subjects, the location? Where are you pointing your camera? What will you and won't you pay attention to? Then you can begin to make the argument, the message, and logistically, begin to think what is the arc, and the structure of the edited video.

Sam Gregory explains:

> The common problem when people begin to make an advocacy film is that often people try and squeeze too many things into one video. The logical thing seems to be the desire to address all the issues, especially if this is the first time you are using video and you're not sure when you will next have the opportunity. But a video really needs to retain a focus. You and the eventual audience need to know what the issue is that matters to you, and what you are trying to communicate about this issue.

Before you begin any editing process, as we discussed in Chapter 2, spend time developing and outlining the central idea. It will make the rest of the process flow better, leading to a more focused and compelling message.

At each stage of the filmmaking process, keep the editing process in mind, so each piece of the puzzle is created and easily put together in the editing suite.

During the editing process, decisions will focus on the structure of the piece, i.e. how your pieces of puzzle will fit together in order to create the desired film.

The postproduction process

In Chapters 3 and 4 we talked about conceptualization and research, preproduction and production. Now we are in the postproduction phase. This stage includes:

- Viewing, logging and transcribing your footage.
- Preparing a paper edit and script.
- Producing an assembly cut of the video.
- Checking the assembly cut against script, and asking yourself if you have stayed true to the original concepts and audience/ advocacy goals.
- Creating a first rough cut, by refining the assembly.
- Testing the film with a select audience for feedback, comments, and suggestions.

- Creating subsequent rough cuts as necessary.
- Creating a fine cut of the video, incorporating constructive feedback from your select audience and script revisions, and possibly adding sound elements including music. This milestone is only halfway through the postproduction stage.
- Creating a final cut.
- Doing the "online," i.e. finishing the video, involves adding graphics, doing a final sound edit, digitizing the film in high resolution, and creating outputted versions. A sample timeline for the editing process is given in Figure 5.1.

A general and ideal guideline for editing in terms of the final length is shown in Table 5.1.

Table 5.1   How long will postproduction take?

Final length of the video	How long to edit it?
5–12 minutes	2–3 weeks
12–18 minutes	3–4 weeks
18–30 minutes	4–6 weeks
30–60 minutes	6–12 weeks

During a real editing process, a film can move back and forth and even in circles throughout the stages described above. One person's assembly edit may be another's rough cut; it's all very subjective. Each film has its own unique journey, and each editor has an individual way of traveling throughout these stages. Furthermore, the time estimates are only guidelines.

In reality, an advocacy video may be under serious time and budget constraints. Perhaps community members may only take limited days away from their families and their work—especially if postproduction facilities are far away in urban centers. Or perhaps, you may need to get your film out fast, in order to respond to political needs in a timely fashion. There are ways to keep postproduction short:

- Make a short final product—keeping your film under 10 minutes may help reduce postproduction time and for many audiences is an effective format.
- Shoot limited, efficient footage in the first place.
- View and log material with your camera in the field.
- Structure a solid paper edit before entering the studio.

FOCUS / CLEAR IDEA	VIEW / LOG / TRANSCRIBE ALL FOOTAGE	PAPER EDIT	DIGITIZE FOOTAGE ORGANIZE BINS	ASSEMBLY EDIT	RE-SHOOT / RE-THINK / RE-SEARCH	ROUGH CUT	TEST SCREEN	FINE CUT (AND ON-LINE)	COPY ZERO
1 day -1 week	1 week - 1 month	1 day -1 wk	1 day - 1 week	1-2 weeks	1 day - 1 month	2-3 weeks	1-5 days	1-2 weeks	
what is the key message, story and advocacy goal(s)?	what exactly do you have on tape?	the blue-print	take only what you need, know where it is	bring it down to the essentials, following your script/ paper edit	will new material make it better?	giving shape to the assembly	feedback and comments	cleaning it up: sub-titles, sound, music narration etc., versions	final master

Figure 5.1   Editing and production timeline

- Book only one or two days in the facility for a rough cut, make a copy of the film, and go back to the community. Do screenings, and make changes on paper. Return to the studio for another day a few weeks later, once you know exactly what changes you wish to make.
- Consider new technologies that allow in-the-field editing (laptop computers with inexpensive editing software). Bring the editor to the community, if resources allow.

Linear vs non-linear

There are two distinct ways of conducting an edit: linear and non-linear.

Linear editing is the old video editing process, in which the images must be assembled in order, from beginning to end. The advantage of linear editing is that it requires the filmmaker or editor to be incredibly organized and detail-oriented throughout the editing process, in order for all the pieces to fall into place. The disadvantages of linear editing are that changes in order or length of segments cannot be made easily. Inserted sequences must exactly match a removed sequence. There is no easy way to make retroactive changes.

Non-linear editing is an editing process performed on a computer, in which the images can be assembled and reassembled in any order. Often non-linear editing is done on a timeline. The benefit of digital, computer-assisted editing is that it allows the editor to make changes anywhere, at any time. You can easily save multiple cuts of one film, and can remember and undo unsatisfactory edits.

Peter Wintonick traces the long history of editing, concluding that:

From tape to virtual cut all editing is done in the mind and not on the machine. Certainly technology can influence the kinds of editing, the aesthetics as well, but I would posit that there is no editing style currently or potentially invented that could not have been used in the 1920s or could not be seen in a film like Vertov's classic of that time, *Man With a Movie camera*. [...] It's not about the technology. Great editing is the absence of editing. Making it invisible, that is. Letting the material speak through you to the audience. Without the necessity of adding too much ego or editing pyrotechnics to distract people from the truth of a scene, a character, a film.

Regardless of what system you use, Franny Armstrong, political filmmaker, notes that "using the software is not editing. It's like touching the keys of a piano: that doesn't make you a musician. Editing is in the mind."

Low-tech and in-the-field editing options

It's important to know that simpler methods of (linear) editing are easy and can create acceptable results. You need only two machines— one player, one recorder, some cables and some time. You can edit a video using camera-to-camera, VCR-to-VCR, or camera-to-VCR, VCR-to-camera.

One filmmaker in Canada proved that you could make a video with just *one* camera, and he called the film *$19.49*, as that was the cost of the tape he used. He literally edited his video as he shot it, filming one shot directly after the other in sequences of how he wanted his video to look. This is called in-camera editing.

Organizing your material

Before you edit, you need to organize and prepare your material. Preparation can save you a lot of time later on.

First, you need to make sure your tapes are labeled properly. If they haven't been named or labeled during the shoot, do it now! Or if you are using material from various sources, create a system for numbering or naming types of material. For example, if you have three sources of material: original footage shot by Juan, original footage shot by Gabriela, and archive footage from the news, then perhaps you could label all tapes from Juan in the 100 series (100, 101, 102 etc.) and all tapes from Gabriela in the 200 series (200, 201, 202). All archive tapes could be 300s.

Now you should sit down and watch all the footage, taking notes (not logs, but notes) of your opinions, ideas, and emotions while watching the footage. You may have to watch the footage several times, which can make this a long and painful process.

If you have 50 hours of original material, it will take more than 50 hours to watch it! The process of screening is to absorb the material into your own brain's "database" so that you can draw from it as you build your video. "Know your footage well. Do not be afraid of your problematic parts," says Liz Miller, filmmaker and teacher. You will also begin noticing the problem areas—what shots don't work (including those you thought would), what sound is bad, what material is just plain missing.

Then, start logging the material, which means transcribing all dialogue spoken, and noting all visuals and sound material available. Using a logging form (see Appendix V), the aim here is to identify and write down all relevant information into logs or databases for future reference. Also, it is important to cite a time code if possible (for more information on timecode, see Chapter 4). Then if you can, print out these logs, and file them in easy-to-access binders or folders. Label the binders properly.

Liz Miller explains:

> During screening through your digital edit suite, you can log and capture tape without digitizing it, meaning you look at your tape, you mark "ins" and "outs" of the shots. You save that imaginary record, and then later on you go through it and you decide which footage you want to capture.

At this point you also need to evaluate the quality of picture and sound. Sandrine Isambert says:

> If you have poor audio, there's basically not much you can do about it. If you have an interview and you can't hear it, even if you subtitle it, the audience won't trust you, because they might have doubts that that is what the person is really saying. Basically, if you have bad audio it's garbage—you can't use the interview because your credibility is in danger. However, if the footage is intended as B-roll, audio may be less important. If you shoot an interview that looks horrible, but the audio is good—the audience will forgive you much more. And once you've established who's talking you can cover it with B-roll. Even if the background is noisy, you can get by with that. But you have to make sure that the [sound] bite is very strong, and very important and essential to your movie.

Structuring the paper edit

A paper edit is your first stab at mapping out the film by using all the elements at your disposal—picture, sound, and perhaps, narration. It is called a paper edit because you write out your sequence on paper or cards, incorporating all the elements and based on your knowledge from logging and screening the footage. You don't need to write the precise details, but here you are creating the links between all the elements. You can shift the cards and scenes around at will.

Comments Howard Weinberg:

You shouldn't slavishly hold to your paper edit, but it helps to structure the video. Don't try and finish your video too fast. You are building a house. You build the foundation, then framework, and only then do you plaster.

While building the "house," some people work with little cue cards to help visualize and organize the material. Gabriela Zamorano, of UCIZONI in Mexico, liked using cards. She mapped out all the picture and sound shots onto different cards and played around with them to construct her videos. "We were overwhelmed by all the material, so playing with the cards helped. It was great to do that before we got to the editing machine."

You may also consider how many different versions of your film you plan to make. Will there be a longer version for committed community members and a much shorter version for lobbying efforts? Keep in mind that two radically different versions may need two distinct edit periods, and will probably even require different kinds of material to be filmed. It is possible to tweak slightly different versions (change narration, for example) and it can be fairly simple to make a basic, shorter version.

In an advocacy context, the beginning of your edit is a good time to check in with advocacy partners involved with the video, and perhaps even find new ones. Sam Gregory suggests:

> It can also be really good to seek out new partnerships at this stage. You can get NGOs and other partners to buy-in during the script phase. That way, you are making sure their issues and input are addressed in the final product, and that they are solid allies in distribution.

For more information, see Chapter 7, and <www.mediarights.org>, a useful website with articles on outreach and planning for outreach during the production phase.

Digitizing, organizing bins

If you are editing on a computer, the next step is to load—redigitize— the shots you think you will need onto the hard drive of your computer or another external hard drive. This creates a digital copy of your material so that you can then work with it in a non-linear editing program.

When you are digitizing, you store your shots in folders called "bins." You can first organize them according to the numbers of your tapes, but you can also create new bins and organize material according to themes, chronology, sections, people, or places.

Liz Miller tells the students in her editing workshops:

> Think of bins as a room you're organizing where to put all your things. When I'm in the field, every tape that I have has a number from 1 to infinity. Your bins are like suitcases where you keep all of your shots. They are file cabinets. You can actually create a lot of file cabinets so that you can organize all of your files in very different ways.

In the edit room

The assembly edit

An assembly edit is a very preliminary edited sequence, which, in broad strokes, shows all the material you think you want to use. Basically, you line up your interesting material from beginning to end, in the approximate order of your paper edit. As you put this assembly together don't second-guess yourself as you go along— create a full assembly then review it. An assembly edit could be two hours long, for a half-hour final video. Watching this edit gives you new ideas of what works, what doesn't. It gives you ideas for the relationships between elements, for the larger structure.

The opening

The opening of your video is important. It will help determine whether audiences want to continue watching your video. A good opening hooks them into the video.

> Use a fact that becomes compelling, something that makes your audience curious to know more, think about what the audience might think, and address the other questions [says Howard Weinberg]. Make your argument not only a strong one, but address the additional reasons and questions. Give context. People need to feel like they've been there. Put people in the middle of the excitement.

Wintonick suggests:

> Never work at the opening at the beginning of the process. Openings change; so don't waste time on the opening. Cut off your first 10 minutes. Many videos take too long to get moving.

There are many options for video openings. Some may open with information that contextualizes the issue, others may provide a summary of facts that gives the viewer a historical perspective, others may consist of a high-impact sequence creating suspense and arousing curiosity. Often programs made for TV will have an opening that summarizes the main soundbites of the whole documentary and gives the viewer a sense of what to expect. Decisions on opening will often depend on the target audience of the piece.

The storytelling tools added in the edit room

Now you have all your elements in one place in the assembly edit. If you are on a computer, don't forget to save versions as you go along! You may want to return to earlier versions later. This is the time to start working more closely with every cut, every edit, and the juxtapositions, to help refine your story, and make it seamless.

"Exercise lateral thinking, work against your own intuition," recommends Peter Wintonick. "Attempt to remove the normal. Flip things around. Break yourself out of formulas."

You will already be working with the interviews, cutaways, B-roll, and verité footage that you shot during the production process (for more information on these elements, see Chapter 4). The following are some of the tools you can now use or think about:

Scratch narration   If you are going to use narration, it's a good idea to begin recording and using a "scratch" (temporary) narration in your video early on, so that you can begin testing and experimenting. You may decide you don't like the voice, or the writing or the narration, and may need to make changes.

Developing narration is a practical exercise in achieving clarity. In Exercise 3.4 (p. 92) we show how narration—depending who speaks it, and how—can influence the reception of your video.

Exercise 5.3: Practice your narration skills
Try this in a group. You are trying to see how to keep your narration clear and explanatory.

Have a colleague carry out a simple series of activities in front of the group. One person in the group is nominated as the narrator, and has to provide a simultaneous narration for the activities where they feel it's appropriate. The rest of the group listens and takes notes on whether the person is using narration at the right times, and if they

Tips on writing narration

- Think before you start writing. If you know what you want to say and what the goal for change and audience for the video is, then the narration, as with the rest of the script, will be much clearer.
- *Don't* describe what is in the picture.
- *Do* ensure that the narration fits the pictures—think of the B-roll you have and how it is going to be used.
- *Don't* overuse narration. Interview dialogue is preferable to narration. Remember that narration has to be covered with B-roll pictures. Often we do not have a lot of appropriate B-roll, and viewers quickly become bored if pictures are dull or relatively unrelated to the narration.
- Make your writing as clear as your talking. Describe succinctly what you are trying to say to someone else—you will probably be clearer, and use language more appropriate to narration.
- Revise as necessary and take advice from others—*but* remember not to lose the freshness.
- Make every word count and also ensure the meaning is clear.
- Avoid too many acronyms.
- Use short words and sentences and cut out the unnecessary—adjectives that describe what is in the picture, phrases that state the obvious or have no inherent meaning ("let's face it"), words that weaken their neighbors ("perhaps, about, maybe") and jargon or clichés.
- Replace *which* and *that* with a dash where appropriate, e.g. *Ocaranza hospital, which was the scene of the worst abuses, was where the first action was taken* could be understood equally well as *Ocaranza hospital—scene of the worst abuses—was where the first action was taken.*
- Make your sentences active. Consider this alternative: *The first action was taken at the scene of the worst abuses: Ocaranza Hospital.*
- Remember you have the option of titles—instead of saying the name of a location on the narration, why not use a subtitle, e.g. a title, *Ocaranza Psychiatric Facility, Mexico.*
- *Read* your narration out loud. Is it clear? Do you trip over words? Is there intrusive alliteration? Is a word repeated too many times? Think about who will be reading the narration—how will it sound with their accent?
- Look through your narration before you give it to the person who will read it. Are there difficult pronunciations of names and places, or technical terms that you should sound out for them before they begin? If they are not a professional voiceover artist or used to recording narration, are there passages that require a special emphasis or pacing?

are keeping it simple and free of unnecessary information. Afterwards, they review their comments with the narrator.

To make this exercise more complex, you can also insist that the narrator speak the narration from a different point of view than their own, or describe the activities with a particular audience in mind.

For examples of possible narrator voices, and of particular audiences, see Exercise 3.2, p. 87.

Music   Music can give emotion, pacing and rhythm to your video, but you should be careful that it doesn't take over the piece. The drama in your video should come from the story, not the music. Some audiences will also respond poorly to what they may perceive as emotional manipulation in overly intrusive or inappropriate musical tracks (note: this is often an issue in cross-cultural transmission of videos). However, as Sandrine Isambert says: "sometimes you need music to energize the piece. Sometimes when people are protecting themselves [from their experience of trauma], they don't seem sad. An audience might not understand this and ask: "Why is this person smiling?" She notes that this may be a good example of where music can help, and that many viewers have an expectation of some music in a video. A traditional documentary without music can become very dry, especially if you have narration.

Stephen Marshall of Guerrilla News network says: "Music targets the heart, it triggers the emotional and the marriage of music and the visual can be a very powerful thing. We use the music both to drive the cuts and build the visual montage." If you want to see how music adds to the impact of a scene, a good classic film to watch is *Psycho*.

If you do want to use recorded music, bear in mind that you must consider copyright issues: licenses for music can be expensive, time-consuming, and slow to get (see "Note on copyright" below). Another option is to follow the example of Joey Lozano, who prefers to use "local home-grown" music that he himself records with local musicians in the field. In these cases, always ask for permission from the musicians to use the music in your video.

Additional media assets—archival footage, stills, animation, and maps   Beyond your original footage there are other resources you can turn to: still photography, images from the Internet, computer or hand-drawn animation, maps, and archival video footage.

Archives can add color, history, and background to your video. Start researching at your own organization or community: are there photographs, even video images around that may be available for your use? What about partner organizations, or even international partners that may have media libraries? Then, of course, there are the established media sources: local, national newspapers, and television stations. They may provide material for free, or very low cost.

During this process of researching additional material, you may learn something completely new about your issue. Howard Weinberg explains:

> When you start editing, you don't necessarily have the argument fully laid out. As you get additional footage, you condense, and you make it sharper. You may start thinking one way, but through continued research, history, and archives you may learn another story. Therefore, the very process of researching footage that you need, you may change your argument and learn something new about the subject itself.

Note on copyright and fair use

If you use or borrow images or sounds that are "owned" by someone else, you may need to consider copyright issues. Before using archives or found material (including music and any material taken from the Internet), check who owns the material. Then ask yourself—how likely is it that you could be sued for using these images or sounds or music? Who will be watching your video? Are you planning to screen only in your community? To judicial bodies? On the Internet?

If your video is for limited, private screenings you may be able to get away without securing all permissions. However, if you intend any kind of public distribution you place yourself at risk of being sued if you do not secure necessary permissions. If you have any desire to get your video on television, the station will require releases from you, proving that you have cleared the copyrights, or otherwise, a lawyer's confirmation that you are in "fair use" of the material.

Copyright can get very complicated and very expensive. For example, television conglomerates such as BBC or ABC charge up to US$400 per second for use of the material they own.

Technically, if you plan on television broadcasts, it's important to know that even logos or brand names have been copyrighted, and are covered by these laws. For example, during the editing of a comic music video, criticizing a proposed hydro-dam project, the filmmaker's lawyer removed all shots that featured the lead singer singing in the foreground, with a Kentucky Fried Chicken sign in the background. The sign had nothing to do with the content of the video; it was simply in the street where the video had been filmed. To go on TV, however, the music video had to do without these shots.

With regard to music, there are many copyrights involved, including writing, publishing, recording, etc. Keep in mind even the song "Happy Birthday" is owned by someone, and if a character in your video sings the song, you may be subject to copyright laws. As attorney Tom Guida says:

> "Fair use," however, is a defense that can be raised against a copyright infringement claim; scholarly commentary, criticism, and news reporting can incorporate copyrighted material, used without permission, if the minimum amount of material necessary is used, the work is not particularly unique, and the proposed use will not deprive the author of a market for their work. Fair use is evaluated on a case-by-case basis, and there is no hard and fast rule for when a particular use will be considered "fair."

In the television world, you'll need a lawyer to back your case, though, and that can get expensive too.

Some images, sounds or work are "copyleft," as there is a growing global movement to stem the dominance of Intellectual Property laws. Some authors, artists, software developers (open source), and creators are labeling their work as in the "public domain," which means their work is free of copyright laws, and is available for free reproduction and use by all.

Transitions, motion effects, and special effects

Most cuts in films are simple "straight-cuts" directly from one image/sound to another image/sound with no overlap. However, there are other transitions you can use. Often these will have a relatively established "meaning" in filmic grammar. Typical uses to be aware of include the use of a fade in or out from black or white to indicate a change in location or time, the use of the dissolve between two scenes to indicate the time passing or an ellipsis, and the use of jump cuts to indicate time passing or deliberate discontinuity. Cross-cutting between two parallel scenes is often used to indicate simultaneous actions. In addition there are special and graphic transitions such as page-turns, wipes, and spins.

You can play with the speed of a shot. Sandrine Isambert says:

> Sometimes you can get an amazing shot out of something you don't think is long enough, just by slowing it down. For example, in *The Price of Youth*, a film about the trafficking of young women from Nepal to India, they used a hidden camera, which was very shaky. It was a color camera, so the colors were great. By slowing the footage down, it became quite beautiful, mysterious. It brought a sadness to the material. Even though we did it for technical reasons, the slow-mo helped audiences to slow down and contemplate too.

Figure 5.2   Undercover footage filmed for *The Price of Youth* (Andrew Levine/WITNESS)

Special effects have a language of their own. At the Guerrilla News Network, Stephan Marshal says:

> we use the "video scratch technique" which comes from the hip-hop style of moving the record back and forth. Kids love this, because it signifies that the material is being handled by someone. Contemporary culture—music, TV culture, DVD culture—is about being handled. It moves at different speeds; it is in the hands of someone. We try and reflect this in our editing style. We also use a lot of compositing effects, we shrink footage (often footage that may be poorly shot, or looks worn out) and we frame it with an animated template around it.

However, beware that the use of certain graphics can easily date a video. In general, unless you are experienced with effects and know that your audience will respond well to them, Sam Gregory suggests not relying too much on these techniques unless you have a very developed style that incorporates them, such as is used by Guerrilla News Network. "The flashy effects," he laughs, "like whirling wipes, page turns, the low end graphics that you can now get on even the cheapest editing program, may seem fun in the edit room or on the computer, but they can date very quickly."

Figure 5.3   Guerrilla News Network uses new interview formats and graphics to communicate with its audience (Guerrilla News Network/Aroun Rashid Deen)

Case study: The editor as fixer

The reality of editing is that much of the time you are troubleshooting, and searching for creative approaches to problems. How do you "fix" the film? How do you create material out of thin air?

Sandrine Isambert identifies some of the common problems she encountered while editing, and goes on to suggest "fixes":

Common editing problems

1. Not enough visual material, and too little B-roll. No sequences filmed, just individual shots that do not "cut" together to form a full sequence.
2. Overwritten scripts that involve a story for which there is no material. Often, a script will feature long historical and political context for which there is no material (archives can be expensive).
3. Too many interviews.

Suggested fix ideas

1. Rewrite the script. Instead of struggling with a script for which you have no material, rewrite the script, sticking closely to your actual footage.
2. Titlecards at the beginning to set the context.
3. If you have some money, you can purchase some relevant news clips from television as archives. The advantage of news items is that they can help set context quickly and efficiently. Cheaper yet is radio, or you can also shoot newspaper headlines to create a historical context section in your video.
4. Make the video shorter! Remember, less can be more.
5. If it's not a pressing issue, or an emergency turnaround on the video, seriously consider reshooting.

The ending

Just as there are multiple ways to open a video, so too there are many ways to end one. For advocacy your priority for the ending will be encouraging people to act, and giving them a concrete sense of what they can do. As we discussed in Chapter 3, this will often mean leaving the audience with a sense that there is room for change, and that the people in the film, they themselves, or people they can influence or persuade can be part of this. This "space for action" usually requires that the video be somewhat open-ended, and that it doesn't leave the audience deflated and disempowered.

Advocacy video endings often include:

- A recap of the situation or survey of the people featured in the video, or testimony from the most articulate or representative.
- A final scene that crystallizes the dilemmas and issues illustrated in the video.
- A call to action or direct request from a person within the video.
- An analysis of the situation, and possible ways to create change, by someone in the video or another person whom the audience will respect.
- Information on other ways that a viewer can get involved after watching the video—often presented in a neutral format via a narrator or end titlecard.

Finishing an edit

The rough cut

Now your video has begun to take shape, you have reached the rough cut stage. Your video is in its first draft form, probably still a bit too long. Perhaps the narration is still scratch, perhaps some additional media are missing, maybe some edits are still rough. At this stage, you are ready to sit back and take a bigger look at the video. During this review process, you need to focus on the structure. Is it working or do you need to restructure?

You might want to show the video to a few trusted colleagues or partners and ask them to analyze the rough cut with these questions:

- Do you get the "message" of the video?
- What are the video's themes?
- Which characters do you feel the strongest connection to? Why?
- Did the video feel the right length or did it drag?
- Which parts were unclear or puzzling?
- Which parts felt slow?
- Which parts were moving or not?
- Do you think this will work for the audience we have in mind? Why or why not?
- If appropriate: Do you understand what action we are encouraging the viewer to take?

Sandrine Isambert suggests that you watch others as they watch your video. "You can learn a lot from their reactions and their faces," she says. Watch how people shift in their seats, and when their attention wanders. Be aware that sometimes the part that people complain about isn't the problem. Sometimes the problem is actually much earlier in the video, and you will have to probe into their reactions to ensure that they are not in fact referring to a structural problem that only becomes apparent at a particular point.

Rough-cut screening groups can quickly identify problems, but don't be too quick to act on their solutions. Think it through and, as Wintonick suggests, "Once you think you're done, go back and watch all your material again. It's refreshing." However, the truth is that the parts you are most attached to, your "pearls," are often the ones that you have to let go.

Fact and translation checking

By this stage, you will need to review your video to check the facts. Ideally, you or someone on your team will verify every fact, statement, and assertion made in the film including quotes, dates, names, agencies, figures, statistics, citations, and other represented facts. This process will help verify the authenticity, and legitimacy of every point made in the film. Fact-checking ensures you don't encounter legal and reputational challenges when you release your video.

But this process is also crucial to make your film legitimate in the eyes of the audiences, whether they are community members or judges on a tribunal. A simple factual mistake may not only detract from the screening of the film, but may also put the whole film's accuracy into question.

Don't count on your interviewees' stories to be accurate in every detail.

Fact-checking can become extremely political. Michael Moore fell under heavy attack for his presentation of the facts in his academy-award winning film *Bowling for Columbine*. For his next film, *Fahrenheit 9/11*, his critical look at US President George Bush, Moore hired an entire team of fact-checkers (who had formerly worked at the *New Yorker*) and lawyers to review every single detail in the film. He even posts all the sources and fact-checking research on his website as further evidence (see <www.michaelmoore.com>).

Fact-checking involves:

- Collecting all facts mentioned in the film.
- Finding an original source for each fact mentioned.
- Double-checking with another, preferably independent and trustworthy source. Some fact-checkers will gather two independent sources. If you are using the Internet, be sure to check the *original* sources.

Note that very few newspapers fact-check the material they print, and are not reliable. Magazines, encyclopedias, academic, and scientific sources are more trustworthy. Sometimes, though, you'll need to conduct further personal interviews.

And if a fact is contentious, or controversial, it may be worth attributing it to your source directly in your video. That means, stating clearly the person or agency from whom you got it.

Fact-checking is also a good process to prepare you and your team to show your film to audiences, who will inevitably have questions for you: "How do you know that?", "Where does that figure come from?", "What is the name of that organization?" etc. Fact-checking is the time to reconfirm your "who, what, when, where, and how" of every point you made, so that both you and the video are solidly set up for the next stage of "going public."

An absolutely critical corollary of fact-checking for content is to ensure that any translation you've used has been checked and double-checked. It is a good idea to go over material several times with native speakers (to ensure that one does not err towards sensationalism— for instance, translating strip-search as sexual assault or rape), and ask them to sit with you as you put in the subtitles so you can ensure that the timing is correct, and that the accuracy is spot-on. There is nothing more damaging for your credibility than a viewer identifying, and then telling others, that you have misrepresented what someone is saying.

Test screenings

Beyond the few screenings you expect to show friends and colleagues, many filmmakers and advocates have done larger "testing" to examine their rough cut, either with advocacy and distribution partners—asking them to critique the representation of the issue, double-check on security issues if they were the documenters on a particular case, etc.—or with target audiences.

Make sure you prepare properly for this—in Chapter 7 you will find more on coordinating screenings. But consider issues like:

- Taking into consideration the subject matter of the piece and the social and cultural customs or political structure of the test audience, who would be best to introduce the test screening? It may not necessarily be the filmmakers.
- How should that person set it up so that the audience knows what to expect or what is expected of them (i.e. encourage them to have a discussion afterwards or to critique the film in particular ways)?
- Will breaking up your audience into small screening groups arranged by some characteristic such as gender or age encourage uninhibited dialogue among peer groups? Or is it more useful to invite questions and discussion across a more varied audience?

Case study: Test screenings

Peter Wintonick has thought extensively about how to use test screening in his work. Here he talks about his process:

> Over the last twenty years of my own documentary practice I have always tried to ask people what they thought. For the film that Mark Achbar and I made about Noam Chomsky, *Manufacturing Consent*, we tested the unfinished film in various stages, for 600 people, in groups ranging from a half dozen to a couple of hundred people. I think it made for a better film and made it into success it has become internationally. .
>
> You should construct a one-page questionnaire, trying not to make leading questions. Make it simple to fill out but make sure it can measure objectively people's objections. Leave room for written-in critique, and provide ways that people can follow up with email or telephone contacts.
>
> On a practical level there are questions you want to ask the audience so that you can see if you are getting things right. On the most basic level, is the story or thesis clear? Is it clearly articulated from beginning to end? Do people like the film, and why? Are there language issues they do not comprehend? Can they see ways the film can be improved?
>
> At a rough cut stage we even went so far as to insert inter-titles to ask test audience questions like: "Do you think a case study example would be good to put here in our structure?"
>
> It is also important to point out that not all feedback is negative: Testing can be very affirmative, reinforcing, and good for the soul.

Go back and shoot

You've reviewed the rough cut. You've collected the answers to your questionnaires. You've processed people's comments. Some of the ideas are new; some ideas you discard; some confirm what you already knew. Perhaps it's time to go back and shoot.

During the editing of the project, *Following Antigone: Forensic Anthropology and Human Rights Investigations*, Sandrine Isambert worked closely with the Equipo Argentino de Antropología Forense/ Argentine Forensic Anthropology Team (EAAF). EAAF uses forensic sciences, including anthropology, to uncover the truth of massacres, disappearances, and other gross violations of human rights so that it can then help the families of victims recover the remains of their

Figure 5.4   The forensic anthropologists of EAAF at work (EAAF/WITNESS)

loved ones and provide evidence to courts. It was a one-year editing project, working with 50 to 60 hours of footage shot between 1992 and 2003 in multiple countries. The film set out to map out the different stages of EAAF's work and explain to audiences in places where such gross violations have occurred and where they are considering using forensic anthropology what the process is and how it could help them.

> It was extremely challenging to make a film that captured all the different facets of their work and the methodology behind forensic anthropology, as often the films at WITNESS are about a specific issue [Sandrine comments]. This is a group that works "digging up skeletons" of the disappeared and murdered, but really the emotional heart of their work is bringing those lost people back to their families.

"We realized that crucial footage was missing," Sandrine recalls. In all the years of using video to document their work, Sandrine found— through the editing process—that the group had been meticulously recording every detail of the exhumations they conducted, but not the emotions of why they were doing the work in the first place, and of how the family members responded to the return of the remains of their loved one. In order to tell a compelling story and engage the viewer—and explain why the members of the team continued to do this work, year on year, at site after site—this human center to the video was crucial.

This is why Sandrine and EAAF decided that the group should go back and film more: this time with the forensic anthropologists turning the camera on themselves, asking more emotional and human questions about their motivations, experiences, and thoughts. "So in the process of editing," says Sandrine, "they learned something too about what needs to be filmed in order to make a compelling video."

The fine cut

The fine cut is another version of your video after you've made all the changes stemming from the rough cut stage. Now it is time to review the finer details and to polish the film: the "ins" and "outs" of specific shots, perhaps the wording in the narration, or losing one or two scenes or shots here and there. At this point it is also appropriate to review the images and material you are using in your film, and ensure that they are appropriate and accurate. Be aware of when it is OK to use generic shots which are non-location-specific or situation-specific, and when it is critical, as an ethical filmmaker, that you do not use footage of one village, one incident, one person to illustrate another different situation.

It's worth showing the video again to some of the people who watched the rough cut. It's also a good idea to show it now to someone who has never seen it before, and compare assessments. You are now very, very close to the final version of the video.

On-line picture and sound

"A video is never finished until you decide to walk away," says Liz Miller.

You've done the best you can and now it's time to create the best looking and best-sounding quality master of the video. This is called the "on-line." This might mean simply redigitizing your material at a higher picture resolution, and mixing your sound so that it is balanced, and the volume levels stay the same throughout the piece.

Or, "on-line" might mean turning to a professional edit studio for color correction (making all the colors "match" each other, and fit into the broadcast standards), and to clean up your sound etc.

Professional edits include several days of sound editing, in which additional sound effects are added and the existing sound is cleaned up by processing it through filters. Resources permitting, you may even decide to record the narration in a professional sound booth. Now is also the time to mix the music with the voices and the sound track.

"Broadcast quality" is a term used in the TV industry to reflect technical requirements for broadcast on mainstream television. While it's great if you can meet these standards, it's important to remember they can (and will!) be dropped if the content is compelling and important, so do not be intimidated by the quality standards. You can only do what is in your means, and that can be sufficient. A video can have a lot of impact even if it's not "broadcast quality."

At this point you may need to make several different language or region versions of your video. In this case, be sure to accommodate for all possibilities. Later, you may not have access to the computer you have been editing on. It's a good idea to make master tapes that allow you to create new versions of the video.

Consider making several different master tapes:

1. Your final original language master.
2. A master that has the sound split between the tracks so that dialogue is on one track, and music and sound effects are on the other. (That way, if you decide to make another language version, you can mix the sound again.)
3. A textless version, with no text appearing on any image—so if you decide to subtitle, or use another language in the text, you have an empty canvas to work on.
4. A master that is both textless, and with voiceover narration and music/natural sound on separate tracks (i.e. a combination of suggestions 2 and 3 above). This master will serve as a generic copy for possible international versions. If it's possible for you to have three audio tracks, it may also be useful to keep the music on a separate track to the natural sound. If you are able to produce this master, the textless version need not be a separate copy.

Your video is complete: Fitting it into a broader strategy

Gillian Caldwell puts the finished video into context:

When a piece is finished, filmmakers feel like they've given birth, but the true work begins when a film is done. What kind of life will it lead? What kind of parent or advocate will you be? Are there stakeholders in the project that will help give the film a life worth living?

Rarely does a video stand alone. Your video will need to be part of a larger strategy of advocacy including meetings, written materials, protests, and other forms of campaigning. As you have been editing the video you should be considering what additional materials—including print and audio—you will need to complement the video. WITNESS projects are accompanied by background material, screening guides, and online information sources with e-action opportunities to send emails to key authority figures. When Shabnam Hashmi toured the USA showing the film *Evil Stalks Our Land* about the atrocities in Gujarat, India she also brought printed documentation—examples of hate-literature, and follow-up material—to the screenings. Ronit Avni, the founder of Just Vision, a project documenting peace initiatives in the Middle East, attended Shabnam's press conference in NYC and said "the sum total of that experience—the film, Shabnam speaking and the printed material—had a huge impact."

For more information, see Chapters 1 and 7.

Exercise 5.4: Watch like an editor and an advocate

This exercise is best done in a group as it is primarily focused on discussing a film you have viewed. For this exercise, you will need to pick a video produced on your advocacy issue: you are trying to analyze your chosen video in terms of story, advocacy intent, and editing.

Now, as you watch your chosen video, try to answer the following questions.

1. Is this an advocacy film? Why? Why not? How could it become an advocacy film?
   If so, what is the film trying to say? What is its goal for change?
2. Who do you think the primary audience is? Can you identify how the film is framed for them?
3. What is the message of the film?
4. How would you describe the editing of the film (i.e. fast cuts, music, transitions, slow, etc.)?

5. What is the structure of the film? Is there a beginning, middle, and an end?
6. From whose point of view is the story told?
7. Is there narration? Was it factual, personal, dry, or emotional?
8. What is the drama, or conflict of the film?
9. How does the film open and get you interested?
10. How does it end? Are you moved to action?
11. At any point do you feel the editing is manipulative or unethical?

Now, the next time you see a film, ask yourself about these considerations—it's a whole new way to watch movies, TV, news, anything on a screen. Peter Wintonick recommends that you begin watching films from far away—for example, the back row of the movie theater. There, you are at a distance from the screen, less drawn into the story. Then you can begin to see and analyze the construction and the editing. Or else watch a film once for the content, and then watch it again immediately to see how it is constructed and edited.

Kat Cizek thanks:

Franny Armstrong	Ronit Avni	Martin Atkin
Amy Bank	Gillian Burnett	Arturo Carrillo
J. and L. Cizek	Sean Dixon	Don Edkins
Sam Gregory	Shabnam Hashmi	Sandrine Isambert
Joey Lozano	Stephen Marshall	Liz Miller
Avi Mograbi	Catherine Olsen	Erica Pomerance
Paul Shore	Atossa Soltani	Amadou Thior
Anna Van der Wee	Howard Weinberg	Peter Wintonick
Gabriella Zamorano		

NOTES

1. Michael Ondaatje, *The Conversations: Walter Murch and the Art of Editing Film* (New York: Knopf, 2002).
2. Ibid.
3. B. Reeves and S.L. Smith, "The Evening's Bad News: Effects of compelling negative television news images on memory," *Journal of Communication* 42, 2 (1992), pp. 25–42.

6

Video as Evidence

Sukanya Pillay

Video can be a powerful source of evidence for lawyers and advocates seeking to right wrongs and create change. You do not need to be a lawyer to film or use video for evidence. This chapter aims to help you think through what you will need to do in order to be effective, including how to think through the filming, editing, and submission of video for evidence.

Many will remember the footage of the Rodney King beating by policemen in Los Angeles. This footage was only 81 seconds in duration but its image was seared into people's minds, and rights groups everywhere demanded justice. Over the course of the 1990s, advocates and lawyers throughout the world developed the use of video footage as a powerful source of evidence.

Video evidence has been used in local and national courts, before internationally constituted tribunals such as the International Criminal Tribunals for Rwanda (ICTR) and the Former Yugoslavia (ICTY), before UN treaty bodies that monitor state compliance with international treaties, and before local nongovernmental people's tribunals such as the People's Tribunal on Food Security in Thailand.

But the use of video evidence has deeper roots than the Rodney King footage. Helen Lennon, a scholar of the use of video in war crimes tribunals, traces the use of film and contemporary video to advance rights causes back to the end of World War II. In 1945, the four Allied Occupational powers—the United States, the United Kingdom, the Union of Soviet Socialist Republics and France—established the International Military Tribunal at Nuremberg to prosecute top-level Nazi leaders. Each country introduced film evidence of alleged atrocities committed by the Nazi regime throughout Europe. Similarly, at the International Military Tribunal for the Far East, established and administered by General Douglas MacArthur of the US Army in 1946, admitted film evidence of alleged atrocities in East Asia. These precedents helped lay the groundwork for the contemporary international war crimes tribunals for the former Yugoslavia and Rwanda (established by the UN Security Council in 1993 and 1994, respectively) to admit video evidence at trial on a regular basis. For example, in the current proceedings against Slobodan Milosevic, the prosecution indicated that it would introduce more than 600 video exhibits.

This chapter focuses on recording and/or using video evidence—both visual images and recorded testimony—in judicial or quasi-judicial bodies, as well as before advisory bodies and commissions. This video can be both video shot specifically as evidence, or found for use as evidence after the fact. Remember that in most cases you will not be submitting evidence directly, but via the prosecution or defense. The legal system will then determine whether your evidence is admissible and how much weight should be assigned to it.

Whenever you may be considering submitting your video evidence to a decision-maker, there are certain rules or themes you should consider to improve the chances that (i) the body will allow your video to be admitted and (ii) the body will be persuaded by your video. Of course, the standards and rules will vary across jurisdictions and venues. Where possible, we have aimed to provide you with a flavor of the sorts of rules that you may encounter. In some instances, we also tell you where you can find the rules that will apply to the court or tribunal before which you are appearing. But you must always ensure that you have obtained the rules of procedure and admissibility that pertain to your video evidence. For example, if you wish to admit video evidence to a tribunal in China, you must obtain any formal rules that govern that tribunal's proceedings; you should also consider how that tribunal has dealt with video evidence in earlier proceedings. We do however believe there are some general considerations that apply to all video evidence. We hope these will be useful as you record, collect, or submit your video evidence.

QUESTIONS TO ASK YOURSELF BEFORE USING VIDEO AS EVIDENCE

Advocates who are recording, collecting or submitting video evidence should consider the following questions.

For what are you using video evidence?

First, identify your reason for using video evidence. Once you know the purpose of the video evidence, you will be able to make better decisions about which segments of your footage to use, how best to present the footage, how to attempt to corroborate or support the content of the footage, and how to take necessary steps to ensure goals for the evidence can be met. If you are collecting video footage for use as evidence, your camera operator must bear this in mind at every stage of recording footage. For example, is the video meant to show a specific incident to prove that a violation occurred? Is it intended to prove the identity of a specific accused person, or to establish a pattern of behavior and/or official acquiescence? Should the video support specific witness testimony or provide geographical and other information that will help clarify witness testimony?

The Rodney King case is an example that illustrates how video evidence may be employed for different uses. The footage in question depicted the beating of a black US citizen by a mob of white police officers. It was broadcast across North America, sparking widespread interest in what seemed to be a clear case of police brutality. However, the defense team relied on the evidence to present a case for justified assault, resulting in the acquittals that sparked the Los Angeles riots of 1992.[1] The same video evidence was used again on appeal, but this time the prosecution reaped the benefits of the footage. An enhanced version of the tape was employed, along with other supporting pieces of evidence, to solidify a guilty verdict for two of the officers involved.[2] The Rodney King case shows how video evidence can be employed in very different ways to achieve very different results. The key is to keep the specific goal in mind when presenting footage to a court, as it may suggest what additional evidentiary support may be required.

What is the intended audience for the footage?

There may be a number of options for the use of a video, and an advocate should strategically determine the best outlet for it. Even the most compelling evidence will be of little use if it does not reach the right audience. Keep in mind the answers to the first question, since the use to which you are going to put the footage may well determine your audience. Providing victims with redress for specific human rights violations, for example, may require that evidence be submitted to a judicial body. Educational initiatives, however, may be better served by reaching the widest audience, in which case releasing the footage through the media could be the best strategic option. For lawyers, the jurisdictional rules of decision-making bodies and past practice will help to determine the correct forum. For other advocates, the potential outlets for video are too varied to be canvassed here.

An advocate working for an NGO documenting patterns of state behavior on torture may wish to submit video evidence directly to the UN Committee Against Torture, the body that monitors state implementation of the UN Convention Against Torture. For more information on the accessibility of these specific human rights venues to video, consult the WITNESS Video for Change manual, online at <www.witness.org>.

How can the evidence be used?

The answer to this question depends on the forum in which the video evidence is to be presented. Different jurisdictions have specific rules regarding what evidence can be admitted, and when such evidence should be provided to the other side. An advocate may find that the procedural rules are dense or vague. A non-lawyer should contact lawyers involved in proceedings before the relevant body for advice. For example, in the case of the International Tribunal for the Former Yugoslavia and the International Tribunal for Rwanda (the ICTY and ICTR), it is possible to contact the respective offices of the prosecutor and defense attorneys.

What is the format of the footage?

Different jurisdictions will use and have access to different technology (i.e. MiniDV, VHS, DVD, Hi8 recording, and playback formats, able to play back either one or both of NTSC or PAL tapes). For further information on production formats, see Chapter 4 and the Appendices. You need to ensure that your video is in a format that can be viewed where you want it to be. The procedural rules may dictate whether you must provide originals, copies, or excerpts. And, as will be discussed further, some formats may be considered more reliable than others.

ALWAYS OBTAIN AND USE VIDEO EVIDENCE WITH THE UTMOST CAUTION

Always obtain and use video evidence with the utmost caution. You must be careful when *recording*, *storing*, and *using* video footage.

You or your camera operator may be taking risks recording footage. In some jurisdictions, human rights abusers may retaliate against people who take part in public demonstrations or who speak out against perpetrators. Governments, paramilitaries, or other authority figures may use your videotape to identify a witness or to identify bystanders and to retaliate against these individuals. Take the utmost care to ensure that the privacy and anonymity of witnesses and bystanders are protected, especially where there is a chance of retaliation. For more details on how to do this, see Chapter 2.

All those involved in creating of video evidence, from the witness to the camera person, should be aware of the risks involved in making the video. They should be given the opportunity to provide informed consent to the risks. See Appendices III and IV for sample release forms that help explain and authorize the ways in which the footage may be used. Be sure this form is adapted as appropriate and translated into the relevant language before use. Whenever possible, consent for use of the footage should be obtained when it is shot. At the same time, you must be mindful that as circumstances change in a jurisdiction, the level of danger to the consenting witness may increase. As a result, you should try to verify a witness' willingness to have their previously recorded statement introduced into evidence. Remember that even if your witness is no longer available because he or she has been given safe harbour elsewhere, or has died, his or her family at home may still be subject to reprisal.

Considerations regarding witness anonymity in video testimony

You must always protect the anonymity of witnesses where necessary. This includes *every* situation where a witness requests anonymity before, during, or after having provided you with information.

However, where a witness has requested anonymity (which may be more common in human rights and war crimes cases owing to the increased possibility of reprisal), a judicial decision-maker may be reluctant to admit video evidence. In some cases it will be impossible or unproductive to use anonymous witnesses. For example, some judicial bodies will require that a witness be identified, or the identity or position of the witness may be integral to the person's evidence. In such circumstances, there may be ways to protect the identity of the witness to a certain extent. The ICTR and ICTY, for example, provided for "closed sessions" in which witnesses in need of protection were able to testify without revealing their identities. It is vital to find, be aware of, and make use of any mechanisms in place to protect vulnerable individuals.

In most jurisdictions, due process and fairness dictate that an accused is entitled to the right to cross-examine his or her accuser, so that he can directly confront a witness who is testifying against him. The cases highlighted below show how some courts view anonymous testimony as being in conflict with those principles and thus may be reluctant to admit anonymous testimony. As video advocates, we must bear these decisions in mind. You may need corroborating evidence to secure a conviction in criminal cases if you are reliant on an anonymous witness.

The European Court of Human Rights (ECHR) considered the use of anonymous witness evidence in a case involving organized crime, *Kostovski* vs *The Netherlands*.[3] Kostovski complained to the ECHR that his right to a fair trial, guaranteed in Article 6 of the European Convention on Human Rights, was violated when he was convicted based on anonymous witness statements read into evidence. The Netherlands argued that anonymous testimony should be admitted because witnesses in organized crime cases were often intimidated, or feared for their safety. The ECHR noted that it understood the importance of struggle against organized crime, and generally permits domestic governments and courts to decide on evidence admissibility issues. However, in *Kostovski*, the ECHR held that the reliance on anonymous statements to secure a conviction in this case "involved limitations on the rights of the defence which were irreconcilable" with the right to a fair trial.

Similarly, the Canadian Supreme Court has cautioned against using videotaped witness statements as the *sole* basis to convict. It cites the unknown circumstances, which may surround the taping of witness statements, the inability to cross-examine a witness, or the inability for a judge to physically view a witness' demeanour before making a conclusion.[4]

LEGAL CATEGORIES OF VIDEO EVIDENCE: DIRECT AND CIRCUMSTANTIAL

Whatever legal jurisdiction you are working in, video evidence generally falls under one of two categories: (1) direct evidence or (2) circumstantial evidence. Each category is explained below, as is (3), refuting (or rebuttal) evidence.

Direct evidence

As the name suggests, you may have "direct" evidence that can be used to prove a particular event occurred or to prove an element of a crime. For example, a video showing X beating Y is direct evidence proving the allegation that Y was beaten by X. The evidence is called "direct" evidence because it specifically establishes a key matter before a court.

Video evidence has been used as direct evidence in domestic jurisdictions. In both Canada and in the United States, video footage has been used as a "silent witness" in situations where there are no human eyewitnesses to a crime, but in which a video camera, such as a security or surveillance camera, records the crime. In *R* vs *Nikolovski*,[5] for example, the video evidence was security camera footage that showed the accused robbing a store. The Supreme Court of Canada held that the video evidence was clear and compelling, so there was no need for any verbal or written corroborating evidence to support it—the accused could be found guilty on the basis of the video evidence alone.

In a case from the United States involving criminal drug charges, a video showed the number of marijuana plants being grown, and the US Court of Appeals concluded that a videotape provided direct evidence to prove the key issue in dispute (the number of plants), and no other evidence was required.

Circumstantial evidence

Unlike evidence that directly proves an incident or element of a crime, circumstantial evidence proves conditions that could reasonably lead to the inference that an incident occurred, or establish elements of a crime. For example, a videotape showing Y injured and X in an agitated state holding a weapon, may be used to prove that X was at the scene of the beating in an agitated state with a weapon. He therefore *could* have carried out the beating. By contrast, a film of the actual beating of Y by X would be direct evidence of the beating.

Circumstantial video evidence has been used by the International Criminal Tribunal for Rwanda (ICTR). In the *Rutaganda* [6] case, the ICTR Chamber considered whether the accused, who was the second Vice President of the National Committee of the Interahamwe (the Youth Militia), would have been aware of the level of violence occurring under his command at the time of the Rwandan genocide. Video evidence was introduced specifically to refute statements by defendant George Rutaganda that he was unaware of the level of violence going on around him. The Chamber was shown a video of two women who were forced to kneel in the street and were executed. In the video, the women were struck so hard by a broom handle that their necks broke; the execution occurred in broad daylight in a crowded street. The video was used to establish that Rutaganda would have likely been aware of this execution, or at least of other similar incidents. The fact that the violence was prevalent and open helped establish, at a minimum, the acquiescence of those in command.

In several jurisdictions, including the UK, the US,[7] and Canada, "similar fact evidence" or "evidence of previously disreputable conduct," may be used to demonstrate that an accused has in the past behaved in a manner similar to the allegation in issue. In each jurisdiction, it is not generally acceptable to submit evidence of prior crimes as proof of a current charge. However, it may be admissible when previous conduct can be shown to be strikingly similar to the conduct with which the accused is currently charged and thus is submitted as circumstantial evidence that he engaged in the same conduct again. The precise standards for admissibility of this type of evidence vary by jurisdiction. The domestic treatment of this type of circumstantial evidence may be instructive at the international level, or in other domestic jurisdictions. If you have videotape that shows a consistent pattern of behavior by an individual, an institution, or a state, you may consider submitting it as circumstantial evidence.

Circumstantial evidence can be extremely important, in two ways: as corroborative evidence, and as contextual evidence.

Corroborative evidence

Video can play an important role in corroborating, or supporting, verbal or written testimony. Video footage can corroborate witness testimony of violations that otherwise may be difficult for lawyers to prove, or even for judges to conceptualize. At the ICTY, in *Stakic*[8] the II Trial Chamber relied upon corroborating video evidence to find that there was selective destruction of Muslim and Croat homes while Serb homes were left untouched. This pattern was made obvious by the video evidence submitted that Muslim and Croat homes were specifically targeted—this was not merely a biased perception of the testifying witnesses.

Corroborative evidence can be useful to strengthen a witness' testimony in the face of skilled or aggressive cross-examination. A witness who has given testimony may be questioned aggressively by opposing counsel who may question the witness' memory, or cast doubt on the witness' motives during cross-examination. Corroborative evidence can help prove that a witness has accurately testified regarding events in issue, thus eliminating any suspicion that the witness is biased or simply incorrect.

Contextual or demonstrative evidence

In many international fora, the adjudicators are not from the location in which the relevant events occurred. As a result, contextual evidence may play an important role in painting a clear picture of what occurred. As the name suggests, contextual evidence provides a *context* for testimony or facts in issue. This evidence is not primarily used to prove or corroborate facts (though it can, see *Akayesu* below), but to help judges and adjudicators to understand the atmosphere, geographic location, or political climate in which events in issue may have occurred.

In the *Akayesu*[9] case, the ICTR was shown footage of rivers clogged with bodies. This imagery did not prove that a specific event occurred, nor did it contribute to establishing elements of a specific allegation. However, it did provide a powerful visual image of an otherwise almost unimaginable scene. In short, the image demonstrated for the court just how bad the situation in Rwanda was. Indirectly, this evidence contributed to the credibility of witnesses who described equally horrific scenarios that an uninformed listener might believe to be exaggerated.

The ICTY has also admitted video to understand the context in which crimes may have occurred. In *Kunerac*,[10] the ICTY was shown footage of Radovan Karadzic and Alija Izetbegovic in a parliamentary exchange. This evidence was used to explain the "ever more aggressive nationalist propaganda, a hardening of the ethnic divide and the organization of political rallies." In the *Tadic* trial, the ICTY was shown footage of the region in which alleged crimes occurred in order to familiarize the court with the geography and layout of the areas.[11] In a similar effort to provide the court with context, the prosecution in *Kordic and Cerkez*,[12] was permitted to submit "dossiers" or "village binders" including video and video stills (i.e. photographic stills taken from the video footage) and transcripts relating to the conditions in, for example, Tulica village. Contextual video evidence was used extensively by the prosecutor to show specific damage to the village, and to assist witnesses who were describing the village.

Refuting (or rebuttal) evidence

This final category of evidence may involve either direct or circumstantial evidence—its distinguishing feature is its *use*. After a witness has testified, opposing counsel or the judge in some legal systems can ask questions and conduct a cross-examination. During cross-examination, a witness' claims can be tested for accuracy and truthfulness. In this process, opposing counsel may use video evidence to contradict, *refute* (rebut), or undermine a witness' previous statements. Outside the human rights context, video evidence has commonly been used to refute other evidence in personal injury cases; for example, in these cases, the refuting video evidence has been used to rebut the plaintiff's testimony regarding the severity of injuries, or to show the plaintiff engaged in activities inconsistent with the claimed injury.[13] For example, someone claims his back is injured and he can't work. But he is captured on video lifting his 5-year old child and jogging.

Video evidence may also be used to refute an allegation, a specific factual finding of a lower court, or another type of evidence.

USING VIDEO EVIDENCE: NAVIGATING THE RULES

You will also need to keep in mind the procedural requirements that also must be met before a court will admit a video in evidence. These requirements are found in procedural rules, qualitative criteria such as clarity, footage quality, organization, and availability of the original source material including raw footage. In this section, we will discuss the general issues you should keep in mind when considering whether and how to use your video footage as evidence.

Remember also that in most tribunals, only the prosecutor or defense attorney may submit evidence, including videotapes. Other individuals and organizations cannot do this. You will need to work with one of the parties and convince them to submit the video evidence.

Once you know the purpose you wish your video evidence to serve, research the likelihood that it will be admitted at the forum where you plan to appear. The forum's rules should guide your filming practices. If you want to use video footage that someone else took, analyze the guidelines and choose footage that is likely to be accepted as credible and relevant.

Here we can outline basic principles that may be instructive when using evidence in any forum. In the event that specific rules of evidence and/or procedure are available, it is important to consult those as well. Each forum generally has its own rules, some of which may be available online.

Whether you are appearing in court, before a tribunal, or even before a village council, customs and practices will determine how evidence is presented to a fact-finder. Courts and tribunals will typically have these rules formally recorded, and the fact-finders or opposing counsel will require lawyers submitting evidence to follow these rules. For example, the ICTR and ICTY both have specific "Rules of Procedure and Evidence," which set out how evidence is to be admitted, and have provisions relating to types of evidence such as witness testimony, expert testimony, proof of facts other than by oral evidence, evidence of a consistent pattern of conduct, evidence of sexual abuse etc., and what must be disclosed to the opposing side.

In general, once you have a copy of the relevant rules of procedure and evidence, look for the following:

- Rules specifically addressing video evidence. Many rules of evidence will not refer directly to video, in which case the general rules will apply. In either case, it is a good idea to look for any evidentiary rule that refers directly to video or visual evidence.
- Rules of evidence that specifically prohibit the use of video.
- Discretion given to adjudicators or prosecutors. It is important to know who possesses discretion with respect to admissibility of evidence.
- Any notice requirements. Many jurisdictions require parties to provide notice to the decision-maker (court or tribunal) and to opposing counsel, of the nature and content and other pertinent details regarding the evidence you wish to introduce. Failure to comply with notice requirements may prevent you from using otherwise admissible evidence.

It is crucial that you comply with the particular rules of procedure relating to video evidence. Before appearing in any forum, you must be sure to obtain a copy of the rules and comply with those rules. Remember that rules of evidence are subject to change, are often quite general, and tend to favor admission of evidence. The unwritten practices of the body may be as instructive as the rules themselves. Be sure to find out about customs and practices in a jurisdiction—for example, decisions to date by judges in the same forum, particularly if there are no written rules that specifically reference video.

USING VIDEO EVIDENCE: ADMISSIBILITY, AUTHENTICITY, AND WEIGHT

While the rules of evidence vary from one body to the next, there are two basic stages at which a decision maker will consider the use of evidence—the admissibility stage, and the weighting or evaluation stage. The first stage will determine whether the evidence will be used *at all*, and the second will determine how much weight, or influence, the evidence will have in the proceeding.

Admissibility stage

In the absence of any rule that specifically permits or excludes evidence, the fact-finder will evaluate whether evidence should be admitted. This determination will generally involve whether the evidence is (1) relevant, including an evaluation of "probative value" against "prejudicial effect," and (2) reliable.

Admissibility: Establishing relevance

The overriding concern in any debate about whether or not to admit evidence is *relevance*.

The party seeking to introduce any evidence must convince the adjudicator that the evidence is relevant to the issue before the court. Relevance can be established by showing that:

- The evidence relates directly to proving an issue in the case (direct evidence).
- The evidence helps to prove an issue in the case as it proves conditions that could reasonably lead to the inference that an incident occurred or elements of a crime exist (circumstantial evidence).

Admissibility stage: Assessing prejudicial impact

In making its determination whether evidence is relevant, a court will also evaluate whether its probative value outweighs its potential prejudicial effect. In this analysis, the fact-finder will balance two basic considerations:

- The *probative value* of the video evidence, which is an assessment of how useful the video is to prove the issue being tried.
- The *prejudicial effect*, which is an assessment of how damaging the evidence is, or if it unfairly plays on the fact-finder's emotions.

Fact-finders such as a judge will generally apply the following considerations to determine the *probative value* of a piece of evidence, including video evidence:

- The strength of the evidence.
- The extent to which the evidence directly or indirectly contributes to findings or potential findings about facts at issue.

Determining the *prejudicial effect* of a piece of evidence is not an exact science. Visual evidence has the potential to be very persuasive or influential, which means that it also has the potential to be highly prejudicial. Video that merely provides "shock value," or serves solely to besmirch the reputation of the accused/opposing side will not be admitted, because it will be considered prejudicial and, therefore, inadmissible.

The following criteria are generally used to determine the *prejudicial effect* of a piece of evidence:

- How damaging or discrediting is the evidence?
- To what extent does the evidence support an inference of guilt or fault solely on the basis of bad character as portrayed via the evidence submitted?
- To what extent may the evidence confuse issues?
- To what extent is the evidence sensational, inflammatory, or injurious?
- What is the ability to respond to the particular evidence?

To summarize, the more the evidence proves an element of the offense rather than provokes an emotional reaction the more likely it is to be admitted. If evidence proves very little, but could unfairly prejudice a fact-finder, it is unlikely to be admitted. Visual evidence, such as video, is frequently found not to be relevant if it is exceedingly graphic and does not shed much light on issues in the case.

Case study: Establishing relevance, a hypothetical case
In the context of a war crimes prosecution, a video depicting dead bodies at the site of a massacre is turned over to the prosecution. The massacre occurred in Plainville on August 1, 1972. The accused in the case is alleged to have participated in the massacre. The footage, taken shortly after the massacre took place, clearly shows the geographic location, provides a panoramic view of the scene, and contains several close-ups of many of the men, women, and children slain. The video shows the condition of the bodies, as well as their position

relative to other landmarks in Plainville. Some of the close-ups are very graphic, and likely to shock the average viewer. Clearly, as the footage shows the immediate aftermath of the massacre at issue, it is factually relevant, but is it overly prejudicial?

The answer depends on the issues in the case. Assume, for example, that the defense claims that (1) the massacre did not occur, or (2) the "massacre" was a military conflict, and did not involve civilians (i.e. women and children). In such circumstances, the video would probably be considered relevant as it contributes significantly to issues that must be decided.

If, however, the defense admits that a massacre of civilians occurred at Plainville on August 1, 1972, and the only fact at issue is the accused's presence or participation, would the video still be relevant and admissible? In such circumstances the same video might not be admitted because it would contain images that could be very prejudicial to the accused (as he/she may be unfairly associated with the evidence), but would not shed light on the fact at issue.

Admissibility stage: Reliability, accuracy, and authentication

In addition to being relevant, evidence must be *reliable*. For video evidence to be reliable, you must be able to establish that the footage is authentic. In other words, the decision-maker will want to be sure that the evidence has not been fabricated, falsified, or tampered with, and that it has not been manipulated in a way that would mislead.

Here we review some of the typical issues that may arise regarding the authentication of video footage.

The reliability of a piece of evidence is a paramount consideration for a judicial decision-maker considering whether to admit that evidence into the proceedings. For video evidence to be considered reliable, the adjudicator must be able to trust what he or she sees. This is a particularly important analysis since video is subject to technological or other manipulation by the filmmaker, who may also, purposefully or inadvertently, film in a way that does not accurately depict a subject. How, then, can one establish reliability? There are a number of ways that reliability may be demonstrated. Depending on the circumstances, consider the following issues:

- Reliable technology
- Filming practices for reliability

- Source of the video
- Chain of custody
- Authentication of footage through an appropriate witness

Reliable technology   Video is susceptible to digital manipulation, such as alteration or the insertion of computer-generated images that can falsify the depiction of events. There are a number of ways to help prove that an existing video is accurate. Witness authentication and careful treatment of the evidence after it is created can help to ensure that decision-makers trust the images they are shown. Some technological considerations can be addressed before and during filming (in the event that you are present or involved in the video documenting) that may aid efforts to establish reliability of the footage.

These considerations include, first, *choice of format.* There are growing concerns about the susceptibility of video evidence to technological manipulation with the increasing use of digital technology (analog formats remain more difficult to manipulate, and, therefore, more difficult to challenge). According to film expert Peter Thomas, digital images are, for now, still very difficult to fake convincingly. Dr Thomas cites the admission of phone taps on CD into the proceedings at the ICTY regarding Slobodan Milosevic, and asserts that, given the relative ease of technological manipulation of that evidence, digital video evidence is not likely to be excluded as a class from judicial proceedings.

A second consideration is *technological authentication.* In some circumstances, you may also be able to use a process called *digital watermarking* to show that the video has not been tampered or falsified.[14] According to Hany Farid, an Assistant Professor in Computer Science and the Center for Cognitive Neuroscience at Dartmouth College, a digital watermark is an imperceptible identification code or signature integrated into a digital or analog medium (sound, image, or video). This technology has been used by copyright owners to identify illegally distributed material. If an imperceptible watermark is inserted into a video at the time of recording, then tampering can be detected by simply verifying that the watermark has been unchanged from the time of its recording. Although digital watermarking is versatile in that it can be used with digital or analog video (or with sound or photographic images), it is a process that is not available in all circumstances, because to insert a watermark at the time of recording requires a special-purpose camera that inserts the watermark as the video is being recorded. There are also questions about the potential for users to remove or manipulate the watermark that have not yet fully been tested. Accordingly, we advise that you ensure you have a witness to testify to the authenticity of your video evidence.

A third consideration is *intentional alterations*. In some circumstances, you may intentionally alter your visual evidence to bring attention to a specific fact or issue. For example, you may enlarge a photographic still from a video recording to show a weapon held in an accused's hand. In such circumstances, draw the court's attention to the alteration, and provide the altered or enhanced copy along with the original, unaltered copy.

Filming practices for reliability   Even the most scrupulous camera-person may inadvertently film in a way that calls the accuracy of an image into question. For example, a debate was sparked by 1992 footage of a Bosnian detention camp. An image of Bosnian internees taken by British journalists was shot from close-up, and it was, therefore, unclear whether the persons depicted were surrounded and in effect enclosed by the barbed wire in the shot, or were simply standing behind it. Any controversy could have easily been avoided had a wide shot been used to establish the scene before zooming in.

Actual and perceived impartiality are important considerations in an assessment of reliability. For video to be considered impartial, it must be free of bias to the extent possible. This means that the footage must be shot fairly, without attempts to mislead the audience. In *Tadic,* the ICTY addressed the issue of impartiality in video recordings of witness interviews. The ICTY concluded that defense counsel had manipulated video evidence by bribing individuals to testify to certain events on camera; he was held in contempt of court and found guilty of professional misconduct.[15] Certainly, this is a most extreme case of an impartial recording, but it illustrates the importance of accurate videography.

Case study: The case of the provocative title

In 2000, the Columbia University School of Law Human Rights Clinic teamed up with WITNESS to document the discrimination against and deportation of individuals of Haitian descent residing in the Dominican Republic. Arturo Carrillo, of the Columbia Human Rights Clinic, explained:

In our case, we needed to do the substantive analysis. We needed to find what rules in Dominican law and their immigration regimes were being broken, as well as within the international system, including the Inter-American system. In our case, there are United Nations instruments that also apply.

They decided they would take their case to three different international institutions: the Inter-American Commission and Court, as well as the United Nations Human Rights Committee.

Two different versions of the video were made. The first video was 13 minutes long and in Spanish for the Inter-American Court. The second was prepared in English for the UN. In both videos they flashed the specific articles of law on screen, followed by testimony provided by specific individuals involved in the case (whose testimony was representative of wider patterns of violations), which corroborated claims of violation of each article. In both videos the articles referenced, along with the overall argument, directly paralleled a written submission that provided more substantive and detailed information on the case.

The first submission was called "El Apartheid Del Caribe: Caso #12.271 Ante La Corte Interamericana de Derechos Humanos" (Caribbean Apartheid: Case #12.271 Before the Inter-American Court of Human Rights). Arturo recognizes that:

Our original title was not strategically a good idea. We had decided to use something someone said from one of our interviews: Caribbean Apartheid… But as a title, this was an exaggeration, and when it came time to go to court, we had a bit of a scare, because we realized that the Dominican Republic could block the viewing of the video on the basis of its biased title!

In the end, the video was admitted in evidence, but Professor Carrillo advises that "in a legal setting the title should appear neutral, with a technical name." The video was renamed and re-edited for the UN screening, "Mass Expulsions of Suspected Haitians in the Dominican Republic: Recent Episodes in a Recurring Practice."

Presenting video in a court setting is like presenting a witness. It needs to appear neutral and credible. Arturo suggests, "make the video look as professional as possible. Use the tools to make it professional." In this case, the video complemented a written submission. The power of the video helped use individual stories to connect with the viewer at an emotional level, and to substantiate the detailed legal argument that related to a broader set of abuses.

Arturo concluded the videos had more impact at the UN level than at the Inter-American Court:

> There are such differences between a judicial hearing (the Inter-American Court) and a briefing over lunch (the UN). The more formal the procedure, the less space you'll have for this kind of video advocacy. But the biggest contribution a video can make is to put a human face on violations.

The following is a list of some considerations to keep in mind as you film to help ensure that your footage is reliable and impartial. Note that in some aspects, this filming style will differ from a style used to film for more traditional documentary where stopping the camera is relatively common, and where you are also focused on gathering cutaways and B-roll. Filmmakers often need to make a conscious decision to film in an evidentiary mode.

1. During recording, keep the camera running: If recording is stopped, you must have someone available to testify why filming ceased, and what occurred during the interruption, especially if you are filming live events critical to the case at hand, or an interview. Frequent pausing or stopping will detract from the perceived authenticity of the footage, and will also make it harder for a viewer to follow.
2. Time and date stamp: Whenever possible, have time and date stamped onto your footage. With most digital cameras, time and date are automatically recorded on the tape. If your video camera does not permit this, then record the time and date verbally and clearly at the outset of recording, along with a brief description of what you are doing.
3. Quality: Ensure that the video you are recording is the highest quality possible. Both picture and sound quality will be used to measure the accuracy of the depiction.
4. Include *all* relevant information: Do not assume that what you are shooting is obvious. Remember that the film may be viewed long after it is shot, and may be viewed by persons who have never traveled to the site. Include all relevant information in your video. When interviewing a witness in a situation that does not present security risks, have them state his or her name, position, location, and time of filming on camera. If filming a geographic location, it is helpful if you can include shots such as street signs

or landmarks that can help to identify the location, in addition to an on-camera verbal statement regarding location. If you are recording footage of an event (e.g. a demonstration), be sure to make sure you have sufficient wide shots of the entire area to give the viewer a sense of the entire relevant surroundings, to properly contextualize other detailed scenes you wish to highlight.

Note: Again, a camera operator must be cognizant of the dangers posed for witnesses and/or for people appearing in video footage. Although anonymous sources may lack the reliability of identified ones and therefore be less persuasive in court, potential risks should be identified and, whenever possible, reduced through careful filming. See discussion earlier in this chapter, and Chapter 2.

5. When interviewing a witness: Make sure the witness is allowed to speak freely and that you are not posing leading questions (questions that suggest a "correct" or specific response), although you can of course ask questions and can ask a witness to clarify an answer. An appropriate question would be: "Did you see anyone at the scene of the crime holding a knife?" A leading question would be: "Did you see Annabel at the scene of the crime holding the knife"—if there were no prior testimony regarding Annabel or her connection to the crime. If you pay attention to this when you are interviewing, the viewer will not feel manipulated, nor forced to see things from only one point of view. They will also have an opportunity to take in relevant contextual information that will enable a better decision regarding the relevance, probative value, and admissibility of the particular incident or event showcased by your video.

Source of the video   Even in the absence of technological manipulation of evidence, all video evidence is susceptible to manipulation during the filming process. A biased camera operator or a filmmaker with a specific agenda may film in a way that does not accurately depict a given scene. It is important to be able to demonstrate the accuracy of the images.

When footage is recorded for purposes other than courtroom evidence, there can be a presumption that the video is unbiased, but this will depend on whether the source is considered to be unbiased. If you are using footage recorded by a third party with the intention of submitting it as evidence, provide the court with written information on the source, including the nature of the work done by the third party. If footage is recorded with the intention of creating evidence, e.g. an NGO recording a street demonstration to capture any evidence of unlawful crowd control, you will have to ensure that the footage is reliable by showing impartiality and accuracy, which are both discussed below.

In proceedings before the ICTY and ICTR, considerable video evidence was obtained from journalists, and in some instances, from civilians. Courts can sometimes be more reluctant to accept video submissions from NGOs who may have an advocacy agenda. There is more work to be done with the judicial system to enhance the perceived and actual credibility of human rights documentors who do their work rigorously and professionally, notwithstanding the fact that it may ultimately be used to support an advocacy position.

Establishing chain of custody   It is often appropriate, or even necessary, to have the person(s) involved in shooting a video testify as to its accuracy and to the circumstances surrounding filming. If the court chooses to question the authenticity of the footage, the source will be the first step and they may be called upon to testify and be cross-examined. If the source of the footage is deceased or unknown, you should provide a reconstruction to the extent possible, of how the footage (or a copy thereof), came into your possession. This is often referred to as a *chain of custody*, which shows who had access to the footage and can help to rebut any allegations of fabrication.

It is therefore important that you are able to detail for an adjudicator the whereabouts of the film *at all times*. In the event that alterations (i.e. editing) occurs, you must retain an unedited master copy, and ideally be able to produce it upon request, as well as to testify as to its whereabouts at all times to allay concerns that it may have been tampered with. You must know, and should limit, the number of people who have access to the master copy. If the master changes hands at any point (including providing raw footage to a duplication facility), you should be able to provide a detailed log of everyone who had access to the footage, i.e. indicating the *chain of possession*, which should clearly indicate the dates and each person in possession of the relevant evidence. And you may have to present the witnesses to support the authenticity and accuracy of the log.

Establishing the accuracy of video footage through a witness   All evidence, including video evidence, must be introduced before a court or tribunal through the verbal (i.e. live testimony) or written testimony (i.e. a sworn affidavit) of a witness that attests to the authenticity and accuracy of the evidence. The process of establishing authenticity is described above. (Note: Some courts will not accept an affidavit and instead will require real witness testimony, especially if there is an objection from the other side.)

Video evidence is most likely to be admitted as accurate, meaning that it depicts what actually happened, if it is introduced through the testimony of (1) the camera operator; (2) another person present at the shooting of the footage: or (3) an expert.

1. The camera operator: The camera operator can be a vital witness. As mentioned, you should have the camera operator available to the court for questioning, or if this is not possible, obtain a sworn affidavit from the camera operator.

2. Other persons with direct knowledge of the accuracy of the footage: Depending on the source of the footage and the reasons it was recorded, the court may take a more flexible approach in admitting video evidence. For example, at the ICTR in the *Rutaganda* decision, journalist Nick Hughes obtained footage from TV Rwanda and compiled an edited montage. The montage was introduced in evidence at the ICTR, through the testimony of Nick Hughes because the journalist at TV Rwanda who had originally recorded the footage could not be located. Because Hughes edited the footage, was present during many of the incidents depicted in the video, and could confirm that the video accurately depicted those incidents, Hughes's testimony was considered sufficient to establish the authenticity of the edited montage and it was admitted into evidence.

Quick tips: General reliability checklist

Use the following suggestions as a checklist to ensure you are recording and submitting the most reliable, accurate, authentic, and impartial video evidence possible:

- *Source information*: You must be able to identify the source of your video footage, meaning the person who did the recording and their institutional affiliation, if any, as well as the date, time and circumstances of the recording.
- *Technology used*: Take all the steps described in this chapter to ensure that you can prove that manipulation has not occurred. You should also be able to attest if necessary, to the type of equipment used to record the footage, and whether it was functioning properly.
- *Never edit the master*: Keep your master copy in a safe, climate-controlled environment (ideally with steady temperatures of 68° Fahrenheit and 30% humidity), and make a copy of the master (a "submaster") that you keep

▶

in a separate, equally safe place and use for editing or screening when necessary. Ensure that the master copy is available to the court, should it be requested. Rules may require that the opposing side may control access to the original.

- *Chain of custody*: You must be able to establish the tape's whereabouts, and who had access to the footage at all times since the time it was recorded.
- *During recording, keep the camera running*: Especially when you are recording an interview or an event in progress, keep the camera running to avoid questions raised by lapses in time.
- *Time and date stamp*: Whenever possible, have time and date stamped onto your footage; if this is impossible, meticulous notes may be sufficient.
- *Quality*: Ensure that the video you are recording is the highest quality possible.
- *Relevant information*: Include all relevant information in your video.

3. Expert testimony: Expert testimony has been considered sufficient in many jurisdictions to introduce video evidence. A person with historical, geographical, or political expertise, for example, may be able to testify convincingly as to the accuracy of a video without actually having been present at filming. The general principle appears to be that authentication through a witness can occur provided that the witness has actual knowledge of the accuracy of the video's contents, either because he/she was present during recording, or because he/she has expertise recognized regarding the depicted events.

Weighting or evaluation stage

In many jurisdictions, once a court or tribunal has decided to admit video evidence into the proceedings, the fact-finder will have to determine how much *weight*, or influence, to give to the evidence. This will typically depend upon the legal use of your video evidence. Many of the same considerations that went into assessing whether the video was sufficiently reliable to be admitted into evidence at all will continue to be important as a judicial decision-maker decides what impact the evidence will have on the outcome.

There is a wide range of possible weightings that may be attributed to an individual piece of evidence:

- It may be of little weight at all, if the counsel submitting the evidence has been unable to establish a legal purpose for doing so (i.e. direct, circumstantial, corroborative, contextual, or refuting), or if problems with the evidence (such as clarity or reliability) were insufficient to bar its use, but still enough to taint its effectiveness.

- Evidence may be considered determinative of a specific issue, particularly if it is viewed in corroboration with other evidence.

Remember that admissibility is not all that matters—getting the evidence admitted is merely a first step, albeit an important one. The "better" the evidence is—the clearer, the more obviously reliable, the more impartial—the better the chance that it will be given significant weight.

Case study: Admitted, but with no weight

Video evidence was admitted, but given little weight, in the case of *Gangaram Panday* vs *Suriname*.[16] Asok Gangaram Panday died while in the custody of the military police in Suriname, and a petition was brought to the Inter-American Court on Human Rights. The petitioner took a videotape of the body in the morgue before it was cremated, and that tape was submitted by the Commission in support of allegations that the deceased was tortured while in detention.

The quality of the tape was poor, and it was taken approximately a week after the death, leading the forensic pathologist, whose report was also submitted by the Commission, to conclude that it was impossible to rely on it to arrive at a precise diagnosis. Both the quality of the tape and the fact that it was shot a week after the death contributed to the weight it was given.

We hope this chapter has helped demystify the ways in which you might be able to use your visual imagery as a powerful source of evidence in court or in another form of legal proceeding. Because of the range of possible venues around the world, we have tried to keep our commentary broad and inclusive, yet suggestive of some of the key practices to keep in mind when considering the use of video as evidence. Hopefully, this chapter has given you some general guidelines and some pointers as to where to go for the information you need to make the difference you have in mind. The bottom line is this: do not feel intimidated by the legal system. It is, in theory if not always in practice, designed to ensure and promote justice. We can all do our part to ensure that it lives up to its powerful potential.

NOTES

1. "The Rodney King Trials," *Seeing Is Believing*, at <http://www.seeingisbelieving.ca/handicam/king/>.
2. *United States of America* vs *Stacey C. Koon et al.*
3. *Kostovski vs The Netherlands*, Application number 00011454/85 (1989) ECHR,. available at <http://hudoc.echr.coe.int/hudoc/ViewRoot.asp?Item=0&Action=Html&X=1214094604&Notice=0&Noticemode=&RelatedMode=0>.
4. *R.* vs *C.C.F.* [1997] 3 S.C.R. 1183.
5. [1996] 3 S.C.R. 1197.
6. *The Prosecutor* vs *Georges Anderson Nderubumwe Rutaganda* (Rutaganda, Georges, ICTR 96-3).
7. See, for example, *Drew* vs *U.S.*, 33i F2d 85 (D.C. Cir. 1964).
8. *Prosecutor v. Milomir Stakic* (Case No. IT-97-24-T).
9. *The Prosecutor* vs *Jean-Paul Akayesu* (Case No. ICTR-96-4-T).
10. *The Prosecutor* vs *Kunarac et al.*, IT-96-23 and IT-96-23/1, "Foca" Trial Chamber II (2001) at para. 17, available at <http://www.un.org/icty/foca/trialc2/judgement/index.htm>.
11. *The Prosecutor* vs *Dusko Tadic* (IT-94-1), available at: <http://www.un.org/icty/cases/jugemindex-e.htm> and <http://www.un.org/icty/tadic/trialc2/judgement/index.htm>.
12. *The Prosecutor* vs *Dario Kordic* and *Mario Cerkez* (IT-95-14/2), available at <http://www.un.org/icty/kordic/trialc/judgement/index.htm>.
13. See, for example, *Vladimir Jamandilovski* vs *Telstra Corporation Limited*, No. NG22 of 1994 FED No. 1012/94 (Federal Court of Australia, New South Wales District Registry, General Division); *Amorgianos* vs *AMTRAK* 303 (2002) F.3d 256; 2002 U.S. App. 59 Fed. R. Serv. 3d, 639 Docket No. 01-7508 (U.S. Court of Appeals for the Second Circuit). Australian Administrative Appeals Tribunal (General Administrative Division) in *Ravi Wickramasinghe* vs *Comcare Australia*, No. A96/401 & A96/444 AAT No. 12465, Canberra, 15 18 July 1997 (hearing), 4 December 1997 (decision).
14. Information on digital watermarking provided by Hany Farid, an Assistant Professor in Computer Science and the Center for Cognitive Neuroscience at Dartmouth College, an expert in this field.
15. *Prosecutor* vs *Dusko Tadic*, Judgment on Allegations of Contempt Against Prior Counsel, Milan Vujin, IT-94-1 (2001), available at <http://www.un.org/icty/tadic/appeal/vujin-e/index.htm>.
16 Gangaram Panday Case, Judgment of January 21, 1994, Inter-American Court for Human Rights (Ser. C) No.16 (1994).

7

Strategic Distribution: Reaching Key Audiences in Innovative Ways

Thomas Harding

INTRODUCTION—MY STORY

In order for your advocacy video to truly make an impact, you will need to ensure that it reaches key viewers with the power to act. This chapter will explain how to choose your distribution method, design your campaign, and ensure your video creates the maximum possible impact.

In the early 1990s I worked as a producer/director on a variety of broadcast television projects. Many of my news features and documentaries were aired around the world on national television networks. However, I was concerned that though these films had a large audience, their impact was minimal. The messages of the films were diluted by the context they were placed in, between advertisements for cars and the latest popular game show.

I left broadcast television and co-founded Undercurrents, along with other video-makers dedicated to using video to bring about change. In the old days as a television director I would ask myself "what film shall I make which will get me airtime on national television?" Instead, I now asked myself "what method of distribution should we use to bring about the most impact in this particular campaign or project?" The difference had profound consequences.

One of my first projects was to assist a community that lived in Wrexham, Wales (see Figure 7.1). Its members were suffering from appalling noise and pollution from the neighboring aluminium factory. For many years they had asked the manager of the factory to do something about the problem, but they received no response.

Here is the distribution strategy that evolved, broken down in stages:

Step 1: Define audience and agree upon distribution strategy

To my great surprise they told me they didn't need a video made about their issues to be distributed by national television. Instead, they told

Figure 7.1   A community activist in Wales uses video to document pollution (Thomas Harding)

me they needed local media attention to build support for the issue in the community. This was a great adjustment for me as a professional producer-director. After all, I was working with a community to bring about change, not making broadcast documentaries any more.

I interviewed various residents, and we submitted these interviews along with recordings of the appallingly loud sound levels to the local radio and newspapers. These were then played on the local television and radio station news.

Step 2: Make adjustments

The residents then asked us to make a video to show to the local manager. But it soon became clear that the manager had no role in resolving the problem. He was never to be seen in the factory and whenever contact was made, he was rude and uncooperative. It was time to rethink our distribution plan.

Step 3: Rethink and build distribution strategy

A few months later the residents told me they were ready to take distribution to the next level. Again I offered to make a great documentary to be broadcast on national television. Again, they told me "no." Why? Because they had done research and had learnt that the owners of the factory actually lived in New York, and would not be watching television in the UK, nor be pressured by UK viewers. We agreed instead to produce a "video letter" that would be made specifically for the owners of the factory. I recorded a series of interviews with the residents, and included footage of the black smoke coming from the factory and a wonderful sequence with one of the elderly ladies wearing ear-muffs while recording the high sound levels on a meter.

Step 4: Maximize the impact

We soon realized that the video letter had become a great story in its own right. Now was the time to get national television exposure. We contacted the BBC and invited their producers to make a film about the video letter. They loved the idea and followed as three of the residents flew from the UK to present the video letter to the owners in New York. The BBC was not only pleased with the story, it was also happy to be able to use large sections of the videotape for its own documentary.

Step 5: Evaluate distribution strategy

As a result of this video distribution strategy, many local community members got involved (owing to local media coverage). The owners dismissed the manager of the factory and reduced sound and smoke pollution because of the video letter that was delivered to them, and the success story was shown on national television, raising the credibility of the local campaign and inspiring others to do the same.

Lessons learned

I learnt many important lessons from this project. Perhaps the most significant was that things don't always go according to plan. And if this happens, take some time to rethink the distribution plan and develop a new strategy. Another is that when a surprising opportunity turns up (like the BBC documentary), grab it with both hands if it will help your overall objectives. Finally, the most important lesson was that there are many different distribution methods available, and knowing what is possible is a critical part of the process.

DISTRIBUTION METHODS

Distribution is important because without it your project becomes a dead-end program. People will say, "I spent two months making video and nothing happened." Distribution gives you feedback on your work and furthers your work. It gives you the impulse to regenerate the process. It is like a fertilizer. (Amalia Cordova, Latin American Program Coordinator, Film and Video Center of the National Museum of the American Indian, USA)

Having read the other chapters, you now know how to design your advocacy strategy. You also know how to produce and edit a video. Now you have to find a way of getting it to the audiences you want to reach.

Remember, you need to create a distribution strategy *before* starting the production and editing process to ensure that the video reaches intended audiences in a timely and effective way.

There are a wide variety of distribution methods available to the video advocate (see Table 7.1 below). In practice, most video campaigns make use of more than one distribution strategy—"multi-purposing." Equally, successful campaigns often target different audiences via separate distribution strategies in a well-thought-out sequence at different times—"sequencing" (see pp. 273–5 for more on these two techniques). Timing and sequencing can be critical in making the difference between success and failure.

Table 7.1   Distribution strategies

1. Public screenings	Community screenings Video vans and mobile screenings Home-based screenings and microcinemas Film festivals Theatrical distribution (movies)
2. Tape/disc duplication and distribution	Self-distribution Via networks Distributor Retail outlets
3. Private screenings	Direct-to-decision-maker Legal process
4. Broadcast media (including cable, satellite and free-to-air television)	Television news Television documentary Radio news and documentaries
5. Internet and wireless	Live streaming Websites Newsletters/campaign alerts Flash animations Video messages via cellphone

In this chapter I identify five basic ways of distributing video. Each requires different technology, different budgets and different amounts of energy. As you may be an organization or an individual with limited resources, think through what is an appropriate choice for you. Remember, it's not necessarily the size of the audience you reach, but being tactical about reaching the audience that will make a difference. With the distribution tactics outlined in this chapter you'll be able to reach, or in some cases, create, the audience that matters, and get around the traditional gate-keepers who prevent audiences from seeing your material.

Make your distribution budget

As you go about designing your distribution strategy, and before you start out on implementation, draw up a distribution budget to find out if you can afford it and if you require further funds. Of course, your aim is to minimize your expenses and maximize your impact.

Key questions to answer before you get to the budget:

- How long will your distribution campaign be?
- How many copies do you want to distribute? How many community screenings will there be?   .
- How will they be distributed and to whom (i.e. local, national, international, via mail or hand)?
- Can you spread your spending across time to allow fundraising to take place?
- How can you reduce your costs?
- Who can help you raise the funds required?

Try to think creatively about how to raise funds as part of your distribution strategy. Don't forget that volunteer time and donations of equipment or venues ("in-kind" donations) count as fundraising so talk to local businesses and individuals who can lend support.

If you can, try to raise money as well. One of your target audiences in your distribution strategy planning process should include potential donors. These can be people on the street who donate a few coins, people who actually buy the tapes and organizations who give grants for important video work (either at the preproduction stage or in order to support outreach). Also, remember that if you are seeking funding for video projects, include outreach funding in this request not only production costs.

You should work with colleagues or advisers to create a budget for your distribution strategy. The sample budget narrative in Appendix VII can guide your thinking, and could also be included in a proposal to a potential funder. It is oriented towards a strategy that primarily includes community and direct-to-decision-maker screenings, as well as distribution of copies of the video. A more detailed resource kit on outreach budgeting is available at <www.mediarights.org>.

PUBLIC VIDEO SCREENINGS

I think it's important to understand the importance of a group experience. Video is an emotionally rich medium, and when people share an experience together, they bond. Also, when you work through organizations, you are building on that organization's strength. People who watch a video with other members of an organization can take action right then and there. (Pat Aufderheide, Director, Center for Social Media at American University, Washington, DC)

A first distribution category is "public screenings." This refers to community screenings, home screenings, video vans and mobile screenings as well as theatrical distribution and film festivals.

Community screenings

A community screening is an event where you show your video in a local setting—such as a school, a town hall, or a store—in front of a group of people. These people might be from the community where you have filmed, or from a community that you are trying to mobilize around the issue. Community screenings can be used to engage people in a specific action, but also as a means to instigate discussion and encourage participatory decision-making.

Multi-community campaigns are particularly useful when you are addressing national issues. One way of reducing the administrative load of this method is to use an existing national network, which will enable you to plug into an already established group of local leaders. This can save considerable time. Of course, for this to work, your issue and your approach must match that of your partner organization. Often, if the organization has been involved from an early stage in the production they will be more vested in it, and more willing to participate in distribution and to shoulder costs themselves.

In some cases you need to bypass local leadership in order to reach a group that is affected by an issue. This is particularly the case with sensitive issues related to women, the gay community, and others affected by taboo policies or practices that local leaders may be reluctant to discuss (such as HIV/AIDS, refugee rights, indigenous land claims, etc.).

Advantages of community screenings include:

- You can make a significant impact on a small budget. You may simply need to find a good venue, invite members of the local population and show them your video.
- A community screening can become a springboard for discussion about a policy or practice that affects the community directly, or for discussion about a sensitive topic that is going to require close attention post-screening, especially if this topic involves trauma or loss.
- If the video is going to present issues affecting the community to a wider audience, the screening provides an opportunity to get the community's feedback first.
- Targeted groups of individuals can be engaged in specific actions in support of a campaign (e.g. student activists on sweatshops).

A community screening can be a one-off occasion, so you don't have to build a massive organization to support the effort. You can even integrate a screening within existing social events. For example, you can show a video at a festival, carnival, or other community activity. This way, you don't have to worry about attracting an audience. You can build on someone else's marketing efforts. If you do this, consider when to schedule the screening. Pick a date that does not conflict with larger social events, such as religious holidays. Coordinate with other organizers to ensure that the timing is strategic.

The steps to organizing your screening include:

- Identify your audience and select the best film or video that suits their needs
- Identify the person or organization who will present the film and facilitate a discussion
- Find the venue and organize the equipment
- Market the screening
- Manage people
- Coordinate an engaging post-screening discussion
- Evaluate

The key to a successful community screening is that the audience will engage with the video—and you can transfer their passion into action.

Case study: STEPS in the community
by Don Edkins, Executive Producer, STEPS, South Africa

The STEPS program in South Africa is an innovative project to create a collection of films about HIV/AIDS for use throughout Southern Africa. The project involves local filmmakers and NGOs throughout the region in the creation of programming.

Our project began when our mobile cinema was travelling in the mountains of Lesotho. At that time, we were showing films about environmental issues, social issues, and political issues. People started asking us for films to learn about HIV/AIDS. There were some films from Uganda, but there were no films in the local language. Then we found in the Western Cape there was the same demand. We had no films to offer them.

So we decided to develop a collection of films—to talk to different audiences. There is so much stigma, so much discrimination around HIV/AIDS, that people don't want to say aloud that they are infected. We knew we would have to work with the characters, the subjects of documentaries, closely, because when they came out and spoke aloud, their neighbors would be prejudiced.

We began the whole project by involving HIV groups in the story lines. We consulted with them, and filmmakers would brainstorm in groups. We have HIV/AIDS experts on the project to evaluate the process all along the way, make sure we are using the right language … that we are going in the right direction. During filming, we also have counseling on hand for the subjects. And the subjects are involved in the screenings.

Each film in our collection stands on its own. This is not a series. Each story has its particular way of telling itself, without making people uncomfortable. When we show the films, we have facilitators there to provide information not contained in the film. For this, we have developed a facilitators' guide to deal with questions relating to the particular film they've just seen—nutrition, gender, or whatever the issue might be.

We conduct workshops with the subjects, so that among themselves they can discuss their expectations, their reactions, both positive and negative. Subjects are part of the whole project, and support each other. They are now going around with the mobile cinemas. We are just completing a film about this entire process. We are also planning a conference next year, to bring all the different screening groups together. ... Our films resonate with the people. They love them because the films are about them.

Identify your audience

As explained in Chapter 1, you will need to identify your audience before you devise your distribution strategy. Once you have done this you will be able to answer the following questions:

- Who do you want to attend the screening (community leaders, people shown in the film, government officials, local residents, human rights advocates, etc.)?
- Do you want to get the most people possible to the screening or are there particular people you want to attract?
- What language(s) does the audience speak? Do you need a sign language expert?
- How long an event will the audience be interested in participating in (e.g. what will their attention span be at the screening)? Do you want to show the whole video or just clips? A trailer?
- Will a video be enough to attract an audience or do you need to organize a social event as well?

Choose the right facilitator

The person who will introduce, contextualize, and facilitate the discussion of the video is critical. A good facilitator will relate to and communicate with their audience, and hold their respect. You will need to brief the facilitator extensively on the film, and watch it with them beforehand. Explain why it was made, and what the advocacy objective was, and discuss how they will open and provide context for the film, facilitate a discussion around questions and issues raised, and move the audience to action after the screening.

Select the venue and the host organization

The wrong venue—too small, too bright, too noisy, too far away— or the wrong host organization—unpopular in the community, representative of a particular faction—could have a negative impact on your efforts. Think creatively about venues—open spaces in community, football fields and basketball courts, churches and other places of worship are all potential screening locations.

Here are some questions to help you locate your venue:

- Is the proposed space one that will be comfortable for your audience? Be sensitive to physical access and security at the venue as well as racial, gender, religious, ethnic, linguistic, and class tensions that may affect an audience's willingness to attend, or to participate fully. Is your choice of venue linked to your facilitator or an ally on the project? Does this mean it's the best choice for a venue or should you look elsewhere?
- Is there enough room for the audience you hope to attract?
- Is there electricity in place? If not, how will you supply it?
- What equipment do they have? What equipment will you need to bring? Is there enough space for a screen if you want to use a projector? Who will set up the equipment and knows how to use it?
- Can everyone see the screen you will use? Can everyone hear with the available sound system? Can you darken the room for daytime screenings?
- If you plan to issue tickets, is there a good place to collect them? How will people pay and do you need to provide a share to the venue?
- Who is in charge of the venue? Can you gain access to the venue two hours before the event to set up? Who will lock the place after you have left?
- Can you provide food and drink at the venue? What will you do with the rubbish?
- What will you do if it rains? Is the venue a dry location? Is there an alternative in case of bad weather?

Organize people and market your event

You will need people to help you organize and market the event. As we discuss in "Networking" below, the more you are linked and allied with other organizations from early stages in the production process, the easier this will be. The following questions will help to assess what support you need:

- Who has direct links to the issues whom you can invite to speak at the event (e.g. people shown in film, campaign leaders, etc.)?

- Who can lend a hand to publicize your event? Who will produce publicity materials and who will distribute them in the community? Who is going to contact local media to cover the event?
- What publicity materials will you need to produce? These may include posters, flyers, brochures, newsletters, information for stories in local media, stickers, and T-shirts. Remember that publicity materials need to be sensitive to local concerns regarding language, modesty, phrasing etc., and may need to vary by audience. Also, many screenings are organized by email, signs or word-of-mouth alone.
- Who is going to organize drinks, food, and other resources?
- Who is going to raise money at the event (sell tickets, collect donations, ask for grants from organizations, etc.)?
- Who is going to manage the equipment during the screening? Do they need training?

Turn viewing into action

In our experience having screenings, we have found that it is best to contextualize the film. We give a brief introduction of our goals and mission, an overview of the presentation, and a short check-in question to get people centred and grounded. Mike Molina, formerly of Books Not Bars, a campaign around juvenile jails in the USA, says:

> The aim of the screening is to turn a viewing experience into action—to transfer the energy and passion that a video provokes into concrete results. How do you do this?
>
> There are a number of ways to mobilize your audience after a screening. Here are a few suggestions:
>
> - Have a facilitator appropriate for the film and the audience.
> - Open by providing context for the film.
> - Facilitate a discussion after the film around the questions and issues raised to help get people informed, and to spark more proactive, invested community involvement.
> - Get the names and addresses of the audience for future networking.
> - Recruit audience members to become active in your campaign.
> - Ask the audience to donate funds.
> - Encourage the audience to take immediate action. For example, you can ask the audience to write a letter to the government or join a march on the town hall.

- Ask the audience to participate in an upcoming action.
- Distribute a sheet with ideas on how to take action, and a list of organizations on the issue.

Making screenings enjoyable

> Viewing can be fun if you are able to connect the issues contained in the film to the lives of your viewers. (Joey Lozano)

Some videos, particularly about human rights, are extremely serious and at times deeply distressing. However, if people feel the connection to their lives, and the opportunity to interact and discuss the issues raised, they are likely to respond to them, even enjoy them. There is also nothing necessarily wrong with introducing additional fun elements to a screening, even if at the core of the event is a focus on a painful topic.

There are many ways to make a community event appealing. Dance, music, food, comedy, poetry, artwork, games, and sport— these are a small sample of what you could provide. The trick is to know your audience. What would they appreciate that would still be appropriate for the subject matter at hand?

Another way to make video screenings fun is to integrate them into street theatre. Show the video as part of the event. Bring a clown or an actor to engage the audience. Film the audience and play back both the video and the "live" footage to keep their attention.

Case study: Structuring screenings with *Operation Fine Girl: Rape Used as a Weapon of War in Sierra Leone*
Lilibet Foster talks about how she and Binta Mansaray planned the screenings strategy for *Operation Fine Girl.*

> With *Operation Fine Girl* we first held a public screening of the film in a town with a broad-based community of people in every age group, ex-child soldiers from each of the opposing factions, and abducted women and girls, to help guide us in setting up screenings across the country. The film was introduced to the village by their tribal chief, and everyone was encouraged to ask questions or give their reaction to the film afterwards, in front of the group. From this, we concluded that a group screening should be followed by separate screenings for different parts of the community. For instance, holding a separate screening for young girls, and a separate screening for child-soldiers without their elders in the room, would generate better discussion amongst them, etc.

Evaluate

Evaluation is critical if you plan to hold future events and want to maximize the impact of your screenings. Ask, why did people attend? How did people react to the video? Will they become involved in the issue at hand? What did your colleagues think? Was the effort it took to organize the event worth the results? Did you succeed in your goals? How could you do better next time?

One method of evaluation is the traditional survey. You can ask people a short list of questions as they leave an event. This might be something as simple as "How would you rate the event: great, fair, poor?" or more complex questions, like: "Has this event changed your opinion/view on X? Much, little, negative, not at all." Be conscious of people's desire for privacy if the screening was about a sensitive topic. Consider how you plan to evaluate the event in the longer run as some people may take a few days, weeks or months to appreciate how the video affected their thinking about an issue. Remember also that change can take many forms—from a clear change in policy, to increased sensitization around an issue, to organizing initiatives among your audience.

If you've set clear goals for your advocacy you'll find it easier to evaluate at every stage.

Case study: Top ten tips for organizing a community screening
Joey Lozano, a human rights activist, videographer and trainer working in Mindanao, the Philippines, offers the following advice:

1. Visit village officials and community leaders days before the screening to explain the upcoming event and determine what requirements you have to comply with
2. Know who your local contacts are. Are they on good terms with those within the traditional political structure? If they are, expect a successful screening. If not, ensure that if you still decide to go ahead with the screening, the event won't be harassed or interrupted
3. Set clear objectives that you want to achieve with the screening, these being your bases in measuring success or failure
4. Ensure that local resources meet your technical requirements (e.g. availability of power supply; enough space to accommodate expected number of participants, etc.)
5. Ensure good attendance by posting announcements or broadcasting them through popular local radio stations in the area

6. Engage the interest of your audience by relating the film to something very relevant to them (e.g. you may want to stress that the film can help them determine the best way to maintain their source of livelihood)

7. Bring other films that could help attract the highest attendance (e.g. you may bring a copy of a popular commercial film, the theme of which falls along the lines of the documentary you want to show them)

8. If necessary, organize an entertainment or talent show that would feature or engage local residents

9. Before starting, give due acknowledgement to local officials, leaders, and others who helped the screening to happen

10. Devise a feedback mechanism that would help you determine the success or failure of the screening

---

Mobile public screenings

Doing in-person presentations is the most effective way to make a long-term impact. The audience meets you, they hear your story and are able to connect the videos to something concrete. The videos then take on a certain intimacy and connectedness for the audience. And many times someone who has attended a screening will buy a tape and show it to someone else who will want to buy copies as well, and so on. (Alexandra Halkin, Chiapas Media Project/Promedios, an innovative indigenous media initiative)

In an ordinary public screening, the audience comes to you to see the video in a fixed location. In a mobile public screening, you take the video from location to location. You can then screen it before many small, targeted audiences, including those who might otherwise have no access to videos at all. You can reach audiences nationwide in the time and place of your choosing.

How to organize a mobile public screening: Video vans

Video vans are simply vehicles (cars, vans) that house the video-related equipment. Typically, they include video players (VHS, VCD, or DVD), sound equipment (amplifier and speakers) and television monitors. Some video vans have projection equipment instead of a television. When going to remote areas, video vans may also include a generator to provide electricity for the audiovideo equipment.

With a video van you can be flexible on timing and location, and build swiftly on momentum. A video van can reach many small audiences in quick succession over a short amount of time. It is, therefore, a great tool for short-term mass mobilization. Within two weeks, for example, you could travel to over twenty communities, providing two screenings a day. With a target audience of 30 people per screening, that's almost 1,200 different people! The key word here is "different." It is fairly easy to build up a small following that will attend a regular video event. It is far more difficult to find different people to come to video screenings. A similar audience might take over a year to target if you focused on one community.

Case study: Video vans around the world

Brazil: Brazil has a long tradition of using video in popular education. One group that has used video vans is the Workers Television Network (Televisao dos Trabalhadores, or TVT). They created a "TV Truck" initiative in which a truck with projection screens on each side would park outside car-manufacturing plants outside Sao Paolo in the early morning as workers were coming to work. Each week they would produce a show called La Jornal on political and social issues in Brazil. Organizers estimated that they reached 3,000–4,000 workers a week, and that greater discussion was generated by the group setting in which the video was viewed.

Kenya: Kakuma Refugee Camp is based in northern Kenya. It houses over 85,000 people, mostly refugees from Somalia and Sudan. FilmAid International has worked with the local community leaders to organize a video-screening program. FilmAid has equipped a truck with a giant screen on the side. Three times a week, the truck tours eleven locations around the camp. The program starts with cartoons for the children, then an educational video, and then a main feature (either a movie or a documentary). The program is changed every month. Typically, 8,000 to 10,000 people watch each evening, and by the time it has rotated the 11 locations, approximately 100,000 have watched each program.

Working with local nongovernmental organizations and the community is the key to success. FilmAid has found that it is important to create a sense of ownership of the program in the community. FilmAid trains refugees and locals and they run the programs themselves. In addition, they have built a "follow-up" schedule, with post-screening discussions during the daytime by members of the local community.

Microcinemas and house parties

Another option related to community screenings is to hold coordinated screenings simultaneously—each in someone's home. The pioneer in this in the USA has been the organization MoveOn, <www.moveon.org>. MoveOn has successfully promoted a series of video screenings across the country by asking its members and supporters to become hosts. For example, around the opening of the political film *Fahrenheit 9/11* MoveOn coordinated over 650 house parties to discuss the film. Hosts with high-speed Internet access could access a live webchat with the filmmaker, Michael Moore, and all attendees learned how to take action on the issues raised in the film. Although MoveOn used a web-based software to help hosts plan parties, and enable people to locate the nearest screening party, it is also possible to organize this via email or even with a circulating paper list of the planned parties. The parties have a host who agrees to coordinate the technical side of the screening, the MoveOn organizers provide a screening guide and in some cases a DVD, and other people attending bring snacks and food, and help clean up.

A variant on this is to try to organize local video parlors or viewing rooms to screen the video, and to reach a wider population. Human Rights Alert did this successfully in the north-eastern Indian state of Manipur, showing their video about human rights abuses committed by the Indian security forces in local video parlors (small, community-based venues showing films), rather than in private homes.

Screenings at film festivals

> Often the press will attend film and video festivals looking for a good story. Some of our best press was through contacts made via film and video festivals. (Alexandra Halkin, Chiapas Media Project/Promedios)

A traditional way to get your videos seen by a wider audience is through the film festival circuit. The scale of a festival can range from fifty people watching three or four videos on a television monitor in a community centre, to a three-week event spanning seventy locations.

Sending your film to an existing festival

Before submitting your video, ask yourself: "Can this festival reach my target audience?" For example, a national film festival may expose your video to national donors, mass media, and other filmmakers, who may be able to help you. An indigenous film festival may attract audiences from within the local indigenous population as well as others working with this constituency. Also ask yourself whether realistically your film has a chance—many festivals are extremely competitive, and you should make sure your film is a strong fit.

Each film festival has different application criteria. Make sure you know their rules before sending your tape. Typical criteria include:

- Good-quality sound and video
- Thematic "fit" with the festival (human rights, labor, etc.)
- Engaging, story-driven narratives
- Type of filmmaker (i.e. "known producers," "first-time filmmakers")
- Potential for TV distributors to pick up

Make sure you don't send master copies, as programmers rarely return tapes. Some festivals require application fees. Only send your video to this type of festival if you are confident your video has a chance of being accepted.

Strengths of film festivals

- Develop a sense of community
- Create a discussion forum for video work
- Allow you to compare the work of various filmmakers and see what other material is being produced on issues you are focused on
- Give you access to a new, large audience
- Enable networking with press, general public and other filmmakers
- Provide media exposure, action, and advocacy opportunities

One way to make festival screenings an effective vehicle for change is, as with a community screening, to engage the audience in post-screening action. An example of this is the work of US filmmaker Judith Helfand and the organization, Working Films (which acts as an intermediary between filmmakers and nonprofit organizations in the US). At the 2002 Sundance Film Festival screening of her film *Blue Vinyl*, about the dangers of polyvinyl chloride (PVC) and vinyl siding, Judith encouraged the audience to write to their lawmakers and to PVC manufacturers. One particular target was the lingerie firm Victoria's Secret. Judith provided postcards for audience members to send to Victoria's Secret letting them know that they cared about the issue. Over 1,500 postcards were sent during one week of the film festival, and the owner of Victoria's Secret called the leading activist organization on this issue, Greenpeace, who had been running a campaign on this topic, to discuss the policy.

DUPLICATION—VIDEO TAPE/DISC DISTRIBUTION

One of the simplest ways of distributing a film or video is by making a copy ("duplicate") and passing it to someone to watch. This method can be particularly successful for focused campaigns such as direct-to-decision-maker distribution and legal process distribution, both of which are discussed later in this chapter.

This type of duplication distribution can be scaled up to mass distribution making use of a print catalogue, retail outlet, website, or other marketing device. It can also be done most effectively, in terms of advocacy, by using networks of allies. A sophisticated example of advanced self-distribution would be Undercurrents' bi-annual compilation that we put together and distributed to subscribers around the world during the 1990s. These tapes were 90 minutes long, made up of ten to fifteen films made by different directors and duplicated on VHS cassette with striking graphics on the box cover. This type of distribution has been copied around the world from Brazil to South Korea to Australia, and is being replicated by compilation video websites such as OneWorld TV.

Once you reach this level you might also be able to use a fulfillment house. This is a company that will "fulfill" video orders for you, sending tapes to purchasers without you having to attend to every order.

Video distribution making use of networks and alliances

Even if you have a distributor it is extremely important that you take a proactive role in getting the work seen. Developing personal relationships with people/organizations who have key constituencies/campaigns is critical so that the network can grow. (Alex Halkin, Chiapas Media Project)

What is networking? Networking is when you make best use of your relationships—the people and organizations you know—to achieve your video advocacy objectives. Networking so that other people help with your distribution will ensure you reach more people in less time with less money being paid by yourself, *and* it will engage a wider section of the community in the project. The key to successful networking is to begin before production so that you cultivate enthusiasm and support for the project early on. By engaging your network in your video from an early stage you can increase the chances they will support it financially and organizationally once it comes to distribution.

For most social justice video, effective use of networking will be the key to distribution, and, most importantly, impact.

One trick to generating a truly large audience by this method is to combine network distribution with screenings for organization memberships, communities, and the broader public. For example, if you distribute 1,000 copies to 1,000 organizations, and each is screened to 100 people, you reach 100,000 people. This is called pyramid distribution.

One of the most successful examples of pyramid distribution is by the video advocacy group Video Sewa in India, who produced a tape, *My Work, My Self*, about the national census, which was distributed to local communities for local playback using television monitors and VHS players. SEWA reached an impressive audience of over 500,000 people through networks, coalitions, and by building on existing outreach activities.

Cash flow: Caution!

It is easy to order hundreds of duplicate copies of a film and then not be able to sell them and therefore not be able to cover your costs. This is a real problem for duplicate-distribution and should be taken seriously by anyone interested in this method of distribution.

Cash flow is a challenge for videotape or DVD distribution. Whereas in a community screening you may sell tickets or ask for donations to raise funds, in tape/DVD distribution, unless you receive a distribution grant, you must pay for bulk copies and then wait to collect income as you sell each one. This can place a big burden on a small organization with limited funds. One solution is to build up a list of purchasers, arrange pre-orders for tapes, and collect the cash *before* you make the copies. Another is to make a limited number of copies at a time, enough to cover you over a short period. This will be more expensive in the long run because per tape/DVD costs for copying decrease as the number of copies increases, but it may save you financial headaches in the short term. Whatever path you take, before you start on the VHS or DVD distribution road, you must think through these finances carefully.

You can also charge different prices for different audiences. Some distribution companies charge more for universities and academic buyers than for nongovernmental organizations who want to use the tapes. Find out about the standard practice and price range in your country or region, and charge accordingly.

Retail outlets

Typically, only the most commercially successful activist documentary videos will be distributed through retail outlets in this way—usually only after they have been released in cinemas. Michael Moore's *Fahrenheit 9/11*, which has become the highest-grossing documentary of all time, is distributed from mainstream retail outlets.

However, the vast majority of advocacy videos do not reach the huge commercial success of this type of movie—and yet there are opportunities for retail outlet distribution. When documentaries become "important" to a local community, it may be possible to persuade local retail owners to sell videotapes "due to popular demand." In the past, campaigns have been organized specifically to persuade such store-owners to distribute these important videos.

Equally, there are opportunities to distribute videos via other retail outlets such as at conferences, fairs, and gatherings.

Distributors

A traditional way of distributing your video is via a distributor. This is an organization, person or company that has built up a reputation and the capacity to distribute videos, either via broadcast media, theatrical release or through retail outlets.

Many producers make use of distributors to help with overseas distribution. Some of these distributors are non-profit and activist in orientation (such as Undercurrents) and have helped many producers gain distribution of their video tape on international news channels such as CNN, MSNBC, Sky News, and BBC. An example of this is when Ken Saro Wiwa took shocking footage of massacres of the Ogoni Tribe in the Delta region of Nigeria. These images were passed to Undercurrents, which was able to get them on to news channels around the world. Other distributors focus specifically on social justice issues, although they hope to find a commercial market for these films. There are also distributors who focus specifically on the educational market, including high schools and universities. If you are looking to engage student activists, these distributors can be a good resource to work with to ensure your video is in university library collections and is used by teachers.

Alternatively, other distributors are run on a commercial basis. These distributors typically provide a service for a fee based on a percentage of the royalties for the videotape sold (see Resources chapter for more information).

Ten tips on duplication distribution

1.   Organize a marketing campaign before you make copies.
2.   Collect orders in advance.
3.   Find a duplication business that will make high quality copies quickly.
4.   The more copies you make, the cheaper the duplication costs will be; fronting costs may be more cost-effective in the long run if you think you can predict the sales or distribution quantities.
5.   Do not make more copies than you think you can distribute.
6.   Check the tape/DVD for the quality of the video and the audio before giving it to someone.
7.   If possible, design an attractive jacket cover for the video box.
8.   Include order and contact information on the cover.
9.   Include issue-related written material with the video, including a call to action such as a sample letter to the relevant authority, and a screening guide.
10. If you had donors for the production itself, return to them for funding with your distribution strategy. They may be as committed as you are to ensuring the video has maximum impact!

TARGETED DIRECT-TO-DECISION-MAKER DISTRIBUTION

Direct-to-decision-maker

One of the most successful forms of video distribution over the past few years has been the direct-to-decision-maker ("D2D") method. This section explores ways of getting your video directly to the people or group you need to influence.

Depending upon the decision-maker's personality, the political climate, the nature of the issue, and the constraints facing this person, the decision-maker may be receptive or hostile to your requests.

Therefore, do your homework in advance to determine whether you need to employ the carrot or stick approach to D2D distribution.

With the "carrot" approach, you may wish to treat the decision-maker as a potential ally and demonstrate why it is in this person's interest to abide by your suggestions. Cooperation in this case is likely to be mutually beneficial.

With the "stick" approach, you will need to apply economic, political, or public pressure on a decision-maker who may not otherwise comply (i.e. publicizing your demands to the public and/or mass media while engaging in D2D distribution).

Here is a list of some methods of D2D distribution:

- *Hand-to-hand*: This is where a campaigner literally places a copy of the video into the hands of the decision-maker. It may also be effective to enlist a respected and trusted intermediary to help convene the screening or pass on the tape for reasons of safety, credibility, publicity, and influence. The benefit of this method is that it is simple. It requires no arranging of meetings or official agreements. The disadvantage is that you do not have a formal meeting to discuss the contents of the video or to resolve issues. And worse, the decision-maker can throw the tape into the garbage bin when the messenger has left his or her presence.
- *Private screening*: A video advocate organizes a private screening of the campaign video for the decision-maker. This may be the only way to show the video to this person. This method has the advantage of confidentiality and trust. It is a gentler method than the public screening method described below. For example, the Comité de Emergencia Garífuna de Honduras, in Trujillo, Honduras, created a video showing community members speaking about economic development and discrimination issues, and asking on-camera for concrete actions in meetings with decision-makers. They then brought this video directly to high-level officials from the capital city and demanded action. Combined with other video strategies, the government is finally beginning to respond to their demands. One disadvantage of this method is that decision-makers can offer you things in private, which they later withdraw. The Brazilian Kayapo tribe's answer to this is to video all private meetings so they have a record of any agreements made.

- *Public screening with decision-maker present*: The video is screened before decision-makers in front of a public audience, often in the presence of people affected by the issue. The advantage of this method is that the audience will remember the reaction of the decision-makers and hold them accountable for their words and actions. For example, CEOSS in Egypt produced a video about a polluted canal that has become a public health threat. Opening with images of the filthy waterway, the tape features interviews with a variety of community members, who each address the problem. The finished tape was shown to over 200 villagers in front of key officials. As a result, filling in the canal has become a priority among local leaders and officials.

  Another advantage of this method is that if any journalists attend, they can record the event and use parts of the advocacy video in their news coverage. The disadvantage is that most politicians will not attend if they have not already previewed the tape or do not agree with its contents.

- *Video letter*: This is where a "letter" is sent to the decision-maker from the campaign group or the local community affected by the issue. The "letter" includes footage of the problem, testimonies from the "victims" or "advocates," and the description of what they want changed. Amazon Watch, a US-based advocacy group working on issues in the Amazon Basin, has had great success with this method. It is usually also publicized to the media, so they can assure that the decision-maker receives the video letter.

Direct approaches to decision-makers are often combined with other forms of distribution. As Table 7.2 shows, D2D is the shortest route to the decision-maker. However, screenings and networking can include a strategy for persuading the audience to contact the decision-maker, and can generate a greater groundswell to complement your direct approach. Screenings can generate community involvement that may make the project/campaign more sustainable. Although the mass media/Internet, because of its broadcast approach, has no guarantee of ever reaching a decision-maker, it can create a political context that adds pressure on a decision-maker. Ideally you should think of using an integrated strategy and "sequencing" the different methods effectively.

Table 7.2 What is the shortest path to a decision-maker?

D2D (direct-to-decision-maker)	Screenings	Media	Tape duplication and distribution	Internet
Group ↓	Group ↓	Group ↓	Group ↓	Group ↓
Decision-maker	Community ↓	Medias ↗↙↖	Network ↓	Internet ↗↙↖
	Decision-maker	Public ↓	Decision-maker	Public ↓
		Decision-maker		Decision-maker

D2D distribution is suitable for:

- Governments and elected representatives
- Corporations and shareholders
- Power-brokers and opinion-formers
- Community leaders
- Human rights commissions
- Intergovernmental and multilateral institutions such as the World Bank and UN
- National and international nongovernmental and civil society organizations

Ten tips for direct-to-decision-maker distribution

1. Research the issue carefully.
2. Identify the key decision-makers.
3. Identify intermediaries who can help you get to these decision-makers.
4. Keep the video short—decision-makers don't usually have much time—and try to make sure they watch it with you.
5. Check the video for quality before you leave.
6. Before the screening cue the video to the best starting place.
7. Check the equipment before any screening.
8. Have follow-up materials including recommendations for change, policy briefing guidelines, and contact details.
9. Leave a copy of the video with the decision-maker.
10. When appropriate, invite the mass media to attend the screening or hand-off and/or turn the screening into an "event".

Video as evidence

Video can also play a powerful role in the legal process. Around the world, video is being used as evidence to assist in promotion of social and environmental justice. From a distribution angle, video used as evidence can lead to wider exposure by the media, by key decision-makers, and by the public because it is associated with high-profile or significant legal proceedings. For more information on using video in legal proceedings, see Chapter 6.

Case study: Community screenings, network distribution and D2D with *Operation Fine Girl: Rape Used as a Weapon of War in Sierra Leone.*
The *Operation Fine Girl* video was launched in January 2002. The video examines the use of rape and sexual assault during the decade-long civil war in Sierra Leone and includes powerful testimonies by survivors, as well as key political actors, human rights experts, and people involved in rehabilitation and support. The underlying advocacy goals were to ensure that gender-based crimes were considered in the transitional justice process, and that communities had an opportunity to begin to discuss what had happened to them. The people who spoke out in the film did so with the hope that their words would make a difference. When they were asked how they would like the film to be used, two of the people featured replied using some form of the phrase "*so people will see.*" Implicit in this is the idea that people will make up their own minds. As one of the young women, Fatmata, says:

> I would like you to show the tape to the international audience for them to see what really happened in Sierra Leone. Most of them have only heard about what happened, so this will make them see that we really suffered—but despite that we are strong and if we are given opportunities we will do better things in life.

Osman, a child-soldier who is featured in the film, hopes that telling his story will lead to understanding, and eventually forgiveness: "I want you to show the tape on TV so that people will see that even though we did bad things we are remorseful."

After an initial broadcast on cable television in the USA (WITNESS leveraged funds from Oxygen Television to produce the program) *Operation Fine Girl* was released in Sierra Leone in January 2002 in a screening to an audience of over 160 NGO representatives and members of the government that was introduced by the country's Attorney General. Word of the film spread quickly through the capital, Freetown, following several radio broadcasts highlighting the film.

More than 100 copies were distributed to national and some international NGOs in 2002 and 2003, and all the groups were encouraged to use it as a tool for further advocacy. Binta Mansaray, the film's associate producer and the local outreach coordinator, advised organizations on when, where and how to use tape for maximum impact, to draw attention to issues raised by the documentary, and to campaign for policies and programs that responded to the special needs of the victims/survivors. She arranged and led many screenings, often in open community settings with large audiences, and in some cases using a mobile generator and TV screen in remote or rural areas. Co-hosting was by a wide variety of organizations ranging from women's groups and investigators of the newly formed Sierra Leonean Truth and Reconciliation Commission (TRC), to schools and churches, women's groups and health clinics, and United Nations organizations.

Operation Fine Girl helped sensitize communities to the notion that women and girls did not voluntarily leave their families to join warring factions but were instead abducted and forced into sexual slavery. Seeing the stories of people like themselves gives community members an opportunity to start discussing their own experiences. Screenings of the film within communities also spurred former combatants and others to come forward with their own testimony about events during the war.

Audiences of up to 500 and 600 people have attended large-scale screenings in communities all over Sierra Leone. Responses range from shock, to tears of relief, to occasional comments that the events belong to the past and should no longer be discussed. But overwhelmingly audiences say that the film should be seen by as many people as possible.

Binta Mansaray also reached out to key personnel involved in the transitional justice process—including investigators of gender-based crimes and violations of child rights—for whom she coordinated screenings to sensitize them on the situation and to provide them with a training tool for others.

Operation Fine Girl was also used to sensitize traditional leaders responsible for administering customary laws that relate to gender issues. Changing attitudes among local leaders is critical, as customary laws promote community stigma and ostracize women who are raped and suffer sexual violence of any kind. In 2002, for example, the National Forum for Human Rights screened the tape for 33 traditional leaders in Kenema Town during its TRC sensitization. The leaders were shocked at the testimonies and said it was painful to watch what women went through. Some of them asked for additional copies to show to their community members.

Key allies and an important source of funding for the efforts in Sierra Leone are the international NGOs and multilateral institutions. The tape has been used as a powerful source of information for international partners to get a clear picture of what women and children went through during the war, including audiences in the UK, Canada, the US, and South Africa. The film's numerous international public screenings have included film festivals, international conferences, and major international media including *The Oprah Winfrey Show*, which aired a one-hour program on sexual violence against girls in Africa, which featured footage from *Operation Fine Girl* and interviews with guest speaker Naomi Wolf and Christiana Thorpe of FAWE, a leading women's rights organization in Sierra Leone featured in the film.

The *Operation Fine Girl* video was effective because the interviewees— everyday victims of the civil war—chose to speak out about the truth of their experience. They told candid personal stories of their own experience—similar to that of thousands of other people across Sierra Leone, yet a collective experience that had barely been discussed. In community screenings, audience members were then able to relate it to their own experience, and start talking about how to respond to sexual violence both as individuals and as a society, in a way that they would not have been able to if they had directly known the people featured in the film.

Another reason why film is so effective is that it reflects the larger process of truth-seeking. Viewers see and learn the names of the women; they also see and hear rebel and military officials confronted about the violence perpetrated by combatants. The inclusion of both perspectives—victim and perpetrator—strengthens the film's credibility and at the same time illustrates a process for uncovering the events of the war, determining responsibility, and preventing similar events from ever happening again.

Many women—and many men—have come forward to tell their stories after seeing *Operation Fine Girl*. Human rights groups were delighted with the three days of hearings of the Sierra Leonean Truth and Reconciliation Commission that were devoted to the war's impact on women and girls, including testimony by individuals, women's groups, NGOs, and international human rights monitors. An additional three days of hearings were devoted to children and youth.

BROADCAST DISTRIBUTION—RADIO AND TELEVISION

A distribution strategy for your film or video is essential. Although you have just completed your film, you're still only fifty percent done, if that. Now you have to find the best ways to distribute your film to the widest possible audience. Isn't that the point? It's of little use sitting on your shelf, so prepare yourself for an all-out distribution assault. (Paul Shore, Guerrilla News Network, an online activist video and media site)

Using broadcast media

The focus of this chapter has so far been on non-broadcast distribution methods of social justice documentaries. This section looks at broadcast distribution, and complements the information in Chapter 1.

Television documentaries

Submitting full-length documentaries to television broadcasters has been a traditional distribution method for socially motivated filmmakers for more than half a century. There have been some great success stories over the years for this method of distribution. Entire government departments have been established based on the notion of mass education through broadcast documentaries. In addition, in some countries, documentary-makers are paid for the right to distribute their work. This, of course, is helpful when raising funds for the next video project.

Many video advocates often think of an eventual TV broadcast—either of their completed video, or of footage they have shot—as the ultimate goal of producing video. However, this may not be the most practical goal, nor actually the place where your video will have the most impact.

Popular broadcast media has obvious advantages—it typically has a substantial, dedicated audience, and a single broadcast could reach millions of viewers simultaneously. Once production costs have been met, the video advocate has to pay little in the way of distribution costs (although it may be wise to invest in outreach around the broadcast), so this can be an extremely efficient means of spreading your message. It is also useful for raising general awareness of your organization and your issue, and changing the context of a political debate, as decision-makers often use mass media coverage as a measure of the standing of an organization, and of what issues matter to the public.

In practice, however, broadcast media distribute few videos explicitly made to bring about social change. This is because television (and radio stations) either:

- Have limited airtime
- Create their own programming about the subject at hand
- Fear alienating their viewers, governmental, or corporate sponsors by devoting airtime to controversial or critical perspectives
- Limit videos regarded as having an ulterior agenda
- Reject an advocate's video because its production values fail to meet station criteria, or standard formats
- Believe their audiences do not care about these issues

Indeed, research shows that in many markets around the world, the number of social issue documentaries on TV has been declining, even in places with public television mandates to cover topics of social concern. Additionally, most documentaries on television in Europe and the USA are commissioned programs rather than acquisitions. Rarely will a television program editor take a finished video from a grassroots filmmaker, particularly one with whom they have not worked previously.

Luckily, as we have discussed in this chapter, television and radio broadcast are not the only ways of spreading your message. Non-broadcast distribution methods can be more appropriate and more strategic in creating change. For example, one advantage of these distribution methods is that you can take your video directly to the audience of your choice, removing the editorial control of another group or organization.

If you do decide to try and produce a documentary for television you should research thoroughly a particular channel's guidelines for submission, assess the cost implications in terms of what you will have to deliver, and consider working with a professional who has experience in negotiating with television channels. Also be aware that television stations typically have standardized lengths and formats for programming. Check with the station you are approaching beforehand to confirm their standards, but the following will give you a starting point:

- Public service announcements (PSAs) are advertisements for issues, and run like standard commercials, usually 15–30 seconds in length. Sometimes, it is acceptable to make 45-second versions, and even up to one-minute versions.
- A half-hour television documentary usually runs for 24 minutes, which allows the station to include a minimum of two commercial breaks.
- "One-hour" documentaries run between 39 and 52 minutes, depending on how many minutes of commercials there are, and whether the station runs news on the hour.

Providing footage to television news

Although it is very hard to get completed documentaries broadcast on television, it is possible in some circumstances to get your footage used in news programs. The key to working with the mass media is contacts. The best approach is to develop good relationships with people who work within the mass media *before* you need to distribute video footage. You can do this by inviting them to events, introducing yourself to them at community meetings, and sending them briefing packs and press releases.

How do you know which journalists to contact? The best way is to watch television, read the papers and listen to the radio. Identify the journalists who cover your issue area and decide if their reporting is generally sympathetic to your way of thinking. Begin building up a contact list. This way you will have the names and telephone numbers ready to hand when you need them. Also tap into trusted networks and allies who may already maintain these kinds of media databases, and with whom you can share information.

Television news can play a major role in your work using video for change. In most countries, television news is the primary or secondary source of information for the public. The news broadcast can give a stamp of "objectivity" to issues that may be hard for activist groups to get, irrespective of the truth of their work. Most news stations are hungry for graphic video footage that accompanies news stories. And once one station picks up strong footage, other news channels are likely to follow suit. However, they are rarely looking for in-depth human rights or community-based stories that are missing the graphic element.

Around the world, human rights and social justice advocates have found they can supply raw footage to television news. Compared to documentary commissioning editors, news editors are usually more eager to take video advocate's footage than documentary commissioning editors. This is because (a) they have editorial control over the content, (b) they have a daily need for footage, and (c) the intake requirements are sometimes less tightly monitored than documentaries.

For example, Brazilian police were videotaped attacking, beating, and shooting 15 law-abiding citizens in a Sao Paulo shantytown. The 90-minute video shot by an independent cameraman, was sent to the national television station, Rede Globo. The images broadcast clearly show an officer hitting one of the men 39 times in eight minutes. As a result of the video, ten of the policemen were charged.

Another example is the footage shot by the Revolutionary Association of the Women of Afghanistan (RAWA) in Afghanistan. RAWA used hidden cameras to document women being executed at the Kabul city soccer stadium. The footage was smuggled out of the country and shown by news outlets around the world. This was, of course, a highly risky undertaking, and this method of creating and distributing advocacy video should be adopted only after exploring the potential risks to the safety of the videographers, those featured in the footage, and the transporters of the tapes. Review Chapter 2 for further information.

Video news releases (VNRs)

> The VNR is a press release in video format. So it says who, what, where, when, and why—very briefly. It is not a documentary or an exposé, or a report. It is designed to make it easy for reporters to cover your issue favorably, or at least cover your message. (Atossa Soltani, Executive Director and *de facto* publicist for Amazon Watch)

A typical way that advocacy groups work with television stations is by providing VNRs, which are short compilations of images and expert testimony relevant to a particular issue you believe the

Figure 7.2   Still of a child soldier in the Democratic Republic of Congo from the video *A Duty to Protect*, distributed worldwide via the internet (AJEDI-Ka/PES/WITNESS)

mainstream media will want to cover. They generally include three to five minutes of B-roll (additional relevant video images that can be used to edit into the material) and brief compelling interviews (ten- to 30-second sound bites) with experts or articulate spokespeople. These interviews should be presented with a separate titlecard including the interviewee's full name and position. Note that news stations don't want to see the titlecards superimposed on the image because they each have their own style regimens. That also goes for the B-roll, so titlecards come first, followed by the interview or image.

Remember that even a VNR requires time to produce and edit, and you should only expend the resources if you have evidence or confidence of the media's interest in your material. VNRs are most effective when they are timely, as for example when there is:

- An upcoming decision or vote on an issue
- A campaign (a boycott campaign, or consumer education, etc.)
- An event being publicized (e.g. "Come to Earth Day")
- An exposé (e.g. on a massacre in Colombia and the role of a US oil company)

- A position statement relating to a pending decision by legislators (e.g. "Why there should be no drilling in the Arctic")
- The launch of a new report, a new project, a new park, facility, vaccine, ad campaign, etc.

The message is the most important aspect of the VNR. After you watch it you should be able to walk away with one core message such as: "Oh, I get it: The group does not want tax dollars to fund the destruction of this tribe or place," or, "More military aid to Colombia is going to increase human rights abuses, so Congress should reject more military aid." If you choose to use a narrator, the narrator should sound as credible as the people interviewed. The tone should be more like a news report than an activist presentation.

Challenges of supplying footage to TV news

- News editors have in the past given video advocate footage to police/authorities, which may endanger the videographer or the subjects, depending upon the context
- News programs will normally use only a small amount of footage (maybe only 15 seconds)
- News programs may misrepresent the story
- News programs are normally only interested in highly graphic and dramatic footage (violence, protests, destruction, arrests)

There are a number of issues you need to decide before going down the television news road:

- What story or issue do *you* want covered?
- Do you have connections in television news? Who do you know in television news?
- Will TV stations take "freelance" or "independent" footage (or footage from NGOs or human rights organizations)?
- Do you have the agreement of your subjects to broadcast their interviews? Under what constraints?
- What part of your story will TV news editors be interested in? Is the story interesting enough for TV broadcast? Is it of good enough quality? Does it contain footage that is typical of the news program? Is it something they cannot film themselves?
- Will the television broadcast help or hinder your campaign? Issues to consider here: do you trust the broadcaster to frame the

issue fairly or supportively? Will the agency of your organization or the community involved be highlighted? Is your tape safe with the TV station?

- How will you get your tape to the television station? What format do they accept (most will not take VHS)? They typically prefer DV standard or higher.
- Will they return it? Will they hand it to the police?
- How will you guarantee that the footage is not used in contexts you have not agreed to? You may need to use a licensing form that delineates a legal contract.

Eight tips for providing footage to TV news

1. Edit your footage, and make it more user-friendly
2. Advertise your footage through web page and email alerts
3. Make your footage available to the communities where you filmed—don't forget about them
4. Label the tape clearly with your name and address for return delivery
5. Include a basic fact sheet about what the story was about—a press release often works
6. Include a rough list of the contents of the tape, in order of action, with approximate times, including the names of all those interviewed, with their titles and, if needed, their organizations. The station will then be able to scan the written summary for potential footage of interest.
7. Include a letter or contract with the terms of your agreement for broadcast, and ask for payment for your footage. It is a useful way to raise money *and* the footage will be treated with more respect. Consider enclosing a proposed license outlining available uses. Is it available free of charge, or for a fee? Do you have all the necessary consents, releases and rights to be able to license the material? Are you offering it for multiple use, for an unlimited period of time, or do you want to limit the period? Are you offering exclusivity or is it a non-exclusive license?
8. If you want the station to work with you in the future, make sure your material is accurate, contains no slander or libel, and is of high quality, interesting for the viewer, and topical.

Outreach in coordination with broadcast

Remember that your work is just beginning once you have a commitment from a broadcaster to do a story or to air your documentary video; to take maximum advantage of a broadcast, you must have a plan in place to capitalize on a forthcoming broadcast. For example, when the national US broadcaster ABC's *Primetime Live* program agreed to produce and air a 12-minute segment on Gillian

Caldwell's investigation into trafficking women from the former Soviet Union (discussed in Chapter 1), she alerted allies within the US Department of State who had the ear of the Secretary of State. She knew that the broadcast would precede the Secretary's visit to the Prime Minister of Israel—and hoped that since the broadcast focused on trafficking from Ukraine to Israel that she might be able to get trafficking on the agenda for the visit. Sure enough, the broadcast resulted in a request from the Secretary's office for talking points, and the topic of trafficking made its way on to the agenda of a top-level bilateral meeting.

Another example of ways to capitalize on a mainstream media broadcast is to use it to drive viewers to your website to take action on what they have learned about. WITNESS worked closely with producers of the internationally televised *The Oprah Winfrey Show* to provide video for a program on sexual slavery in Africa. As part of the licensing contract to provide the videotape at reduced rates to the program, they negotiated for an onscreen and Oprah-narrated reference to the WITNESS website. Then on the WITNESS homepage, they created an online action resource for people tuning in after *Oprah* to capitalize on their momentum and desire for engagement.

A third pre-broadcast strategy is to network and encourage house parties when you know a broadcast important to your issues is scheduled to take place. Be sure that your house party host volunteers are equipped with background information and concrete calls to action so that they can ask their visitor viewers to get involved on the spot.

The web can be a great location to provide further information and provide ways to act in locations where Internet access is widespread. In the US, programs produced for public television often have extensive websites that are worth looking at as examples. For further resources on off-broadcast outreach and lessons learned (in the US, but potentially applicable elsewhere), visit <www.mediarights.org>.

Community television alternatives

There are a number of alternative television distribution strategies. They range from managing a program on community television to owning a television station itself! Some of the benefits of this option include:

- High degree of editorial control

- Building a long-term institution that can serve all the diverse issues of a community
- Becoming a forum and a focus for the community

Running a community program

Many communities around the world manage social justice programs on their local television stations. This happens in much the same way as an independent producer would provide a documentary to a traditional television broadcaster or make a regular series. The great advantage of this approach is that you don't have to worry about running a television station.

One of the lessons learnt from cable access television in the US, which had no quality control, was that the poor programming attracted a near-zero audience. However, it is also true that niche programs on cable can have a very strong and loyal following. As with a community screening, a committed, even if small, cable access audience may be useful.

Running a community station

The second, far more ambitious option is to establish your own television distribution station. This gives the great prize of controlling your own schedule. Of course, the problem is that you must first find a way to establish your operation (which may or may not require governmental approval). Many countries will not give permits for community television. And if they do, they often limit what can and cannot be broadcast.

You must also raise the considerable resources to maintain your operation. A small, low-powered community TV station has a start-up cost of anywhere between $10,000 and $200,000 (including transmitter, camera kits, edit suite, playback). And then you must cover the annual running costs (staff, tape-stock, electricity, repairs, telephone, rent etc.).

One of the burdens of owning your own television station is that you must fill the airtime every day, every week, every year. This must be balanced by the need to attract an audience to your programming.

The trick, therefore, is to fill the airtime with programming that is going to appeal to your audience and that you can afford over a long period of time, and to mix this with material created to support your advocacy or social change goals. One solution to this is to mix acquired programming (attractive shows that other people have made) on a low-cost basis, with programming that you have made by yourself.

The great advantage of low-powered television is that the social organization owns the broadcast distribution itself. For example, the Kurds in northern Iraq ran their own low-powered television network after the First Gulf War in 1991. At first this was a low-tech operation. Recently, as funding has increased, the Kurds have been able to distribute a great amount of high-quality programming. This television network has been key to building the sense of community within Northern Iraq and unifying the region around certain issues.

Case study: Soap opera—using fiction for social change advocacy

A feminist group in Nicaragua called Puntos de Encuentro wanted to use media advocacy to address some of the post-revolution social problems in the country. First, they created a newsletter called *Boletina*, which spread like wildfire through the countryside. The newsletters became famous for running political stories directly beside readers' favorite recipes. Then Puntos de Encuentro turned to radio, with hit programs about social issues affecting women.

Soon they began considering television. They decided to create a soap opera called *Sexto Sentido* that would run every Sunday afternoon. It is a fictional series—which they describe as a "politically correct" version of the American sitcom, *Friends*. The show follows the lives of six young people living in a section of Managua.

Amy Bank, executive director of the show, points out:

> Our TV show is the centrepiece of a multi-pronged advocacy strategy. It's not just a TV show for the sake of a TV show. We want to reach a national level audience. It's a fairly sophisticated organizational strategy, with the newsletter and the radio. The TV show is the hook to get people interested in the issues... The advantage of an episodic soap opera is that it allows you to make the problem much more complex. There are no neat solutions in half an hour. No instant solutions. The situation can stay complex, and the problem can deepen—like in real life. You have to trust the audience.

After they air each episode, all week long, they program related material on the radio show, linking in to the relevant issues. "It's a powerful way to address human rights, creating characters that through daily life confront conflicts and find remedies," says Liz Miller, who made a documentary about the project. "They engage in the daily practice of exercising human rights."

Amy insists:

> what we do is advocacy, but it's important not to preach. We have a point of view, we have a distinct way of seeing the world, but we try and focus and making people relate to the characters. Minds don't open with one TV show, but it can spark dialogue, and that's what we're trying to do. Real social changes are a long-term messy process.

Radio networks

Strange as it may seem, radio can provide an excellent forum for distributing video footage. Radio stations typically have smaller budgets than television stations and are often looking for good sources for stories. They also have the advantage of reaching a number of new audiences—the "captive audience" of car commuters in urban areas, as well as people in rural or remote areas, which may not have good television coverage, and where people are unable to afford a television.

You will be providing the audio track only to the stations. Therefore, they will be looking for high-quality sound recording, descriptions of surroundings, background sounds, and interesting interviews. They will not be interested in footage that relies heavily on the visual component.

When providing footage to radio stations, you can simply take your camera to their edit suites and copy the audio track to one of their audio recorders. Bring along your cables in case they don't have ones that fit your camera sockets.

Make sure you sign a license agreement with the station (similar to television agreement above). This will limit their use of your audio recordings, and it will also detail if you are to be paid or not.

DISTRIBUTION USING THE INTERNET

Over the past ten years or so, the Internet has become a powerful tool to advance advocacy initiatives across the globe, despite unequal access to technology worldwide. From women's groups in Afghanistan to news portals in Dubai, it is now possible to distribute video on the Internet. The global network of Indymedia sites has demonstrated the democratic potential of the Internet to become a space for expression for many.

For video advocates with access to limited Internet equipment, there still remain some important distribution opportunities for your work.

Strengths of Internet/web distribution

- *Mass audience*: The Internet can be a mass media outlet. You can reach a large number of people who have access to the Internet with little effort. From an online audience you can also generate an offline audience, as the MoveOn.org example above (p. 248) shows.
- *Global exposure*: Theoretically, people around the world will be able to access the material.
- *Targeted*: You can build up a database of people who are interested in your work, who can then be informed quickly of new material online and action they can take. This then becomes essential to mobilization and fundraising.
- *Low-cost*: The Internet can be cheap, compared to similar mass media distribution outlets. These costs may depend on if you are being charged for the server and to stream video.
- *Quick distribution*: You don't have to wait for an organization to distribute your material. You can do it yourself, immediately.
- *International distribution*: Via email, it costs the same to email someone in the next-door village as to another country. This is very useful for international networking.
- *Viral potential*: An email link to an appealing or compelling video is often forwarded on to others. On the web, an email to thirty people, who each send the email to thirty people, who each send an email to another thirty people, who send to another thirty people, etc., would eventually reach one million people.

Choosing an Internet-based strategy: Your material, your capacity and your audience

The Internet is NOT a good distribution strategy for everyone. Before you use this strategy answer the following questions

- Does your target audience have access to the Internet? Is it familiar with using the Internet? Is their access fast enough to watch video?

- Does your material work for the Internet? Review the guidelines in Chapter 3 on what works well for the Internet.
- Do you have the ability to put video on the Internet? Will your Internet service provider accept your footage? How much will they charge to stream it?
- Is there an effective way to take action or mobilize people using the Internet? If you are going to use an e-action format, will you need to pay for it in order to use an efficient system?
- Is there a better strategy for reaching your audience? Consider creating a flash video, for example, which can accommodate much slower bandwidth.

If you do decide to stream video online:

- Pick a technical format and stick with it, so viewers will return and not have to get new software.
- Make sure that your Internet service provider will not take out, edit or reject any controversial content. If possible, establish your own streaming server.

It is also useful to know that some organizations dedicate themselves to the distribution and publicizing of grassroots, alternative, progressive, and human rights videos via the Internet. For more information, see the Resources chapter.

Case study: Broadband-based mobilization in South Korea
by M.J. Kim, Korea Daewoo Workers Video Collective
South Korea has the highest level of broadband Internet access in the world. Labour unions have utilized this to broadcast meetings and actions live to their members.

On April 10, 2001, several hundred workers of Daewoo who had struggled against mass layoffs two months before gathered together in front of the factory gate to enter the union office located inside the factory. They had got a warrant from the court that they had the right to use the union office space and marched peacefully. Suddenly, the riot police attacked the workers and violently beat them. On the spot, there was one cameraperson who was a member of Daewoo workers' video collective and he shot every detail of this incident (see <http://dwtubon.nodong.net/english/>).

Figure 7.3   South Korean video activists in action
(Labor News Production)

Immediately, people around the country came to the website and saw how the government was violently oppressing the workers—most of whom were seriously wounded and some paralyzed. This incident and the subsequent Internet webcast had a real impact on the politics of the day and people's attitude towards the government.

MULTI-PURPOSING AND SEQUENCING

An advocacy campaign can develop and implement several distribution strategies for the same video—"multi-purposing" an investment in video for maximum effect. Often, these different distribution approaches complement one another.

An important facet of distributing the video to multiple target audiences is "sequencing." This is the strategy of using the momentum or attention generated by one successful distribution method to open·

the doors to further distribution. For example, a legal decision may generate attention that can be leveraged into a television broadcast, which may then give the opportunity to hold a private screening with senior government decision-makers in which they are convinced to take action.

Case study: Behind the Labels

Here is an in-depth example to show you how this process can work. The example is *Behind the Labels: Garment Workers on US Saipan*, a 45-minute documentary produced by Tia Lessin for WITNESS and Oxygen Television in the US. The video tells how, lured by false promises and driven by desperation, thousands of Chinese and Filipina women pay high fees to work in garment factories on the pacific island of Saipan—a US territory exempt from normal minimum wage laws—and about the labor and human rights abuses they are subjected to on the island. There was an unusual element to Oxygen's involvement. Unlike the majority of television documentaries, they actively encouraged the film to be developed with an advocacy audience and usage in mind.

Figure 7.4   Global protests against sweatshops from *Behind the Labels* (Oxygen Television LLC/WITNESS)

There were multiple change objectives for the film including:

- Pressuring the US Congress to take more legislative action.
- Building consumer pressure on Gap and other clothing retailers to settle a lawsuit related to the situation in Saipan.
- Providing a more general campaign and educational tool for groups working to curb sweatshops globally.

The distribution strategy employed by this campaign is described in Table 7.3, showing how the project unfolds, the audience changes, and the campaign builds.

The *Behind the Labels* video was part of a campaign led by Global Exchange and United Students Against Sweatshops, and including UNITE!, AFL-CIO, WITNESS and other groups that resulted in major clothing company, Gap and other manufacturers settling workers rights claims in a landmark lawsuit. Workers received back pay and damages from a $20 million settlement fund and an independent factory-monitoring program is getting underway. Legislation in the US Congress is stalled at the time of writing, in the face of strong opposition from powerful politicians with links to the garment industry.

Five tips for sequencing and multi-purposing

1. Plan your distribution strategy before you start production. Work out which distribution strategies will build on others. Which strategy should you carry out first?
2. Contact your key allies as early as possible. Involve them in the process and ask their advice.
3. Be flexible—things don't always go according to plan.
4. If you see a new distribution opportunity, take it!
5. Remember, distribution is about having an impact on a targeted audience.

Bearing all these ideas in mind, I hope you will be able to use and learn from the ideas, case studies and experiences in this chapter, and develop your own effective distribution strategy.

Taken together, the tools we've provided in this book should help take you down the road to successful video advocacy. With good planning, careful production, effective and ethical editing, and strategic distribution you can achieve the change you seek. Good luck!

Table 7.3　*Behind the Labels* distribution

Target audience	Action sought	Method of distribution	Timing
General public, particularly in the USA	Direct viewers to online advocacy campaign, lobbying legislators in the US to take action to reform the situation, and asking garment manufacturers to improve conditions	Broadcast television in USA and in Australia	First eight months of campaign
Solidarity and activist groups in the US working on sweatshop, labor and human rights issues	Take part in protest and letter writing campaign to pressure companies involved in legal action on Saipan to settle, and US government to enforce existing law and implement new legislation	Community screenings around the country, with supporting materials to facilitate taking action in protests, and letter-writing. Video embedded in existing campaign, and complementing other advocacy. Also screenings hosted by key allies and leadership of community allies	First eight months of campaign, with community screenings focused on one week in lead-up to Congressional screening
Law-makers in Washington, DC	US government to enforce existing law, and implement new legislation. Put pressure on companies involved in lawsuit	Face-to-face meetings, and screening of film hosted by speaker with personal experience of conditions	After community screenings around country
General public in US	Contribute to global campaigns to raise awareness on sweatshops	Broadcast television and film festivals in US. Via distribution to 300+ libraries in the USA with screening packs	During initial broadcast of the video, and in years 2 and 3 after production of video
General public globally, as well as anti-sweatshop advocates in Asia	Contribute to global campaigns to raise awareness on sweatshops	Via translation into Chinese language version for use in China, and broadcast and film festival distribution in Australia, Israel, across Europe, and in other countries	In years 2, 3 and 4 after production of video

Glossary

Assembly—A rough ordering of clips prepared at an early stage of editing.

B-roll—Additional (non-interview) footage, which will serve to complement interviews and help tell your story. In any filming situation you should always be looking to gather images/footage relevant to the story—e.g. if an interviewee is talking about life in a refugee camp you would take shots of the living conditions, of people working, of people preparing meals, of the conditions in the schools. These will be used to "cover" (i.e. provide visuals while someone speaks) both interviews and narration.

Bracketing—Holding the shots in the beginning and end of a camera move to provide a range of different options in editing.

Burnt-in timecode—See **timecode**.

Close-up (abbr. CU)—A shot framing with the subject of the shot very large in the frame, revealing a detail only (i.e. the human face, or hands).

Crabbing—The slightly crouching movement made by the camera operator when filming (and moving) sideways.

Cut—In editing, the point where one shot ends and the next begins. Edited films are made mostly of "straight cuts" but may also include different kinds of **fade** and **dissolve**, as well as special effect transitions such as **flips** and **wipes**.

Cutaway—A cutaway is a shot that the camera "cuts away" to from an interview or dominant scene, to allow for explanation of the character and the context of their story, or to "cover" edits and help to build a sequence. A cutaway is usually a detail of the scene that is not visible in the preceding or subsequent shot—in the case of an interview it could be the character's hands, say, or the face of a person listening. Or, for example, if someone is talking about a gold mine in an interview, you may use cutaways of the goldmine while the audio of the interview continues underneath.

Dissolve—A gradual merging of the end of one shot and the beginning of another produced by the superimposition of a fade-out onto a fade-in of equal length.

Establishing shot—A shot used near the beginning of a scene to establish the interrelationship and context of elements to be shown subsequently in closer shots. Also termed a **general view** (abbr. GV), which is an establishing shot that places you in the environment. It is often a wide shot of an exterior of a building or of the location the scene is about to take us into next, and is also used as a transition shot from one location to another alongside music or narration.

Exposure—The amount of light allowed through the lens.

Extreme close-up (abbr. ECU or XCU)—A shot framing in very close to the subject (closer than would be necessary for a close-up), revealing extreme detail (e.g. part of the human face).

Fade-in—A gradual appearance of an image from black (or another color) or gradual increase of audio levels to audibility.

Fade-out—A gradual transition of an image to black (or some other color, known as a fade-to-black, fade-to-white etc.), or gradual reduction of audio levels to inaudibility.

Fine cut—An edit stage after you've made all the changes stemming from the rough cut stage. At this point the focus is on fine-tuning cuts, timing, and shot choices.

Firewire cable—The cable (technically known as an IEE94 cable) used to transfer digital data from a camera to computer, camera to camera, or computer to computer.

General view (GV)—see **establishing shot**

Headroom—The space above someone's head in a shot.

Hose piping—The term used for "roaming" camera work where the camera indiscriminately moves like an eye, and is largely uneditable.

Iris—The eye of the lens, which opens and closes, and decides and controls the exposure.

Jump cut—A jarring **cut**, which breaks the continuity of time by jumping forward from one part of an action to another, without substantially changing the angle or size of shot or the location of the subject within the frame. For example, you use one section of an interview, and then you cut to a different part of the same interview still at the same angle. The person will "jump" in the transition. Often jump cuts are "covered" by **cutaways** to make the transition look smoother, though they can also be used for effect.

Log—A list with details of audio and visual content of all the shots on a tape of footage.

Long shot (abbr. LS)—A shot framed so that the subject and their surroundings can be seen. Often the long shot serves as an **establishing shot**.

Medium close-up (abbr. MCU)—A shot between a medium shot and a close-up (e.g. a human figure taken from the chest up).

Medium shot (abbr. MS)—A shot between a long shot and a medium close-up (e.g. a human figure taken from the waist up).

Montage—(1) The juxtaposition of seemingly unrelated shots or scenes, which, when combined, achieve meaning (as in, shot A and shot B together give rise to a third idea, which is then supported by shot C, and so on); or (2) A series of related shots that lead the viewer to a desired conclusion (as in, shot A leads to shot B leads to shot C... leads to shot X; shot X being the outcome of the sequence).

NTSC—There are two different video standards: NTSC or PAL. Cameras record in this format, and televisions and VCRs are equipped to play back in a particular standard unless they are multi-standard. In general, NTSC is used in the Americas and a few African and Asian countries, while PAL is used elsewhere. Brazil uses a PAL variant known as PAL-M. SECAM is an older standard, which has generally been replaced by PAL.

Omni-directional microphone—A microphone that is equally receptive to audio from all directions.

PAL—see **NTSC**.

Pan—To turn the camera left to right or right to left on a horizontal axis.

Paper edit—The process and result of ordering sections of a text script in the order that you intend to edit them together into a rough cut of the video.

Point of view (abbr. POV)—Point of view (sometimes given with hyphens) describes the perspective from which a video is being told. It is also a term for a shot taken from a person's point of view (as if in their shoes).

Postproduction—The filmmaking process after shooting, including logging/transcribing, the paper edit, and the editing process including assembly, rough and fine cuts, and outputting of a final video.

Preproduction—This stage includes preparing and researching an outline, initial script and a shooting plan, logistical planning (budget, schedule etc.) and fundraising.

Production—The period of time when a video is shot.

Rough cut—The first assembly of a film, which the editor prepares from selected takes, in script order, leaving the finer points of timing and editing to a later stage.

Scene—Action that occurs in one location at one time.

Sequence—Series of shots that fit together to encapsulate a particular idea or action.

Shooting plan/schedule—The document, written in advance of the shoot, that details who/what is being shot, when, where, and how.

Shotgun mike—A directional microphone that attaches to the top of the camera.

Shotlist—The list of shots a filmmaker knows in advance he/she will want to film on location.

Storyboard—A series of sketches of the shots in a sequence.

Streaming video—A series of video files sent in compressed form over the Internet, then uncompressed and played by a computer's media player as it arrives.

Tilt—A shot movement tilting the camera up or down.

Timecode—A special track on videotape that marks each video frame with a unique numerical value so that editing systems find and track footage precisely. Each frame of video will have a timecode in the format HH:MM:SS:FF (Hour:Minute:Second:Frame). With a **burnt-in timecode** this number is part of the visible image of the tape and appears on the screen as you play back the tape.

Title—Onscreen writing overlaid on a picture (or against a black background).

Tracking—A shot that follows a moving subject by having the camera move with the subject.

Uni-directional microphone—A microphone that is most receptive to sound coming from a particular direction.

VCR (Video Cassette Recorder)—Machine that plays and records videotapes.

Verité—Observational footage of activities and "life happening in front of the lens," which the camera observes with no or little perceived interference into what is occurring. Also known as **observational/actuality**.

White balance—A function on a video camera, which is set to make sure that colors are represented accurately. It is set by pointing the camera at something that is pure white and pressing a white balance button for a few seconds.

Wide shot (abbr. WS)—A shot that shows the full context of a scene. Similar to an **establishing shot**, but used more integrally within a sequence rather than at the beginning of the scene.

Wipe—A type of transition from one shot to another. The image wipes across the screen like a blind or curtain.

Wireless microphone—A microphone that is not attached directly to the camera, but sends audio from a remote microphone and transmitter to a receiver attached to the camera.

Zoom—Increasing or decreasing the magnification of a lens, making it look as though you are getting closer/further away (zooming in/zooming out).

Resources

ON SAFETY AND SECURITY

1. **The Committee to Protect Journalists** is an independent, nonprofit organization founded in 1981. It promotes press freedom worldwide by defending the right of journalists to report the news without fear of reprisal. It publishes an excellent safety manual for journalists ("On Assignment: Covering Conflict Safely"), downloadable at no charge on the Committee's website, as well as a manual about journalists working in areas of "sustained risk."

To report attacks against journalists, or to review previous cases, contact:

330 7th Ave., 12th floor
New York NY 10001 USA
Tel: +1 212-465-1004
Fax: +1 212-465-9568
<www.cpj.org>

2. **Reporters Sans Frontières**
To report attacks against journalists, or to review previous cases, you can also contact:

Reporters Sans Frontières
5, rue Geoffrey-Marie
75009 Paris, France
Tel: +33 1 44-83-84-84
Fax: +33 1 45-23-11-51
<www.rsf.org>

3. The Brussels-based **International Federation of Journalists** publishes a useful safety manual <ifj.org/hrights/safetymanual.html>

4. The **International Committee of the Red Cross** helps detainees in conflicts, including journalists. The main number in Geneva, Switzerland is +41 22 734-6001. The emergency after-hours number is +41 79 217-3204.

5. The **Rory Peck Trust** promotes the work, safety, and security of freelance media workers in news and current affairs broadcasting worldwide. The Trust subsidizes training in hostile environments for freelancers, advises them on insurance, and provides financial support to the families of those killed or seriously injured during the course of their work.

The Rory Peck Trust
7 Southwick Mews,
London W2 1JG, UK
Tel: +44 (20) 7 262 5272
Fax: +44 (20) 7 262 2162

6. The **Dart Center** is a global network of journalists, journalism educators, and health professionals dedicated to improving media coverage of trauma, conflict, and tragedy. The Center also addresses the consequences of such coverage for those working in journalism.

Dart Center for Journalism & Trauma
Department of Communication
102 Communications Bldg.
Box 353740
University of Washington
Seattle, Washington 98195-3740 (USA)
Tel: +1 206 616-3223
Fax: +1 206 543-9285
<info@dartcenter.org> <www.dartcenter.org>

7. **Human Rights Watch** (HRW) is one of the world's most important and influential human rights advocacy organizations. In certain cases, HRW may be able to offer solidarity and support on the ground, with international awareness.

350 Fifth Avenue, 34th floor
New York, NY 10118-3299 USA
Tel: +1 212 290-4700
Fax: +1 212 736-1300
<www.hrw.org>

8. **Amnesty International** (AI) is a worldwide campaigning movement that works to promote internationally recognized human rights. In certain cases, AI may be able to offer solidarity and support.

Amnesty International—International Secretariat
1 Easton Street
London, WC1X 0DW, UK
Tel: +44 20 7413 5500
Fax: +44 20 7956 1157
<www.amnesty.org>

9. **Privaterra** is an organization that trains human rights and social justice groups on electronic security.
<www.privaterra.org>

WEB RESOURCES FOR EDITING AND ADVOCACY

WITNESS <www.witness.org>
The following information is available from WITNESS. Copies can be downloaded at <www.witness.org/training> or ordered at <www.witness.org/store>:

- "Video for Change"
- "Tips and Techniques"

Amazon Watch (USA) <www.amazonwatch.org>

Chiapas Media Project <www.chiapasmediaproject.org>

Chicago Video Project <www.chicagovideo.org>

Freespeech TV (USA) <www.freespeechtv.org>

Guerrilla News Network <www.gnn.tv>

The **Independent Media Center ("Indymedia")** <www.indymedia.org> is a network of collectively run media outlets for the creation of radical, accurate, and passionate tellings of the truth. We work out of a love and inspiration for people who continue to work for a better world, despite corporate media's distortions and unwillingness to cover the efforts to free humanity.

MediaRights <www.mediarights.org> a nonprofit organization, helps media makers, educators, librarians, nonprofits, and activists use documentaries to encourage action and inspire dialogue on contemporary social issues

OneWorld <www.oneworld.org>

Undercurrents <www.undercurrents.org>

Video Activist Network <www.videoactivism.org>

Working Films <www.workingfilms.org> is a national organization that links independent documentary filmmaking with community education, organizing, and direct action to support social, economic, and civil justice.

Appendix I
WITNESS Video Action Plan

Organization Name:
Your Name:
Your Position:

Date:

This is a version of the WITNESS Video Action Plan (VAP) – a questionnaire designed to assist our partners in developing a plan to integrate video into their human rights advocacy work. This VAP should guide you through the process of thinking about the advocacy tactics, logistical preparations, skills, and the visual literacy required to successfully create a video advocacy project. It should be used as a starting point for thinking through a project, as well as setting realistic expectations and timelines to successfully meet your goals.

For guidance in filling out this document, please refer to the following documents:
- WITNESS training materials at www.witness.org/training.

Finally, please note that the tables and charts throughout this document are meant as a guide. You need not use them if you'd prefer to write/print on a separate sheet of paper.

PART 1: Overall Video Advocacy Framework

Outline of Objectives and Audience

Remember, the most successful video advocacy is generally implemented to support a specific campaign where video is strategically and tactically used in tandem with other advocacy activities and tools such as written reports, briefings, events etc., and in support of a specific, defined advocacy objective.

1) Across your organization, what are your key advocacy objectives and the tactics you will use to pursue them over the next two years? Are there specific key advocacy events of relevance to your objectives? If so, please list them, and note why they are important.

OBJECTIVE	ADVOCACY TACTIC	KEY EVENTS	NAMES AND DUTIES OF PEOPLE INVOLVED	OTHER NGOs OR STAKEHOLDERS INVOLVED IN THIS PROJECT
1.				
2.				
3.				

285

4.

5.

6.

2) Please expand on what are the specific objectives for change in policy and practice that your video will advocate for. Be specific on how you would know if you had been successful in achieving these objectives. Note that you can have both primary and secondary objectives. Add additional rows to the table as needed.

SPECIFIC POLICY OR CHANGE OBJECTIVE	MEASURE OF SUCCESS?
1.	
2.	
3.	
4.	

3) For your video project, who are your audiences? Audiences should have the ability to influence your advocacy objectives, either directly or indirectly. Please list in the table specific organizations and/or individuals you would target for distribution.

Use the guide of possible types of audiences below, but feel free to add any audiences that you feel are relevant to your issue.

TYPE OF AUDIENCE	LOCAL	NATIONAL	REGIONAL	INTERNATIONAL
Courts, tribunals and other judicial bodies				
Legislative and Executive bodies				
Human rights bodies, Commissions, Special rapporteurs, Working groups, etc.				
Key decision-makers with influence on human rights issues (financial institutions, corporations, aid agencies, etc.)				
NGOs, solidarity groups and community-based organizations				
Press and media (including television, internet and radio)				
General public				
Other?				

4) Please analyze your audiences, ranked in order of significance, in the table below. Use the example provided in the table as a guide.

AUDIENCE	ACTION SOUGHT	AWARENESS	PERSPECTIVE	MESSAGE	STORY/VOICES	DISTRIBUTION
What is the specific audience (individual, group) that you want to reach?	What do you want this audience to do? (please relate to objectives for change in question 2)	Audience's current level of awareness of issue	Audience perspective on issue (negative, neutral, positive etc.)	What you are trying to convey to this audience so that they will take action?	What story and what people in a video will persuade or move your audience to action?	How and when would you reach this audience? Is there a strategic moment to reach this audience? (e.g. via public/private screenings, legal hearings, conferences, direct contact, the mass media). Be as specific as possible with dates and opportunities.
Senegalese President	*Financial and policy commitment to support landmine victims*	*High, we have been doing a lot of advocacy work directed at the Senegalese government on behalf of landmine victims*	*Neutral but no policy/legislation or action has been made to assist these victims*	*You have the ability to provide support to landmine victims by adequately funding support services.*	*The human impact of landmines, the urgency of the need to assist victims and the illegality of non-assistance. Voices of victims, as well as informed neutral experts recommending action.*	*Via a private screening on December 12, 2004 organized with other NGOs in our anti-landmines coalition.*

5) What length, stylistic approach and language do you think will be optimal for your primary audience? If you are choosing to target multiple audiences, will these require a different language, length or style of video? If so, please give details.

6) What other organizations, networks and alliances have you worked with, or do you plan to work with in this video advocacy campaign? Please describe how you have worked with them in the past or envision working with them.

7) Are there any security risks associated with filming and then widespread dissemination of the video footage outside or within the country, either for the person who has filmed the footage or the people featured in the video? If so, please elaborate.

8) Please list any existing or in-progress videos or documentaries related to your advocacy focus. How will the video project that your organization proposes add to this video material? What can you learn from existing videos about what you want to include and what you want to avoid? Please be specific in naming any videos that exist, or indicate if there is no current related video material.

9) How has the media portrayed the issue (if at all)? Has that helped or hindered your advocacy strategy? How would you want the approach of your video to be different?

PART 2: Planning the Video

Strategy: Message, Story and Storyteller

1) Write a paragraph that describes the story that viewers will see in your video. This should not be a summary of the video's message or an analysis, but a description of how you visualize the story unfolding.

Two examples would be:

– "In the Casamance region of Senegal we see a fertile, prosperous city and countryside contrasted to the plight of landmine victims. We follow the lives of four landmine victims of differing ages, genders and social classes, each of whom is trying to continue living and working. They explain the lack of medical assistance, and the socio-economic and psychological effects of landmines on their lives. Their personal experiences are reinforced through expert interviews, culminating in an appeal, voiced by the victims, to the government and the international community to meet their obligations to provide assistance to victims of landmines, cease the use of landmines and to de-mine the region, as is stipulated under the Mine Ban Treaty to which Senegal is a signatory."

– "First we see images of the offensive by the Burmese military government that took place at the end of 2004, and then the continuing life of the villagers in the war zone in 2005, in which they are always faced with the fears and possible threats. They stay in small groups near their fields, living in temporary homes, and avoiding their villages in the plains. They have limited food, access to healthcare and education, and security. Villagers of all ages as well as children show us how they live, talk about their experiences and personal stories, and talk about their hopes and fears, and hopes and fears for their children. The video shows the continuing insecurity faced by people, and that additional support is needed for internally displaced people in Burma, as well as pressure on the government to stop attacks on these people."

Think visually and verbally – every word should describe something you see in the video.

2) Among the messages you identified in your Audience chart, what will be the most important messages of the video?

3) Who can tell your story most compellingly for your audience? Remember that compelling and memorable individual, personal stories are part of most powerful videos and stories, and that an "expert" interview may give credibility and help

elaborate nuanced legal or policy obligations. You may consider how you would tell "both sides of the story" or explain why this is infeasible or ill advised. Consider that 'who' tells the story can also include the narrator.

4) If you plan to use a narrator in the film, who would be your first choice of narrator and how will you get access to this person? Narrators can play a very useful role in helping to structure the film, and fill in the gaps in information. However, for some audiences, narration may be perceived to be manipulative or indicative of a particular point of view/opinion. Issues to consider in the choice of narration include credibility of the narrator, gender, national origin, celebrity recognition and their availability/accessibility etc. In the event that this person may not be available to provide narration for the video, please also draft a list of other potential narrators.

PART 3: The Pre-production, Production and Post-production process.

There are essentially three phases of film-making: pre-production, production and post-production. In this section, you will explore the fundamental character of each of these phases and begin to think about how your video advocacy plan translates into an actual video. Pre-production includes researching the issue at hand, fleshing out the themes to be explored, preparing outlines for what you want to cover in your video, making logistical arrangements and fundraising. During the production phase, the filming will take place. At the postproduction phase the footage (video material shot) will be logged, transcribed and edited into videos appropriate for the target audience(s). [Logs are written details about the footage on each tape and include descriptions on the location, length, visual and audio content of shots. Transcripts are detailed notes of the content of each tape.]

Pre-Production and Production

1) What questions and background research will you need to address before shooting? Common key questions are noted below, and you should include additional ones that are relevant to your specific organization and video advocacy plan.

Questions	Required Research/Notes
1. What are the security risks for people appearing in the film if it is shown locally/regionally/internationally?	
2. What kind of consent document will you require of people filmed?	

3. What permissions will you need to film in different locations where you would like to film?	
4. Are there any rules of submission for video at venues where you plan to show the video for your target audience?	
5. How will you identify additional funding for the video production and distribution?	
6.	

2) What is your organization's policy on security and on consent as it relates to people interviewed or filmed for your human rights documentation?

3) What are the audio and visual components that you hope to include in the video? Please use the list in the Appendix to this Video Action Plan as a guide.

a) Existing Materials
NOTE: Archive video and photo material, as well as music, can be difficult and expensive to license.

WHAT IS THE MATERIAL?	HOW WILL YOU OBTAIN ACCESS TO IT?	WHAT RIGHTS NEED TO BE OBTAINED IN ORDER TO USE THIS MATERIAL?
Existing video interviews		
Existing footage shot by your organization		
Existing television or video footage		
Existing photos		
Existing music		

Existing sound sources (not music or interviews)	
Printed materials related to the video	

b) Interviews: List the interviewees you want to video. If you do not have a specific person in mind, give a general description of the type of interviewee you are looking for. Use the example below as a guide.

NAME AND FUNCTION OF INTERVIEWEE	OBJECTIVE OF INTERVIEW	LOCATION (AND ANY PERMISSION REQUIRED)	LANGUAGE	POSSIBLE SECURITY CONCERNS WITH THIS INTERVIEWEE
Example: James Brown, ex-child soldier	Child soldier talking about how he was recruited, his life as a soldier, when and how he was demobilized, how he feels about the war, what his civilian life is like and what his hopes and fears are for the future.	Transitional reintegration center, Monrovia, Liberia. Need to request access from center director	Gbande/English	Cannot show face, or use real name

c) Sequences: Prepare an outline list of the sequences you wish to shoot to tell your story. A sequence is a series of shots that fit together to encapsulate a particular idea or action. Include the locations needed to acquire this material and the reason to include them.

SEQUENCE (DESCRIBE WHAT WE SEE AND HEAR)	LOCATION (AND ANY PREPARATION/PERMISSION REQUIRED)	PURPOSE: WHY IS IT TO BE INCLUDED?
Example: Group of ex-child soldiers playing football.	Transitional reintegration center, Monrovia, Liberia. Need permission from center director.	Show the child soldiers as children.

4) Choose an interviewee from the list above and draft a list of questions you wish to ask. Please note that interview questions must be open-ended to allow for your interviewee to elaborate the fullest response. For more guidance you should review WITNESS training materials. This is an exercise that you should complete as preparation for each interview you conduct.

NAME:
LOCATION:

Questions	
1	
2	
3	
4	
5	
6	
7	
8	
10	

Plan a production timeline

Outline a timeline for the pre-production, production, post-production and distribution of your first video project. Sample activities are listed below. However, the time required for these will depend on the nature, scope and strategy of the particular project, as well as on the time and energy you are able to commit to the project.

STAGE IN THE PROCESS	ACTIVITY	DATE TO BEGIN	DATE TO FINISH	LOCATION	PERSON RESPONSIBLE/ADDITIONAL INPUT REQUIRED
Pre-production	Research on security constraints				
	Research on existing audiovisual materials and other background research				

295

	Development of video action plan	
	Logistical preparation for filming	
	Fundraising for the production and distribution/advocacy	
Production		
	Filming – Location A	
	Filming – Location B	
	Filming – Location C	
	Filming – Location D	
	Filming – Location E	
	Filming – Location F	
	Filming – Location G	
Postproduction		
	Logging and trancribing footage	
	Preparing a script	
	Reviewing script with co-workers and allies	
	Edit video	
	Key advocacy events to launch video	

PART 4: Implementing the Outreach and Advocacy using your Video

In video advocacy, tactical and strategic distribution of the video is the key element in achieving change. It is often not the number of people who have seen the video that is most important but rather whether the video has reached key audiences with a power to make a difference. Distribution can be effected in a number of ways, including face to face meetings, screenings at key events, private screenings, conferences, hearings, briefings, distribution to key advocacy/campaign allies and partners for use in their advocacy etc.

1) Will it be useful to develop accompanying materials such as a briefing pack, action kit, fact sheet or screening manual to go with the video? If so, what would they contain?

2) Who will be your allies in getting the video to your intended audiences both nationally and internationally (including NGOs, networks, allies, media organizations etc.)? Are there groups who already have the connections to reach your intended audiences? How can you involve these groups from an early stage in your video advocacy process in order to secure their commitment?

3) What level of media exposure are you looking for with this campaign? Please note any concerns to be aware of in terms of the presentation of the issue in the mass media.

4) If you intend to use the mass media, which media organizations would you target nationally or internationally? Do you already have contacts within these organizations? Please note that media organizations may be reluctant to broadcast your advocacy footage or video for a variety of reasons. However, they may still be willing to use some of the material as B-roll for a specific news item or to instigate their own investigation based upon the material presented to them.

MEDIA ORGANIZATION	CONTACT EXISTING?	WHAT DIMENSION OF THE VIDEO'S STORY MAY INTEREST THIS MEDIA OUTLET? WHAT WILL BE THE CHALLENGES IN SECURING COVERAGE THAT RETAINS YOUR ADVOCACY MESSAGE?

5) Based on these considerations expand on the audience distribution chart you created in part 1 to create an outreach plan, with additional clear timelines and division of responsibilities.

AUDIENCE	ACTION SOUGHT	CONTACT DETAILS FOR AUDIENCE	DISTRIBUTION	TIMING	PARTNER STAFF MEMBER/ OR ALLY RESPONSIBLE FOR OUTREACH	STATUS OF OUTREACH (TO BE UPDATED AS YOU PROGRESS)
Example: Senegalese President	Financial and policy commitment to support landmine victims	Via Private Secretary at xxxx phone/email	Via a private screening on December 12, 2004 organized with other NGOs in our anti-landmines coalition.	- Coincides with launch of international advocacy campaign around implementation of landmine convention. - Prior to public launch of video and media release.	Partner advocacy coordinator	Screening venue identified and booked; planning meeting scheduled with allies

6) The most successful campaigns incorporating video advocacy rely on using different video strategies in sequence, so the impact of one action builds on another? For example, you might coordinate the release of your material to television to build and increase pressure after you have had the opportunity to engage grassroots networks via screenings, and to show the video in a private meeting with decision-makers in tandem with written reports and other advocacy tools. Please consider where there are the possibilities for doing this and incorporate them into the chart above.

7) Looking at the distribution audiences you have identified, how many copies of your video will you need to distribute internationally, regionally, nationally and locally? What format is optimal for this distribution (VHS Pal/NTSC, DVD, VCD etc.)

	VHS-NTSC	VHS-PAL	DVD	VCD	BROADCAST-QUALITY COPIES FOR MEDIA USE
Local					
Regional					
International		,			
USA					

APPENDIX: AUDIOVISUAL COMPONENTS

All video is made up of combinations of visual and audio elements. Think creatively and expansively about different kinds of sound and images. What will make this story visually interesting? Can you tell your story using different combinations of visuals and audio components? What will have most impact on your audience? What do you have access to given security, budget and time constraints? Can you make a virtue out of necessity?

Some kinds of visuals and audio to think about:

1. Visuals

* Visual and audio documentation of events happening – People *doing* things, without commentary.
* Landscapes, locations and inanimate objects that are part of the story.
* Interviews – One or more people answering questions, posed to them by an interviewer on or off-camera who may be edited out of the final film.
* Conversations observed – People aware of the presence of a camera, but not being interviewed directly.
* Conversations or people talking to each other, with the camera unobtrusive or hidden.
* Re-enactments – Factually accurate recreations of scenes that could not be filmed, or are in the past. Remember that there may be credibility problems with this in the human rights context, particularly if the reasons are unclear to the audience why a scene could not be filmed, or needed to be re-enacted.
* Expressionistic shots – Often symbolic or artistic, to represent a concept or provide visuals where you do not have access to the location, e.g. in historical interviews.
* Manipulation of imagery via slow-mo, fast-forward, motion-capture etc.
* Still photos or documents – Either static or shot with the camera panning/tracking or zooming in or out.
* Text including on-screen titles, headlines, and graphics – Used for creative and informational purposes, including subtitles for foreign languages. These are usually added in the editing.
* Library, news and archive footage –This could be from a professional archive, but also personal memorabilia, and possibly material from other films. Remember footage from a commercial source is usually expensive and complicated to get permission for.
* Blank screen – Causing the viewer to reflect on what they have just seen or heard, prime them for what is next, indicate a change of sequence or location, or to emphasize sounds.

2. Audio or Sound Elements

* Interviewee – You can use audio only, or audio from a picture-and-sound interview with audio only used, or both picture and audio used.
* Conversations – Either recorded with the participants' knowledge or unobtrusively/secretly.
* Narration – Could be a narrator, the filmmaker or a participant.
* Synchronous Sound – Sound shot while filming.
* Sound effects – Individual sounds shot while filming, or at a later point.
* Music – This is usually added in editing.
* Silence – The absence of sound can indicate change of mood or place, or cause the viewer to refocus on the screen.

Appendix II
WITNESS Footage and Tape Description
Part 1 : Summary

(NOTE: This form may be used for a single tape or for a group of related tapes. Please use the Part 2 : Log or Transcript to shotlist or transcribe each individual tape.

Partner / Source Name_____

_____

_____

Tape Number / Title_____

Date(s) video was shot_____

Location(s)_____

_____

_____

Number of Tapes_____NTSC or PAL?_____

Raw footage_____edited footage or productions_____

Camera Originals or copies?_____

Should originals or copies be returned to partner?_____

Is there a contact person for questions regarding permissions or content?

_____

_____

Videographer(s)_____

Language(s)_____

Summary of video content: please describe the events on the tape, the background or context, any significant events leading up to these events, the people or groups involved; or attach or reference any relevant documentation: _____

_____

_____

_____
_____
_____
_____
_____
_____
_____
_____
_____
_____
_____
_____
_____
_____
_____

Are there any quality problems with the tape? (e.g. damage, camera malfunction, audio dropout, ambient noise, etc.)_____

_____
_____
_____
_____
_____
_____
_____
_____
_____
_____
_____

Are there any security or safety concerns or restrictions, specific or general, relating to this footage? Please describe in detail._____

_____
_____
_____
_____
_____
_____
_____
_____
_____
_____
_____
_____

Summary of Interviews   Please list the names and affiliations of any persons interviewed on the video; if there are security limitations on the use of any interviews, please explain.

Name, Affiliation   **Use of Name?**   **Use of Face?**
Signed release?
and Notes

1._____

_____

_____

2._____

_____

_____

3._____

_____

4._____

_____

_____

5. _____

_____

_____

APPENDIX: WITNESS Footage and Tape Description
Part 2: Log or Transcript

Tape Number: Title:

Time-code   Description

(please see shot abbreviations and examples below, and use as many pages
as necessary to complete the log.)

Appendix III
Sample Personal Release Form
(Short-Form)

I give my unconditional permission to _____, its successors, sponsors, employees, distributors, licensees and assigns _____ to record and film me, my voice, and/or my appearance, and to make unrestricted use of these recordings and films in any way the Producers see fit in perpetuity. I understand that Producers shall own all rights in all such recordings and films.

   I understand that the Producers are relying on this permission and, therefore, I am making it permanent. Furthermore, I give up any and all claims against Producers in connection with their use of the recordings and films.

_____

Signature:

_____

Printed Name

_____

Date

_____
_____

Address

_____

Telephone Number

Appendix IV
Sample Personal Consent and Release
(Long-Form)

I hereby grant to _____, its successors, sponsors, employees, distributors, licensees and assignees (the "<u>Producers</u>"), the unrestricted permission, right and perpetual license to use my name and make still and motion pictures of me and sound recordings of my voice (the "Materials"), and to reproduce, exhibit, broadcast, advertise and exploit all or any part thereof, in and by any media now known or hereinafter to come into existence, throughout the entire world, in connection with their film, the working title of which is _____ (the "Film") or any derivation thereof.

The Producers shall own the copyright and all extensions and renewals thereof and all rights in the Film and in the Materials, which shall be deemed a work made-for-hire for the Producers pursuant to United States copyright laws.

I understand and acknowledge that the subject matter of the Film will deal with issues and events of a personal nature to me and members of my family, which may be depicted in a light favorable or unfavorable to me or my reputation, at the sole discretion of the Producers, and I hereby waive any claim to any moral rights or any violation of my rights to privacy, publicity or confidentiality pursuant to statute or common law in connection with the Film or any other use of the Materials.

As the Producers propose to act in this Consent and Release forthwith, I hereby declare it to be irrevocable, and hereby release the Producers from any and all claims, liability, actions or demands whatsoever in connection with the use of the Materials of the Film.

_____
Signature

_____
Printed Name

_____
Date

_____
_____
Address

_____
Telephone Number

Appendix V
Preproduction and Production Checklist

PREPRODUCTION RESEARCH	NOTES
Key messages?	
Outline of story and style	
Archive footage?	
Music?	
Previous films/books about subject?	
Contacted potential interviewees?	
Organized where and when interview filming will take place?	
Any security threats to consider?	
How will you/subjects travel to and from interview and filming sites?	
Will you film alone?	
Fundraising?	

PRODUCTION CHECKLIST	NOTES
Camera equipment	
Camera	
Lens cloth	
Tapes	
Pen to label tapes	
Silica gel/desiccant for camera bag	
Waterproof cover for camera (may be an umbrella or a real cover)	
Charged batteries	
Charger	
Batteries and extra batteries	
Tripod/tripod head	
Audio equipment	
External microphone(s)	

Batteries for the microphone(s)	
XLR cables	
Headphones	
Boom pole	
Camera adaptor to hold external microphone	
Lighting equipment	
Light kit (lights, gels, diffuser, clothes pins, stands)	
Reflector	
Gloves	
Forms/Lists	
Producer's list	
Consent/Release forms	
Location permit	
Interpreter/translator confirmation	
Equipment insurance	
Directions, maps of area	
Call-sheet (schedule)	
Shooting plan	
Questions for interviewees	
First aid kit	
All medical, passport information on crew	
Equipment list (with serial numbers)	

Appendix VI
Script Formatting for Video Documentary

In a typical documentary script video and audio are placed in separate columns:

VIDEO	AUDIO
WS—View of Salween valley, a remote area near the Thai–Burma border MWS—Track along the shore of a village located on the Salween river MWS—Shots of people harvesting crops CU—Women sifting rice	MUSIC: Karen traditional music NARRATOR: This is the Salween valley, located in the hills near the border between Thailand and Burma. It is mainly home to villagers from the Karen ethnic group, who live from fishing and cultivating fields on the slopes
WS—Looking downstream on the river MS—Village leader working with his nets in shallows of river	NARRATOR: Taw Say is a leader of one of the villages that line the Salween river NAT. SOUND of river and harvest noises
MS—Village leader sitting outside of house; with river in background	VILLAGE LEADER: (talks to camera) My name is .... And for many centuries my family has lived here in the Salween valley

Usually in the script you will indicate shot size, and camera movement/action.

In the audio column you list narration, or natural sound, or music cues. It can contain narration or a transcript of what the people onscreen are saying, or at least their first and last words to use as cues to begin and end the shot.

Appendix VII
Costing-Out Your Video
Distribution Strategy

"Project X" outreach and distribution	Expense detail	Cost
Costs		
Staff time (outreach)	X% of producer's time/salary; Y% Full-time outreach coordinator	
Development and printing of relevant accompanying documentation	X sets of materials at $Y	
Targeted screenings	Number of conferences and/or special screenings	
Dubs (includes tape stock and dubbing)	$X per tape x Y tapes	
Post and packing	$X average (assuming Y domestic/Z international distribution)	
Marketing costs	X sets of material at $Y	
	Total costs	
Income		
Volunteer time	X volunteers at $Y equivalent	
Tape sales	X copies at $Y	
Sales of T-shirts or other items	X sales at $Y	
Donations		
Ticket sales	X sales at $Y	
Grants		
	Total income	
	Total surplus/loss (Total costs—Total income)	

Budget narrative guide

- Staff time: The budget for this proposal will include staff time to coordinate outreach and distribution of "Project X," including preparing accompanying documentation, identifying appropriate audiences, coordinating outreach, organizing and co-facilitating broadcasts, screenings and conferences, and supporting organizers to hold their own screenings.
- Development and printing of relevant accompanying documentation: Includes the costs of copying/printing accompanying materials and reports, as well as the costs to develop screening materials including staff time.
- Targeted screenings: We are budgeting for X conferences and/or special screenings to be conducted by our staff at relevant venues either with key mass audiences or specific decision-making audiences. Costs in this budget line include domestic/international transportation, conference fees, and lodging for screening facilitators, as well as costs for renting space for screenings where necessary.
- Dubs: We have a target list of some 150 groups/institutions who will benefit from access to free copies of "Project X." This distribution list is based on a detailed breakdown of target groups and outreach strategies.
- Post and packing: Estimated to include envelopes and mailing costs.
- Marketing costs: Including posters, flyers and paid advertisements.
- Volunteer time: Include this in your calculation, but remember that its cash value is only relevant if they replace a role or function that you would otherwise pay for.

Notes on the Editors and Contributors

Sam Gregory is a human rights activist, advocacy trainer, and video producer, and currently the Program Manager at WITNESS <www.witness. org>. He has worked in collaboration with human rights groups in the Philippines, Guatemala, Argentina, Thailand/Burma, and the US, supporting international advocacy and outreach campaigns, and has led a range of international human rights training workshops.

Videos he has produced have been screened at the US Congress, the United Nations and at film festivals worldwide. In 2004 he was a jury member for the IDFA Amnesty International/Doen Award.

Gregory currently focuses on WITNESS' training initiatives, and on work in Asia, including extensive campaigning with the grassroots organization Burma Issues, recently including the videos *Entrenched Abuse: Forced Labor in Burma* (2004) and *No Place to Go: Internally Displaced People in Burma* (2002).

He was a Kennedy Scholar at Harvard University, where his Master's focused on international development and media. He has worked as a television researcher/producer in both the US and UK, and for development organizations in Nepal and Vietnam.

Gillian Caldwell is the Executive Director of WITNESS <www.witness.org>, which advances human rights advocacy worldwide through the use of video and communications technology. She is also a filmmaker and attorney with experience in the areas of human and civil rights, intellectual property, contracts, and family law.

Caldwell was formerly Co-Director of the Global Survival Network, where she coordinated an undercover investigation into the trafficking of women for forced prostitution from Russia. She produced and directed the video *Bought & Sold*, based on the investigation, garnering widespread media coverage, including BBC, CNN, ABC, the *New York Times*, and the *Washington Post*. She lived in South Africa during 1991, investigating hit squads, and has worked in Boston, Washington, DC, and New York on issues related to poverty and violence.

She is a recipient of the 2000 Rockefeller Foundation Next Generation Leadership Award, was named one of 40 Outstanding Social Entrepreneurs by the Schwab Foundation, a 2003 Tech Laureate by the Tech Museum, and a Special Partner by Ashoka: Innovators for the Public. She speaks English and Spanish.

Ronit Avni is the founder and Director of Just Vision <www.justvision.org>, which uses digital media to highlight the efforts of Israeli and Palestinian civilians working for a rights-respecting, lasting peace. She is currently directing a feature-length documentary, *Blind Transmission*, due for release in 2006. Avni recently received the Auburn Theological Seminary's 2005 Lives of Commitment Award. From 2003 to 2005, she was a Joshua Venture Fellow. In 2005, she and her colleague, Joline Makhlouf, appeared on *The Oprah Winfrey Show* as an Israeli–Palestinian duo.

Prior to launching Just Vision, Avni was the Program Associate at WITNESS. She has co-produced short videos with NGO partners in Senegal, Burkina Faso, the US, and Brazil. She wrote and produced *Rise* with the Revolutionary Association of the Women of Afghanistan. *Rise* premièred at Makor and screened at the Women's Film Festival in Seoul, South Korea, and at the GlobalVisions Film Festival in Canada. Avni has lectured at universities across North America.

Thomas Harding has worked for over 15 years in the media as TV executive, producer, and director. He co-founded Oxford Channel, a free-to-air local television station in Oxford, England, with his wife Debora Harding. He is also the co-founder of Undercurrents <www.undercurrents.org>, the award-winning environmental production company.

Harding has worked as a documentary and news producer for many of the world's leading broadcasters, including BBC, Times-Warner, Channel Four, ITN, and TF1. He has written for newspapers and magazines, is the author of *Video Activist Handbook* (Pluto, 1988 & 2002) and contributed a chapter in *DIY Culture: Party & Protest in Nineties Britain* (Verso).

CONTRIBUTORS

Joanna Duchesne is an independent filmmaker, who spent seven years heading the production of video and radio materials for Amnesty International. She has traveled extensively for her work, has filmed undercover, and worked with many human rights groups and media outlets internationally. She has also trained individuals and groups in many countries in video production techniques and media skills.

Duchesne is currently dividing her time between running the video unit at VSO (Voluntary Services Overseas) in London, UK, and working in a freelance capacity.

Katerina Cizek is a Czech–Canadian filmmaker whose films have not only documented the handicam revolution, they have become part of the movement. Her films have instigated criminal investigations, changed UN policies, and been screened as evidence at an International Criminal Tribunal.

Cizek's film about new technologies and human rights, *Seeing Is Believing* (co-directed with Peter Wintonick), won the prestigious Hamptons Festival Abraham Prize, and toured at festivals and on television internationally. She has also made films about the Czech velvet revolution and the Rwandan genocide, worked in Aboriginal gang territory; investigated global human trafficking, and directed a series about the battle over water in Kazakhstan, Uzbekistan, and Kyrgyzstan. These films won awards at New York World,

INPUT, Golden Gate, IDFA, Banff, and Biarritz, and the European ECHO Humanitarian Award. Cizek has twice been a Canadian Gemini nominee, and the recipient of a Montreal New Talent Award.

Cizek lectures widely, has co-founded an Aboriginal news magazine, and has contributed to various publications including *HorizonZero* (an avant-garde digital arts and culture web publication) and *Walrus Magazine*.

Liz Miller is a documentary filmmaker, community media artist, and professor of new media/video/film production. Her video works include *Novela, Novela* (30 min, 2002), *Parkville Portraits* (2000), and *Just Here* (1999); web projects include *Moles* (1999), and *Memories Under Construction*.

Miller's work has been exhibited and broadcast at venues including Herter Gallery, Real Art Ways Theatre, Brooks Gallery, and New York Hall of Science. She has won awards from the International Association of Women in Radio and Film, Latin American Studies Association, and the National Educational Media Network; and has won fellowships from the National Endowment of the Arts, Paul Robeson Fund, and Frameline.

Miller is currently working on a feature-length documentary, *Marvelous Resources*. This film examines diverse perspectives on water privatization across the Americas.

Sukanya Pillay obtained her LLM in international legal studies from New York University, and currently teaches commercial and international law at the Faculty of Law, University of Windsor, Canada.

Her international law experience includes coordinating WITNESS when it was a project at the Lawyers Committee for Human Rights (now Human Rights First) in New York, and directing the Law and Human Rights Program for TVE, London. During this time Pillay worked with NGOs worldwide to produce videos to protect human rights. She has also conducted more than 20 human rights missions to conflict zones including Haiti, Northern Ireland, Israel/Palestine, and countries in Asia and Africa.

From 2000 to 2002, Pillay was in-house counsel at Hutchison, responsible for legal operations in India. Since 2002, she has been teaching law, with a focus on transnational law, corporate social responsibility, and human rights. Her 2004 documentary film, *Robbing Pedro to Pay Paul?*, examined the effect of US agricultural subsidies and NAFTA on Mexican corn farmers.

Index

Compiled by Sue Carlton